EPSOM & EWELL AT WORK

JEREMY HARTE

AMBERLEY

First published 2017

Amberley Publishing
The Hill, Stroud
Gloucestershire, GL5 4EP

www.amberley-books.com

ISBN 978 1 4456 7258 8 (print)
ISBN 978 1 4456 7259 5 (ebook)

British Library Cataloguing in Publication Data.
A catalogue record for this book is available from the British Library.

Origination by Amberley Publishing.
Printed in the UK.

CONTENTS

ACKNOWLEDGEMENTS

The pictures used in this book came from the collections of Bourne Hall Museum, built up by many hands over fifty years. I am grateful to everyone who has been part of this process – not least Ian West, who came up with some much-needed postcards at the last minute, and Edred Tims, for the use of photographs taken by his grandfather. For the text, I have – like anyone who undertakes historical research on Epsom & Ewell – been indebted to the superlative website managed by Peter Reid at www.epsomandewellhistoryexplorer.org.uk. And for contemporary pictures of the racing world I am grateful to Caroline Baldock, who is as talented with a camera as she is on horseback. If her attempts to train me to recognise winners have not always been successful, it is the fault of the pupil and not the teacher.

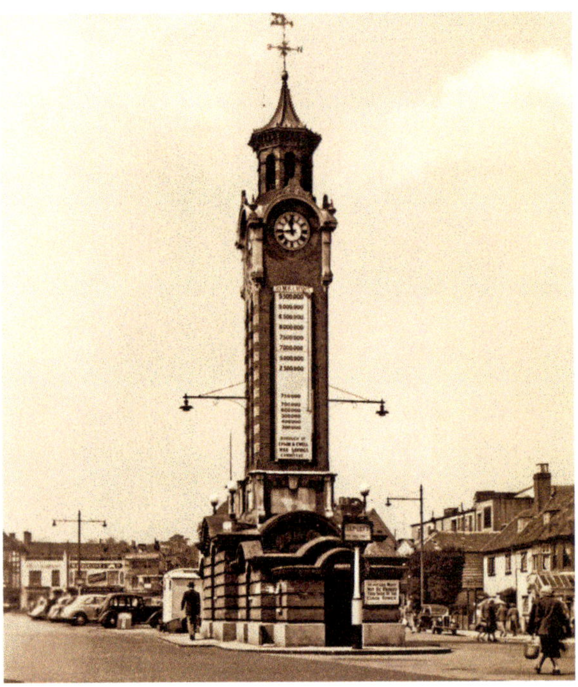

Built in 1848 to reflect Victorian self-confidence, the Clock Tower is a symbol of Epsom. After the Second World War it bore a banner of the town's achievements for War Savings.

INTRODUCTION

Where Roman bullock carts and medieval waggons once carried wares from London, lorries now sweep down the A24 towards the edge of the North Downs. Lying at the foot of these chalk hills, the twin settlements of Epsom and Ewell drew trade from the junction of roads to Hampshire and Sussex. If you follow the old roads uphill, you can look back and see the City in the blue distance below you, set in the flat London basin below the Downs.

This long sweep of chalk hills from east to west has determined the geography of settlement in northern Surrey. Chalk is a dry rock, and rainwater drains quickly through it, until it meets a more impervious stratum. So the natural springs all break at the foot of the hills, and it is along this narrow line that the ancient villages were founded. Ewell, where the strongest spring breaks out to form the headwaters of the Hogsmill River, was also the largest settlement. The parish boundaries ran north to south, capturing the prized fields of light, easily tilled chalk topsoil and above it the downland grazing, while meadows and enclosed fields followed the course of the river downstream. The core of old Epsom, centred on St Martin's Church, was a similar settlement but to the west the soil was very different – a heavy clay. That simple geological

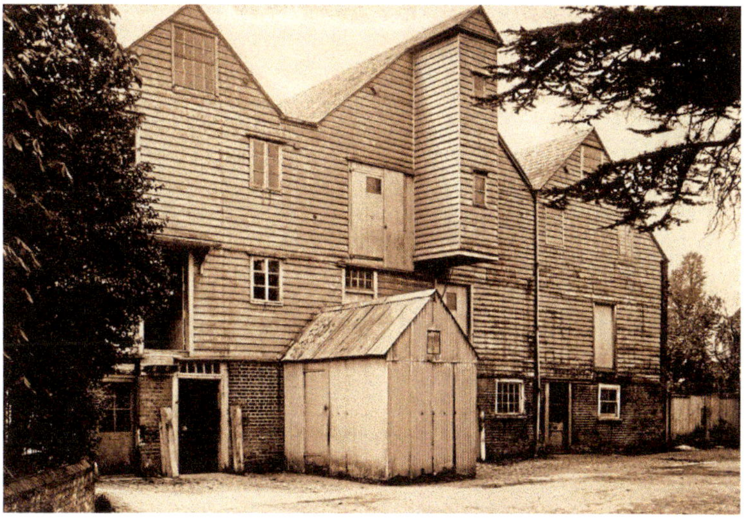

The Upper Mill at Ewell had run since Domesday Book when it was extended under Charles Hall in around 1810. By 1929 it relied on a gas engine when water was low.

difference would determine the diverging future of the two villages when the magnesium sulphate trapped under the clay was found to be the active property of Epsom Wells.

One summer day (tradition places it in 1618) farmer Henry Wicker discovered this mineral spring on the otherwise barren land of Epsom Common. Wealthy Londoners, made constipated by a meat-rich diet, soon found relief in taking Epsom Salts. Until then Ewell had been the larger and wealthier of the two but now it was Epsom which became known nationally as a centre for leisure and entertainment. The fashion for taking waters died away, as fashions will, but the days of the spa left Epsom with a legacy of dignified buildings that enabled it to gradually overtake its neighbour as a public centre and a location for trade.

Ewell still had its river, which at that time was the only source of industrial power. London's demand for this was growing and since the Hogsmill had enough water for multiple mills, it ran a paper mill as well as the old corn mill through most of the eighteenth century, with one set of gunpowder mills between Ewell and Ruxley, and another further downstream along Worcester Park Road.

Between the 1820s and the 1840s, the go-ahead inhabitants of Epsom provided it with all the trappings of a small Victorian town: a Local Board of Health, municipal supplies of water and gas, a school and workhouse, rebuilt churches, a landmark Clock Tower and (thanks to the rivalry of railway companies) a choice of two stations. At Ewell, the influence of two or three dominant landowners ensured that the agricultural interest would prevail; there were no such figures in Epsom, so land was for sale to build villas for the City businessmen. Like many other places on the urban periphery, Epsom had hosted horse races since the seventeenth century; but unlike the rest, it could draw on a sympathetic lord of the manor as well as the managerial skills of the Dorling family, who provided successive entrepreneurial Clerks of the Course. With the building of a Grandstand in 1830, the fiftieth year that the

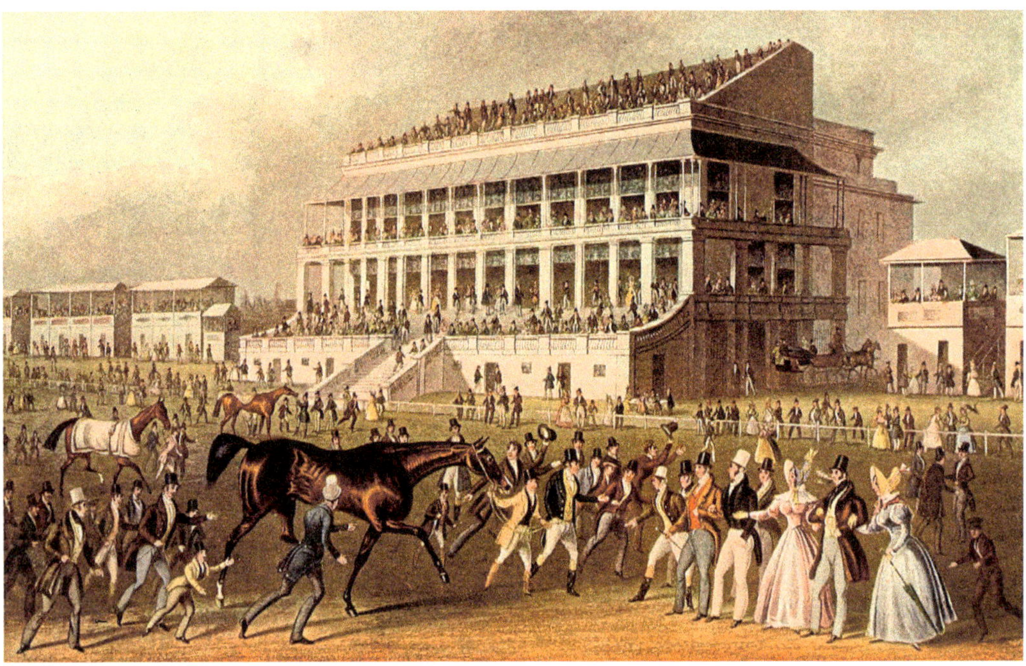

Bay Middleton being led in after the 1836 Epsom Derby. The newly built Grandstand in the background had a stone staircase with Doric columns, and room for 2,000 people on the roof.

Derby had run, this race grew from a niche aristocratic event to a national festival, and crowds of up to half a million surged through Epsom every June.

For the rest of the year the close-cropped turf of the Downs provided ideal gallops for training horses, and so racing stables were established on the roads leading southwards. The contrasting clay soils of Epsom Common also influenced the development of the town: too poor to farm, they were colonised from the seventeenth century onwards by squatters and smallholders who supplied the growing town with its own proletariat. The bricks that built Georgian Epsom came from here, in a seam of the Reading Formation, which was later exploited further north at Kiln Lane, the Organ Inn and Worcester Park. The clothes of the town were washed by laundresses on the Common, where the rows of furze bushes provided a natural drying ground.

Epsom and Ewell remained traditional communities. Wills made by residents up to the mid-nineteenth century show that agriculture remained dominant, followed by the food trades – butchers, millers, bakers, dealers in corn, and the ubiquitous victuallers and innkeepers. The next most important sector was costume, mostly tailors and shoemakers, while the general retailers were outnumbered by those who manufactured the goods they sold, such as blacksmiths and tallow chandlers. Next came the housing sector with its carpenters and builders, and transport relying on wheelwrights, saddlers and coachmen. Epsom's gentry customers could support clock and watchmakers along with a bookseller and, of all things, a herald painter; but most manufactures remained local. From field to corn to flour to bread, from grass to ox to meat for roasting or tallow for candles – these were steps in the industrial process which everyone could see happening in front of them.

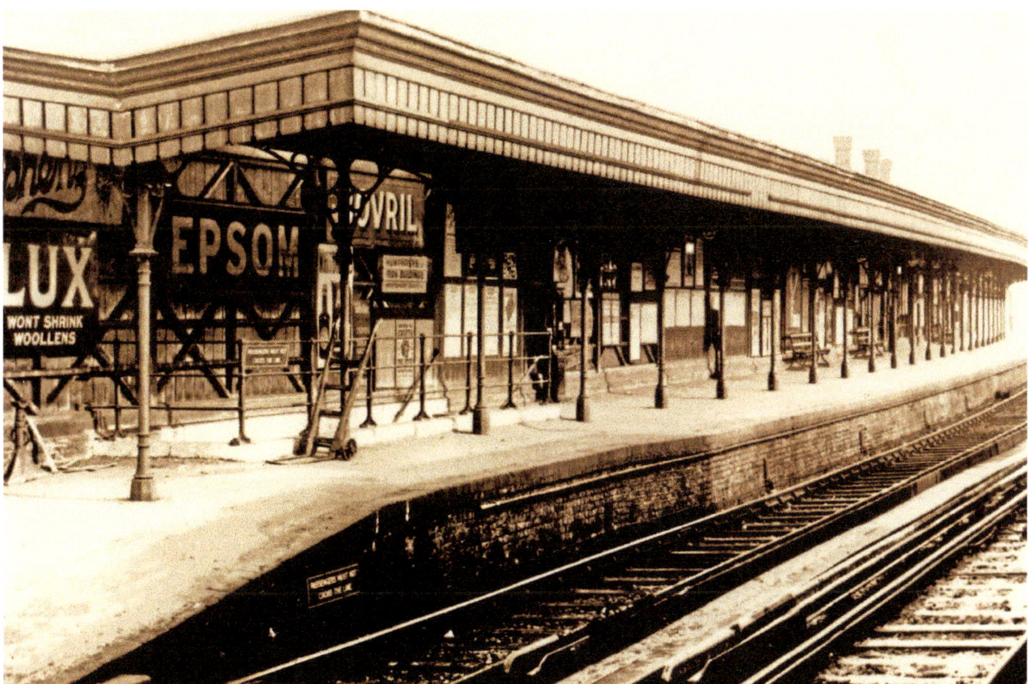

Epsom's first station was built at the top of Upper High Street in 1847 by the London Brighton & South Coast Railway. The existing station came twelve years later.

It was a small world: Epsom had just under 3,000 inhabitants in 1820, and 11,000 at the death of Victoria. All the trading families were connected. Cropley's son from the builders married Miss Polhill from the butchers, whose sister had married the founder of Page's motors, who took over premises from Skilton the vet, who was the brother of Skilton the dairyman, who married Miss Hope the butcher's daughter ... and so it went on; a closed circle but an effective one. More than half of the councillors in post during the First World War were local businessmen: an auctioneer, baker, bootmaker, builder, plumber, printer and victualler who steered the town through the worst conflict the world had yet known.

Everything was changed by the suburban development which began in the 1920s and reached its peak in 1939: a tide of housing that reached out to the edge of the Downs and would have gone further if it had not been for the Second World War, followed by a more rigorous planning policy and the imposition of the Green Belt. The changed character of Ewell was recognised by its incorporation with Epsom as a borough in 1937. In the same year a quarter of Epsom High Street was demolished and built 30 feet back to facilitate traffic, and the names on the new storefronts were no longer local but national: Woolworths, and Burton the Tailors.

Sixty years later, the organisers of the borough's Diamond Jubilee decided to showcase family firms that dated back sixty years in Epsom and Ewell. There were only three: Giles the nurserymen, Lester Bowden the tailors, and Epsom Coaches. Another twenty years on, none of these are locally owned. Commercial logic has led to moves, transfers and buy-ins which make no concessions for family sentiment.

But every morning, the strings of thoroughbreds still ride out on the Downs. They, at least, are following a tradition which has not passed away.

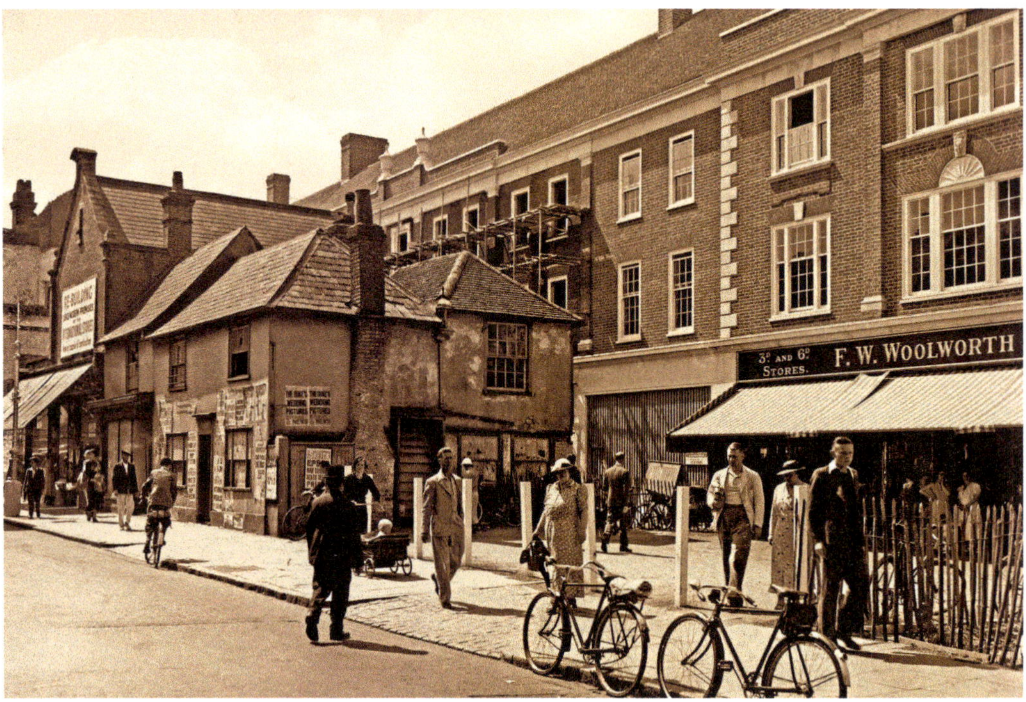

In 1937 the north-eastern sector of Epsom High Street was widened to smooth the flow of traffic to Brighton. A neo-Georgian shop façade was built behind the old street.

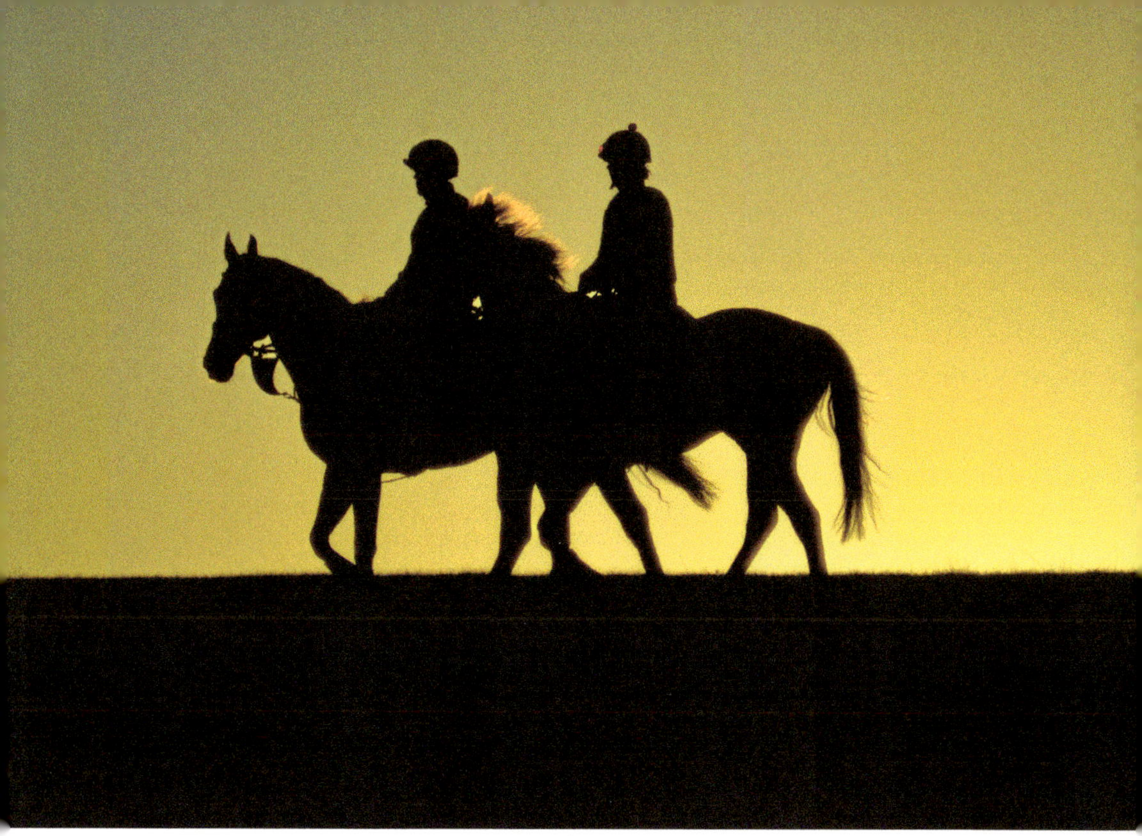

Above: From opposite the Grandstand, horse-friendly traffic lights lead to the Downs. This is Lee Carter's string with Paddy Bradley on Follow Me and Michelle Allen on Bongo.

Below: After twenty years of planning, Epsom got its own indoor shopping centre in 1985. The Ashley Centre was built to fit in without compromising the character of the town.

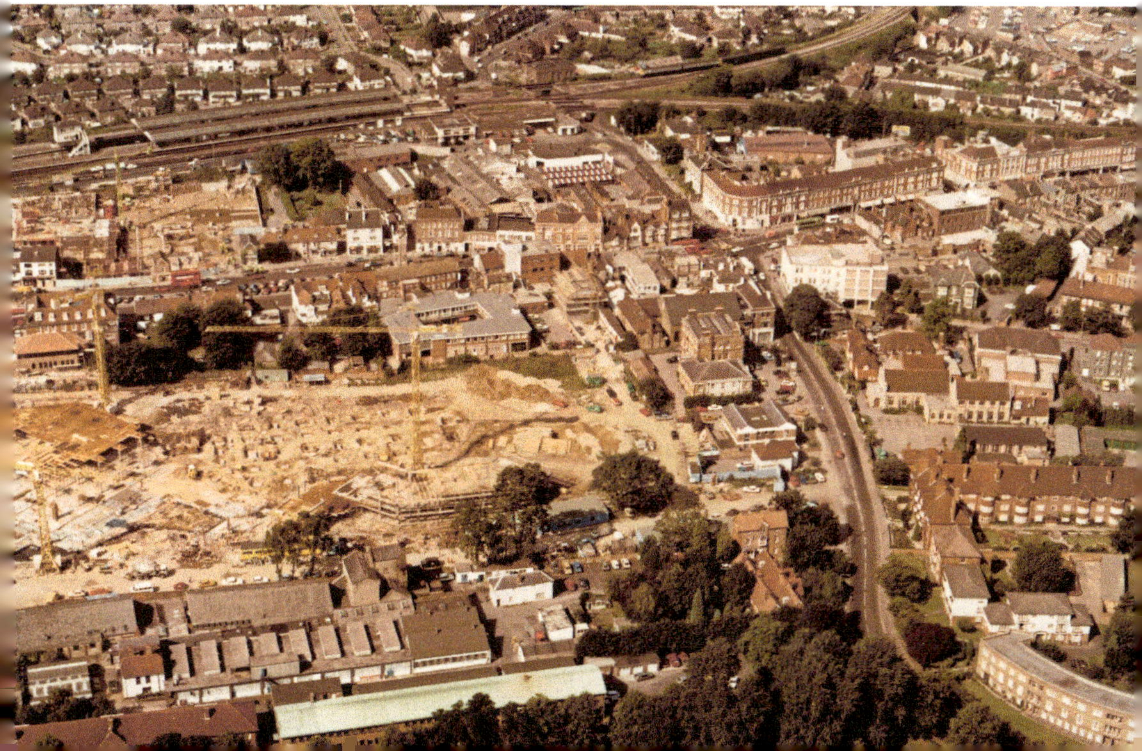

HORSE SENSE

Col Dennis O'Kelly was a dark horse. Nobody knew where he had acquired his military rank, or the wealth which enabled him to entertain visitors at his show house at Epsom, and rumour had it that the money came from a questionable partnership with a London madam. But one thing was certain: he owned the fastest racehorse of the day – probably the fastest of all time. Until his death in 1789 the great Eclipse was at stud on West Hill, where he could be seen among hundred acres of paddocks and stables.

Eclipse was born too early to run in the Derby, which was founded in 1780, but Epsom had been a racing town before that. The training stables in Church Street may not have been built, as legend claimed, by Charles II for Nell Gwynn, but they were well-established by the 1770s when Bob Bloss, the jockey, set up business there and at the Old King's Head next door.

Success at the races usually came to landowners whose estates, and income, were large enough to train the best. At the Durdans, Sir Gilbert Heathcote bred Amato, the 1838 Derby winner, and this was remembered by Lord Rosebery when he bought the property in 1874. In 1881 he commissioned George Devey to build an indoor riding school with a dais at one end from which he could inspect and judge the horses. The earlier stables were supplemented by the Cicero yard, named after Rosebery's Derby winner of 1905. Cicero is buried in the grounds nearby along with Ladas and Sir Visto, who had won for Rosebery in 1894 and 1895.

Breeding counted for people as well as horses. When John Nightingall, the trainer of South Hatch, was asked about his sons, he said, 'Young Jack will be the best of the lot, his mother is Robert I'Anson's sister.' In the end, despite kinship to the man who trained Austerlitz to win the Grand National, Jack didn't do as well as his half-brothers William and Arthur. William's son Walter succeeded his father at South Hatch and won the 1930 Irish Derby with Rock Star, going on to train for Winston Churchill. He married Bessy, the daughter of George Hyams who trained at Downs Cottage; she had previously been married to George Duller, the hurdles jockey turned trainer whose wartime years were spent in what may have been the Home Guard's only mounted division.

As this might suggest, the horse world was very much an extended family. Jockeys became trainers and stable lads were encouraged to become jockeys with skills passed down from father to son (later daughter), or from master to employee. When Richard Wootton arrived at Treadwell House from Australia in 1906 he was a new face and the acrimony which he aroused led to a libel suit with *The Morning Post*. But his son Stanley became the principal trainer of the town, buying Six Mile Hill Gallops in 1926 and tutoring a string of winning jockeys. Discipline was strict but then these were the years of the Great Depression and any job was welcome. Besides, you couldn't criticise an academy which turned out pupils like Charlie Smirke, who rode four Derby winners as well as four for the St Leger and two for the 2,000 Guineas.

The last locally trained Derby winner was April the Fourth, owned by actor Tom Walls. His horse almost failed to make it to the course in 1932 despite starting from the Looe on Reigate Road, only 2 miles away the Derby crowd was so dense that he had to walk the last half-mile through the crowd.

Generally, however, Epsom trainers did better with steeplechasers than with horses racing on the flat. Between the 1950s and 1970s the town was at its height as a training centre, with two of the largest stables in the country based in Burgh Heath Road. After that the location of Epsom on the fringe of the London urban area began to tell. The potential value of land for building outweighed its use for horses, and employment legislation altered the old hierarchies of management in the yard. But there are still stables around the Downs, with ten of them participating in the annual Trainers' Open Day in August.

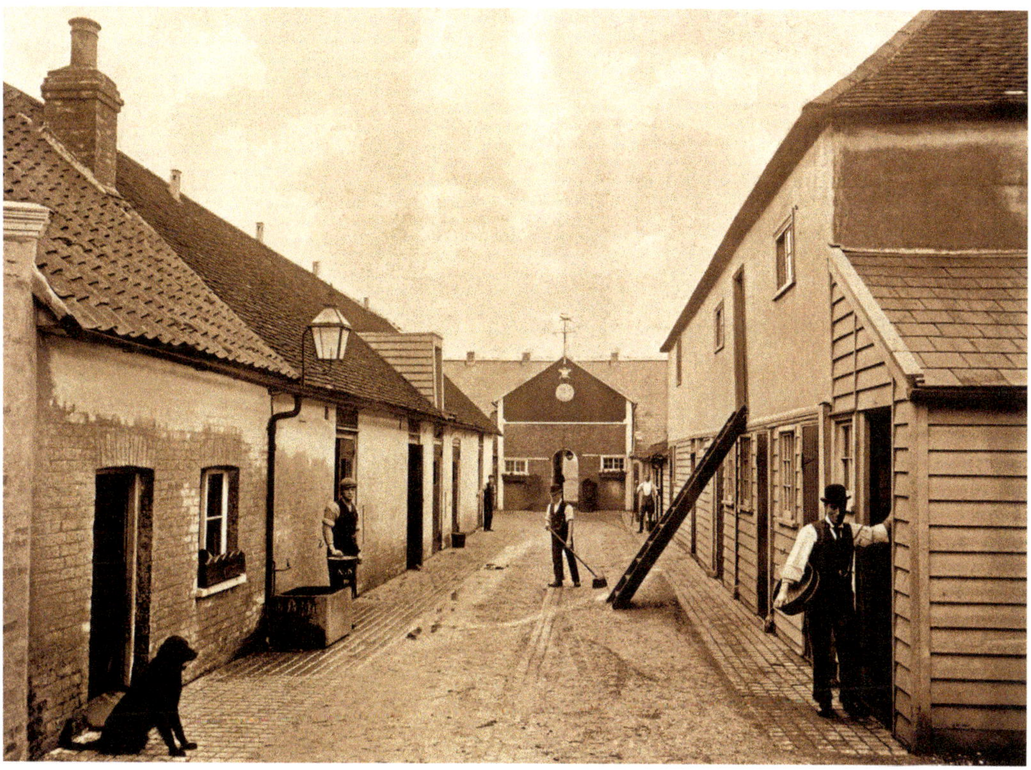

Arthur Nightingall's yard at Priam Lodge in 1896, with Don the dog on duty. John Jones used to train steeplechasers for the Prince of Wales here – hence the triple feathers.

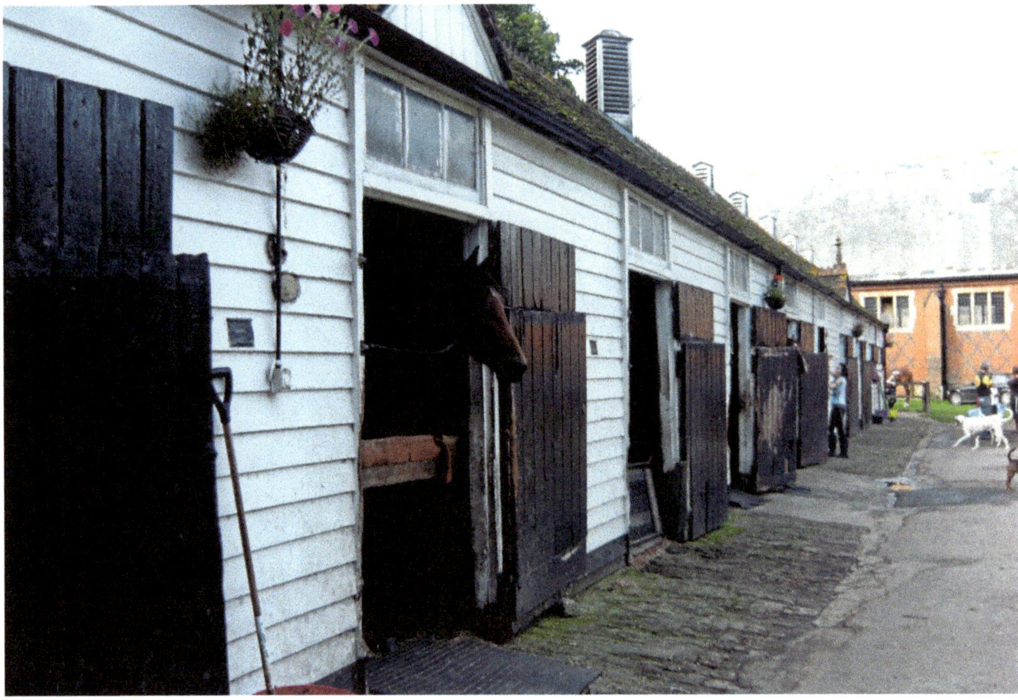

The old foaling stables at the Durdans in 2009, three years before Philip Buckman moved in. At the back is the indoor riding school built for Lord Rosebery in 1881.

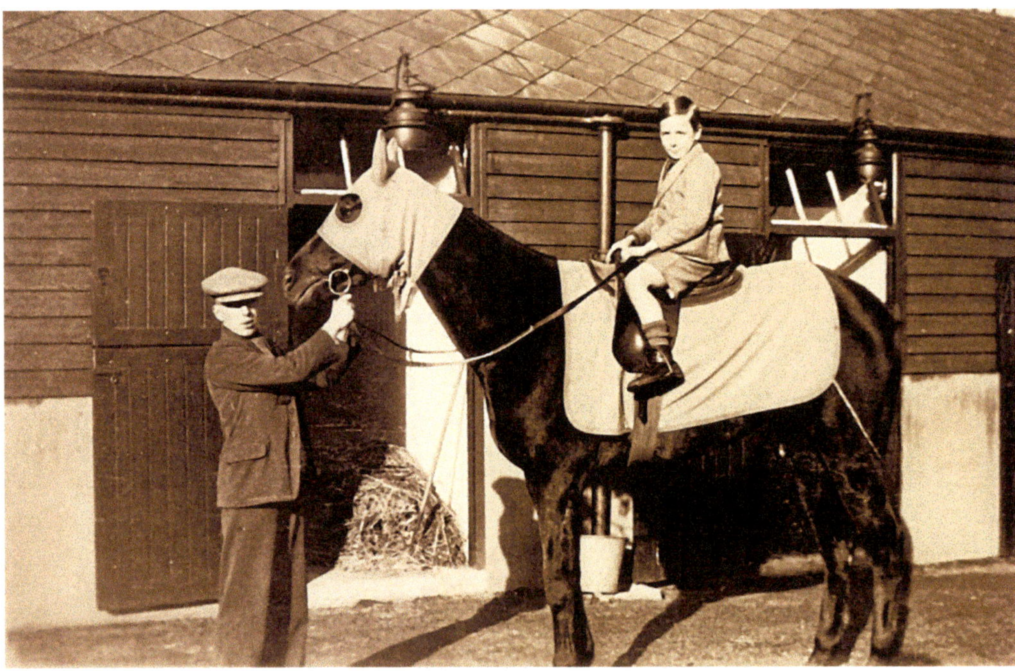

A young Vic Smyth at Tattenham Corner Stables. Apprenticed to the Woottons at Treadwell House, he retired as a jockey in 1925 and trained at Mospey and Priam Lodge.

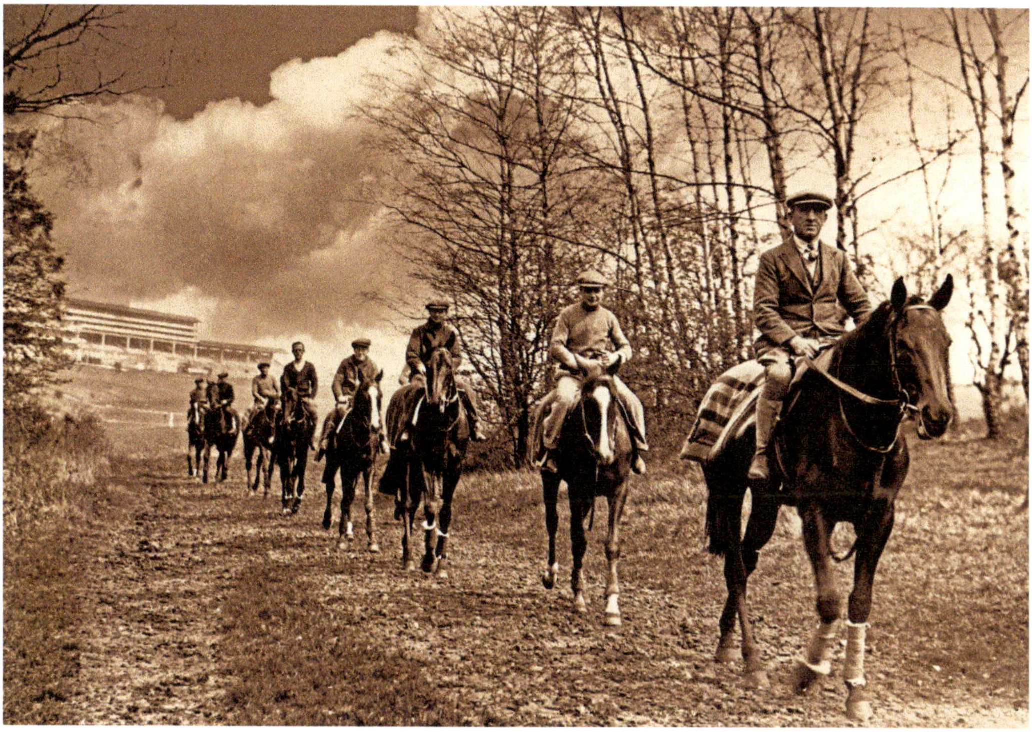

Walter Nightingall's string from South Hatch exercising in April 1938 in preparation for the Spring Meeting. Five years later he won a wartime Derby.

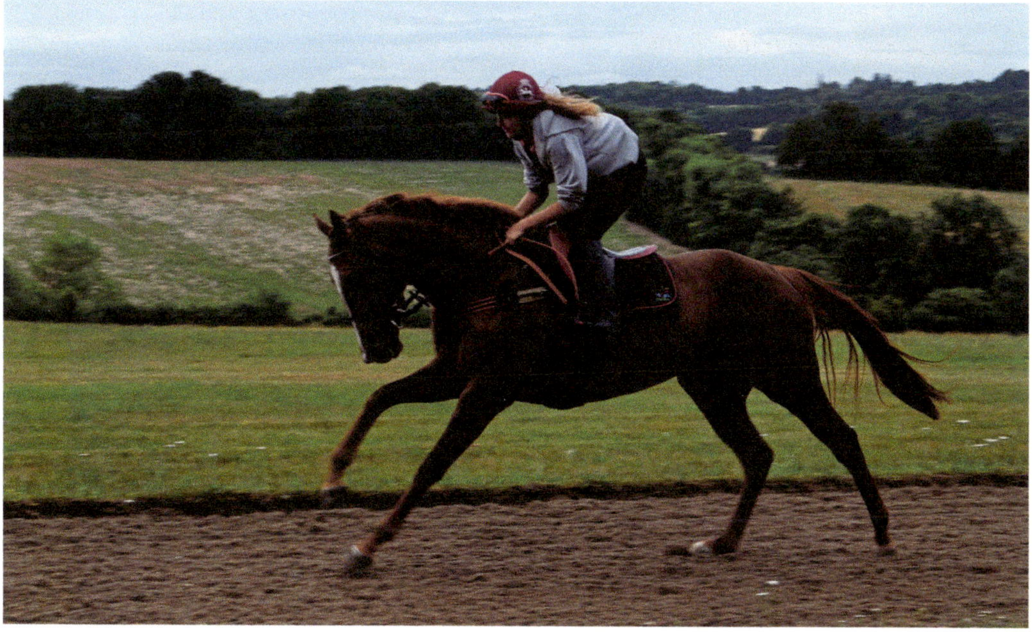

Libby Halls from Laura Mongan's yard at Condover Stables cantering on the top poly, one of the three all-weather surfaces extended to 5½ furlongs in 2016.

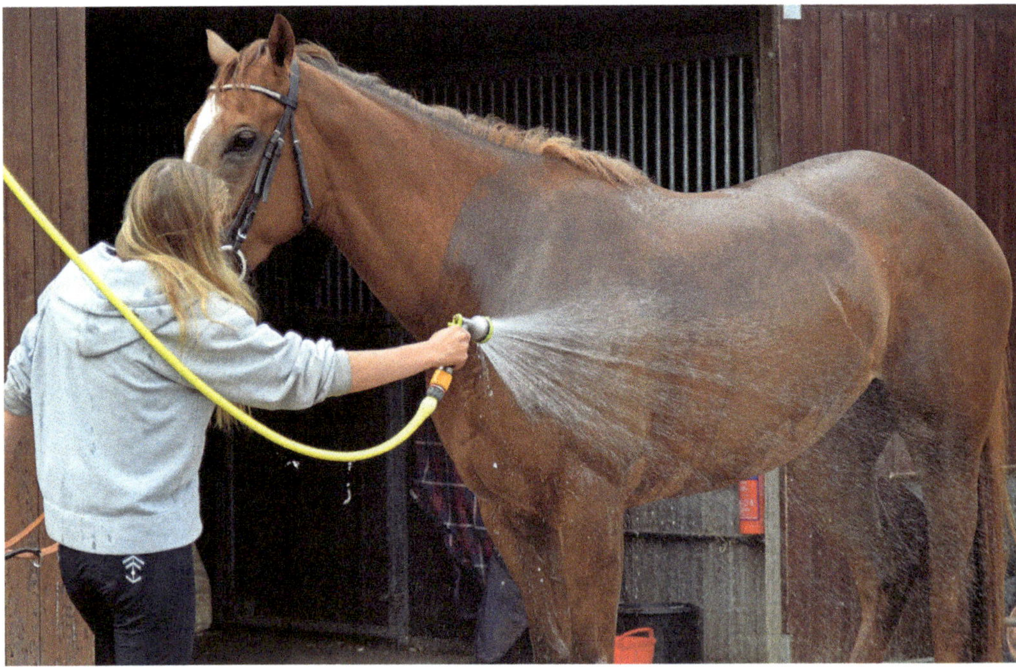

Washing the horse down at Condover Stables after a gallop to remove sweat and cool down. Laura Mongan sent out her first runner and winner from the stables in 2004.

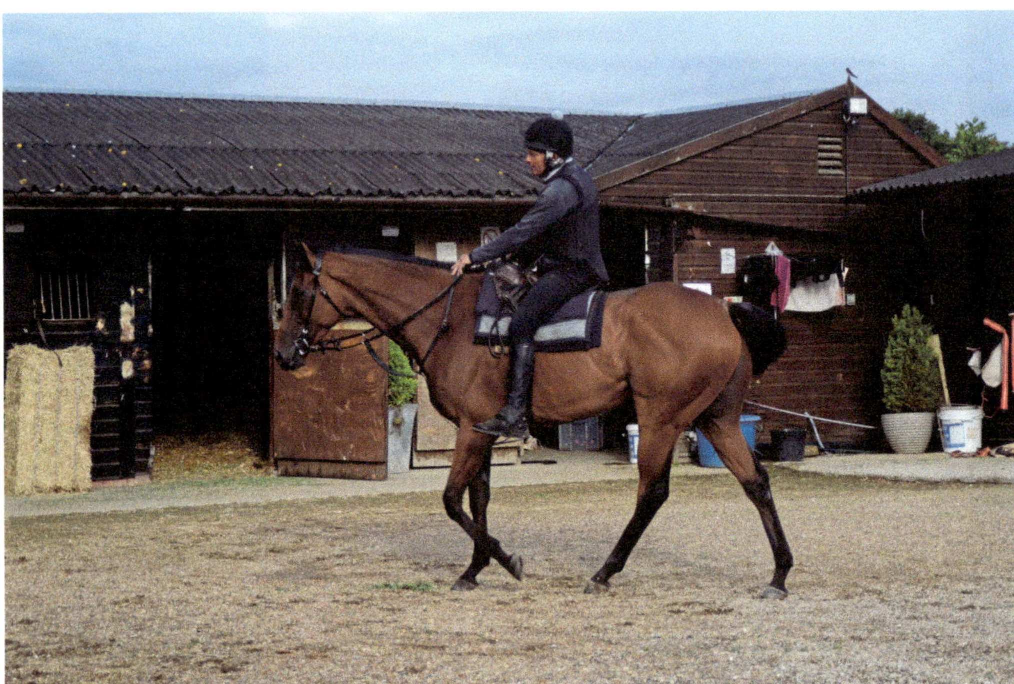

Simon Dow riding back through his yard at Clear Heights Stables. He started training in 1988, and became chairman of the fifty-year-old Epsom Trainers Association.

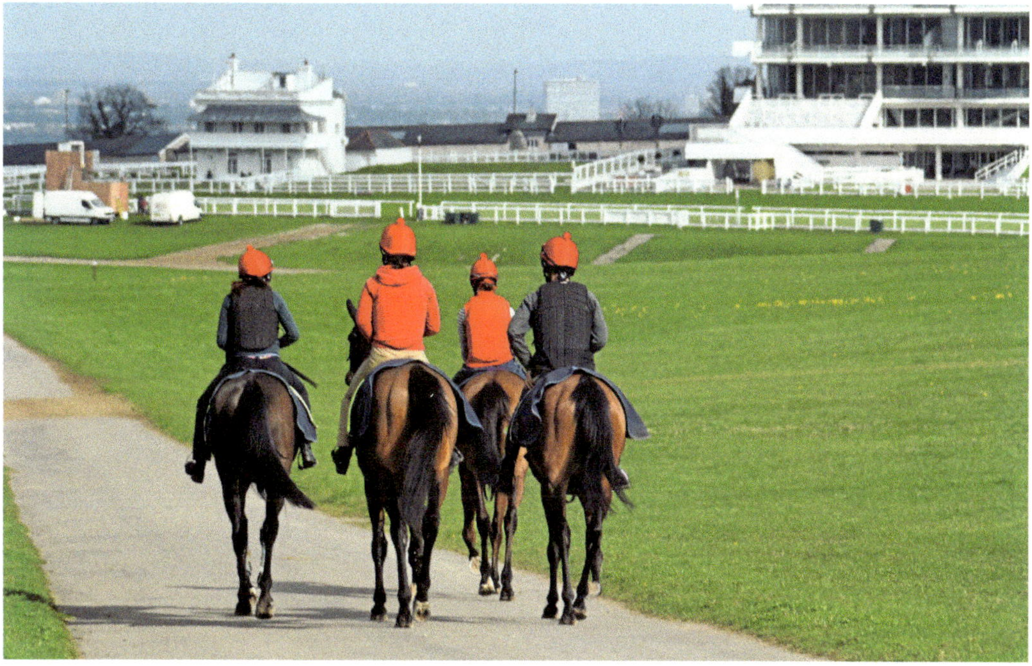

Lee Carter's string from the lower yard at Clear Heights, where he took over after John Akehurst's death in 2012. In the background are the Prince's and Queen's Stands.

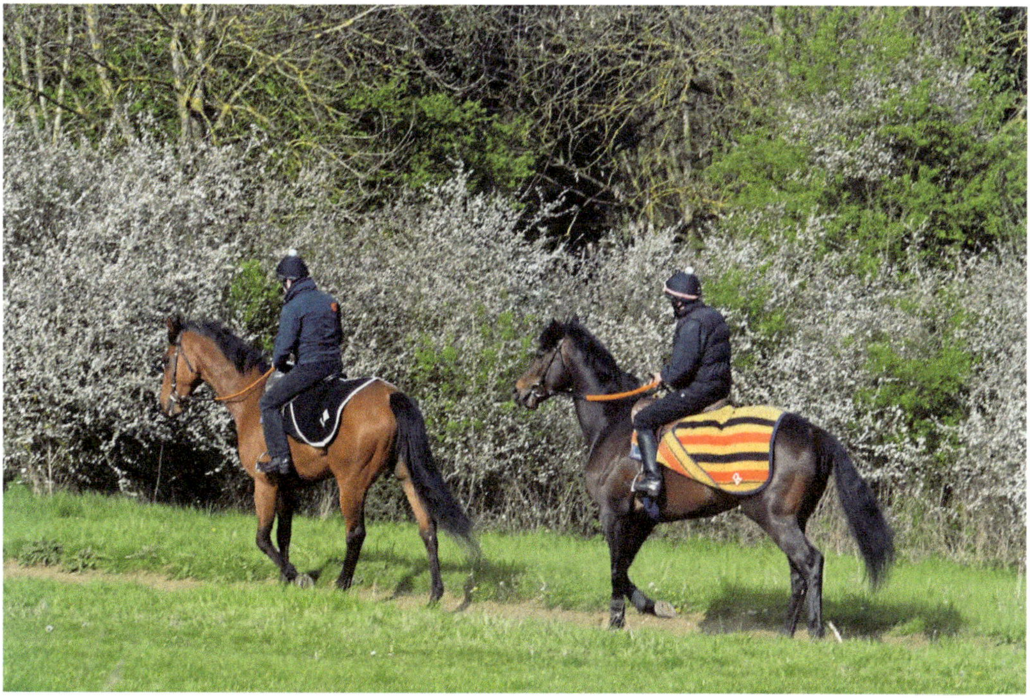

Ian Mongan on Morgan's Bay rides to the fibre sand. Behind is Ollie Jago on Harbour Law, who in 2017 became the first Epsom-trained horse to win the St Leger.

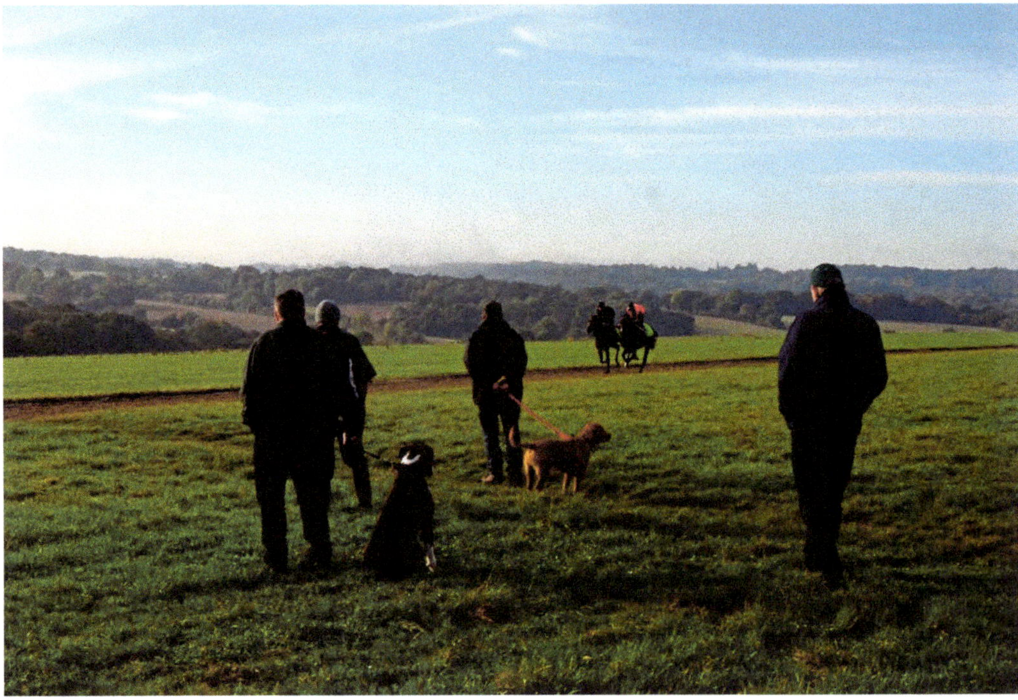

Roger Ingram on the Downs in autumn 2016, watching his horses working. He trained at Southwell, before moving back to Shifnal Cottage and then Wendover in 1994.

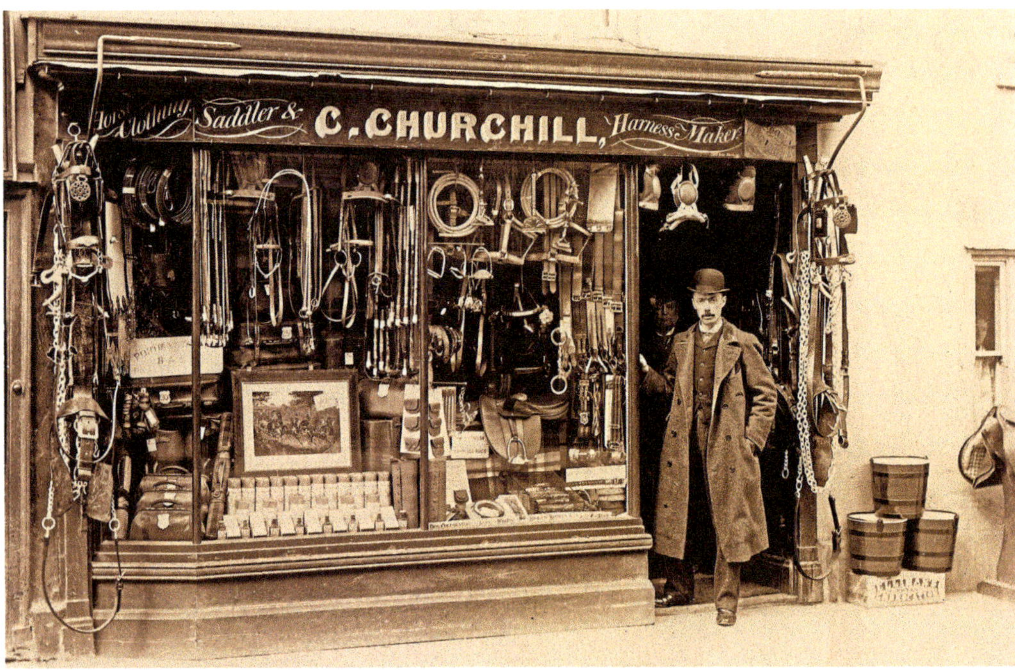

In 1880 Charles Churchill had followed his father as a master saddler at No. 30 High Street in Epsom. His grandfather and great-grandfather had been in the same trade.

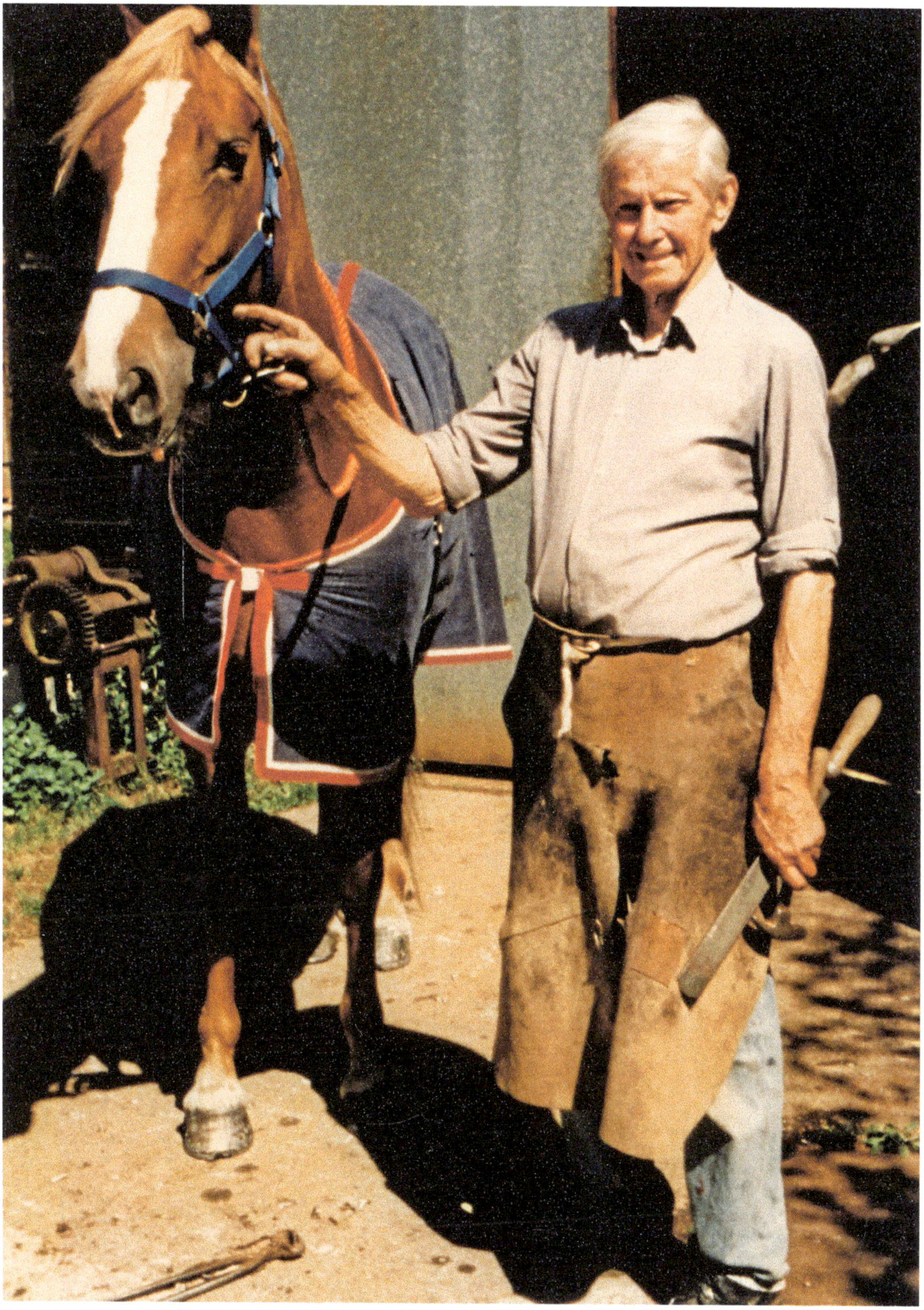

Gordon Ralph was brought up as a farrier by his father. In a long career, he was only ever kicked twice. When he began work, shoeing cost 3/6*d* for a Shire; at the end, £90.

FARMS AND FIELDS

Until 1802 the agricultural land of Ewell was farmed in the time-honoured ways, in a vast open field divided into unfenced blocks. But after a Parliamentary Act for enclosure, the old landscape was fenced up into separate holdings. Some medieval farmhouses remained in use, among them Fitznells and Rectory Farm. Others, such as Longdown and Priest Hill, were built on the newly enclosed land. The Great Park of Nonsuch Palace, which extended across the London Road into what is now Stoneleigh, had already been divided into separate farms in 1731. Epsom continued under the old system, although piecemeal enclosure took place as landowners acquired contiguous strips, and the old fields were not enclosed until 1870.

Victorian Epsom was still very rural. The Surrey Agricultural Association was founded here in 1829 and continued to meet in the town throughout the rest of the century, holding livestock shows and sheep-shearing competitions on Fair Green. At West Street School in Ewell, the children were regularly excused so that they could go gleaning after harvest. They also absented themselves for haymaking, potato picking and gathering acorns for the family pig.

The nearby suburbs of London relied on support from agricultural land. Sparrow Farm in Worcester Park provided winter pasture for the delivery horses of R. White's, the soft drinks manufacturers. There was a market for specialist crops like herbs, Edward Martin grew and distilled mint at Nonsuch Court Farm, where local people used to buy his strong mint water to stave off winter colds. Joe Lavender of Cherry Orchard Farm did some market gardening, kept pigs and took a dairy cart around the village. The most successful dairy farm was run by the Curtises, who had moved to Horton in 1886 where they eventually ran all three of the farms into which the estate was divided. By 1910 they had moved to Fitznells Farm on the edge of Ewell village and their herd of fifty Guernseys provided top-quality milk, despatched for outer London by pony cart every afternoon.

North Looe Farm was bought up by Surrey County Council for conversion into smallholdings, and these were made available just after the First World War, when many ex-servicemen hoped to make an independent living, although increasing mechanisation was making it difficult for the small farmer to compete. The first tractors in the area, which only had one wheel in front, on a steering pole, were demonstrated at Ewell Court Farm in 1919. But over the next ten years it became obvious that the future for land lay in speculative building and not in agriculture.

The Second World War interrupted the spread of development as a home supply of food became vital. Girls from the Women's Land Army gathered every morning at the Clock Tower for the lorries that would take them to farms as far apart as Ashtead and Wimbledon. Others felled trees on the Surrey Hills, and there were attempts (not very successful) to grow potatoes on Epsom Common.

Meanwhile horticulture was increasing in importance. In the 1820s nursery gardens had been laid out by Messrs Young at the foot of East Street, where they grew the first commercial bananas in England. In 1860 these grounds had been taken over by the Scotsman George Dods, who built new greenhouses – some for the cultivation of Australian and South African exotics, some for geraniums and specimen plants.

At the local mansions, gardening was carried out on a grand scale: at Bourne Hall in the 1870s, James Child was responsible for a cucumber house, melon house, fernery, pineapple pits and four vineries. There was competition among gardeners to grow the best and earliest fruit, and at Woodcote Park the vineries had rack and pinion arrangements on the windows, so that these could be winched up and down to control temperature. At Nonsuch Mansion House two gardeners were kept busy stoking fires for the orchid house.

But the future lay in the small gardens that were springing up with suburban development. Frank Giles, the son of a carter at Green Man Farm, took over the old nursery site in East Street after serving in the First World War. He had thirty-six staff who carried out street planting for the council on the new estates at Ewell Downs and Woodcote, while shrubs and bedding plants were grown for landscaping their gardens. Many of the men were called up for the Second World War and the nurseries were made over to food production. But Frank's son Maurice revived the firm in 1948 and it remained active until the end of the century.

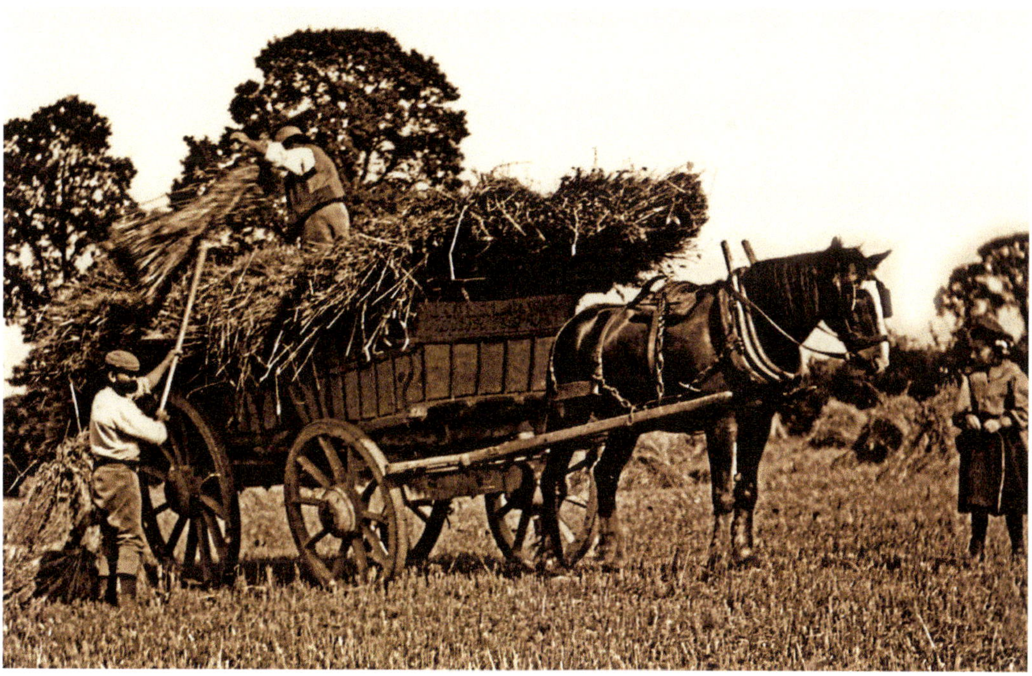

Harvest at Ruxley Farm. A younger man is pitching the sheaves; his older companion stacks them on a box waggon borrowed for the day from Epsom.

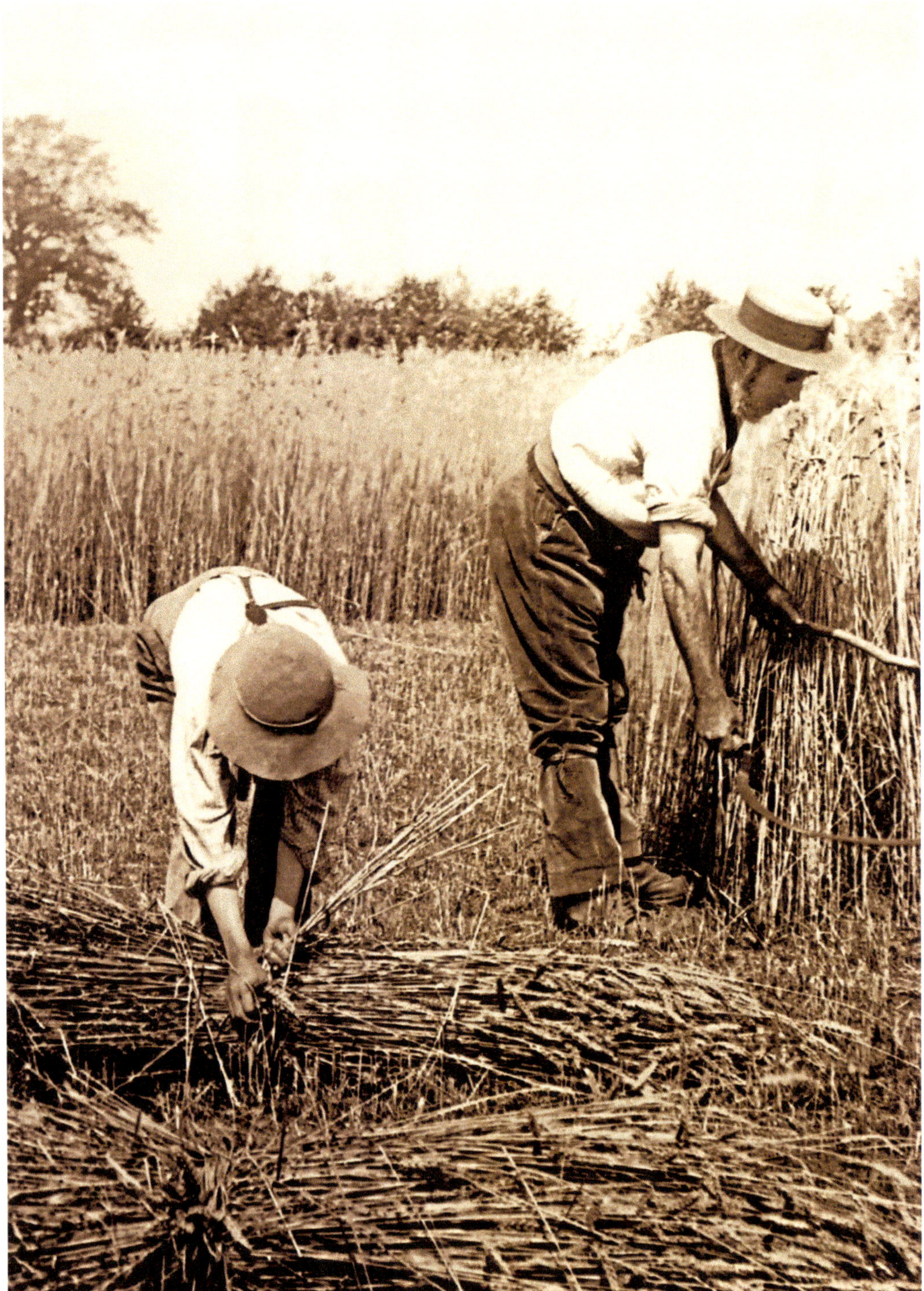

Harvest at Ruxley Farm, c.1890. The man in front is gathering wheat with a bent stick and cutting it with a fagging hook, while his companion binds the sheaves.

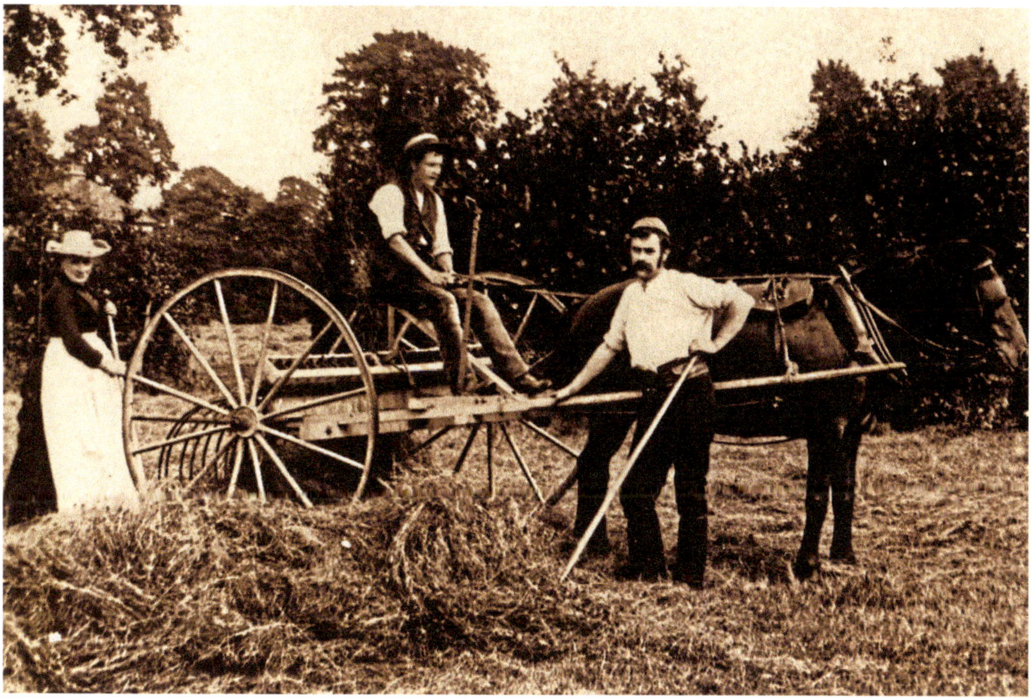

Haymaking at Poplar Farm off Chessington Road, c.1890. This looks like a family effort, helped by the horse-drawn dump rake – an early make with more wood than metal.

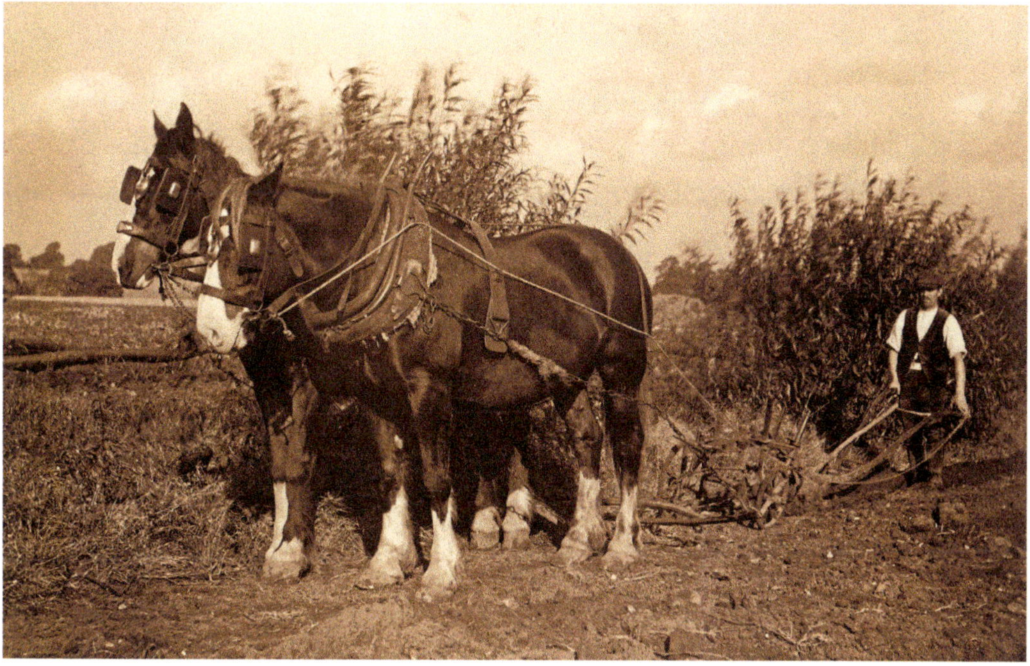

Trevor White with a two-horse plough at Poplar Farm, 1913. Hundred acres of poor strong clay, originally common land, were farmed here by Walter Hemming.

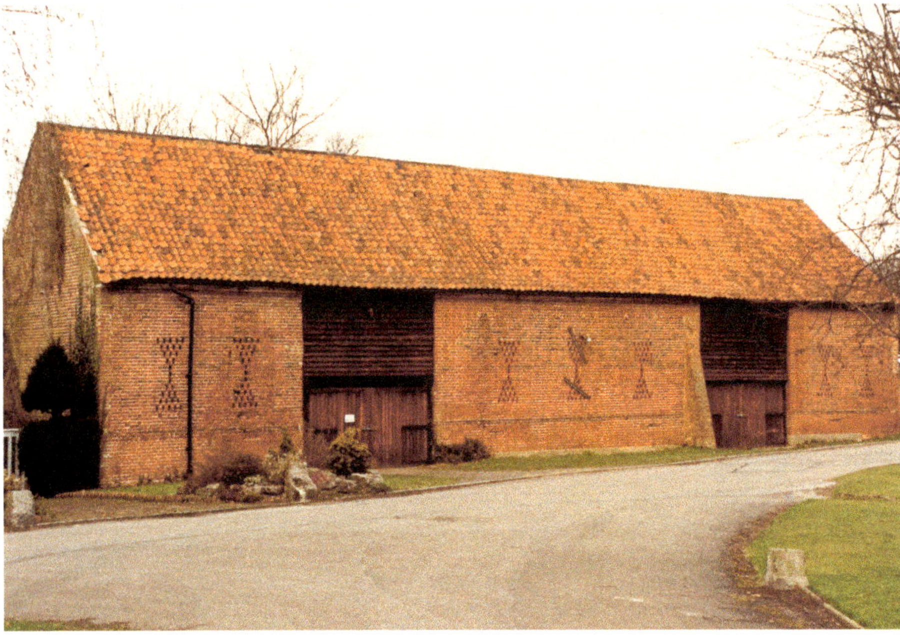

The estate barn at Woodcote Park was built in 1770 for George Nelson, who had just purchased the mansion house. It is five bays long with a catslide roof at the back.

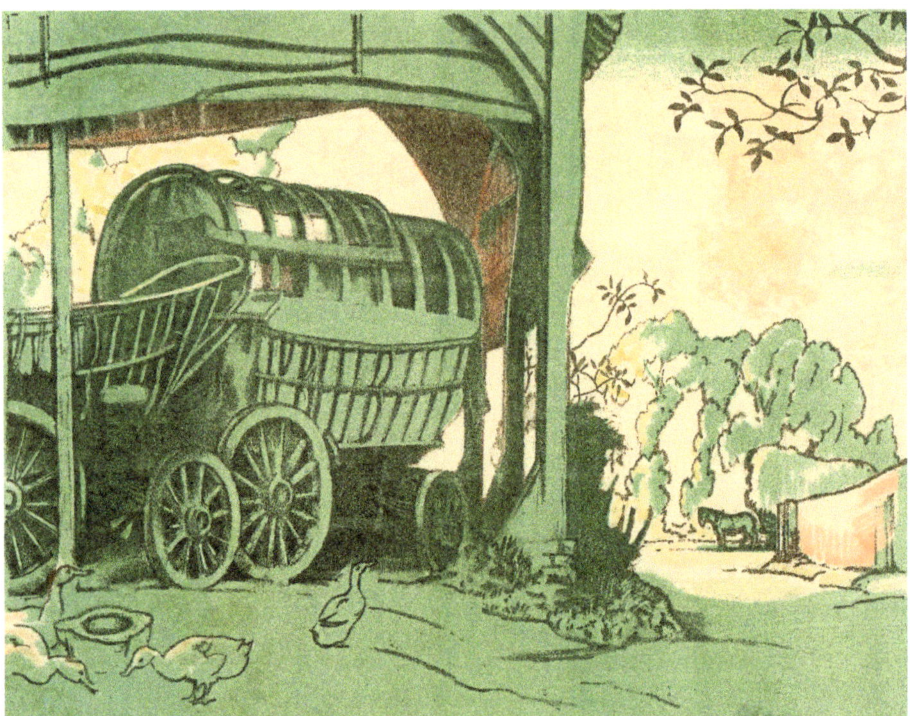

Waggons from the Upper Mill in Ewell, drawn by Arthur Laird in the 1920s. Ducks feed from an old stone mortar, while a loaded haywain is coming up Kingston Road.

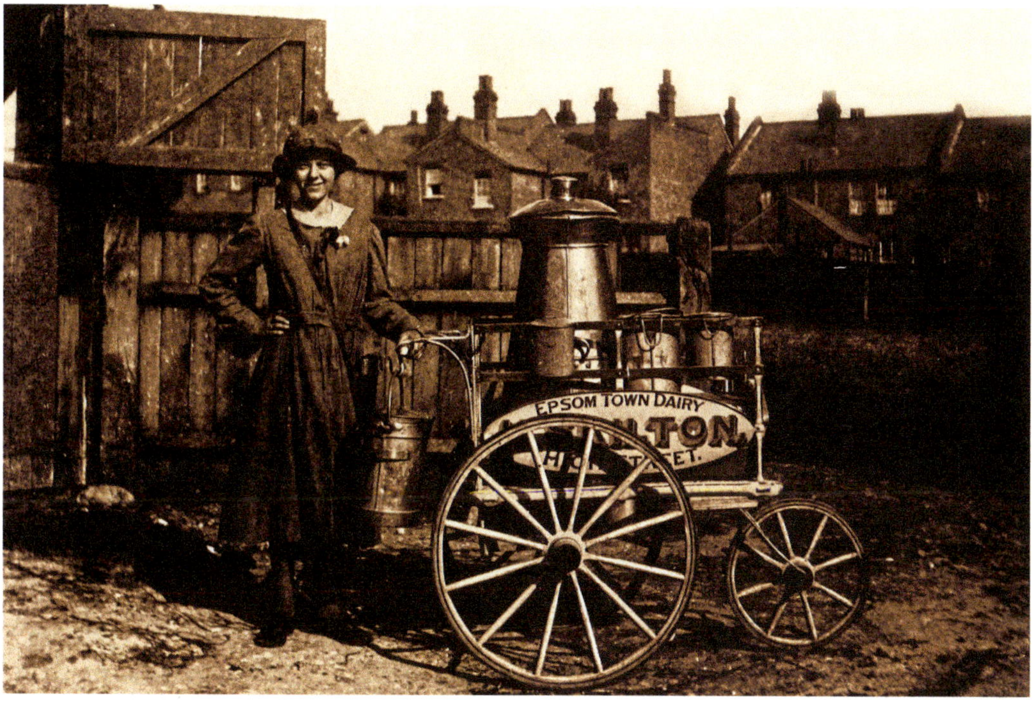

During the war, women took over milk deliveries: Nellie Herridge worked for Skilton's dairy in Alexandra Road. She got up at five o'clock each day for £1 a week.

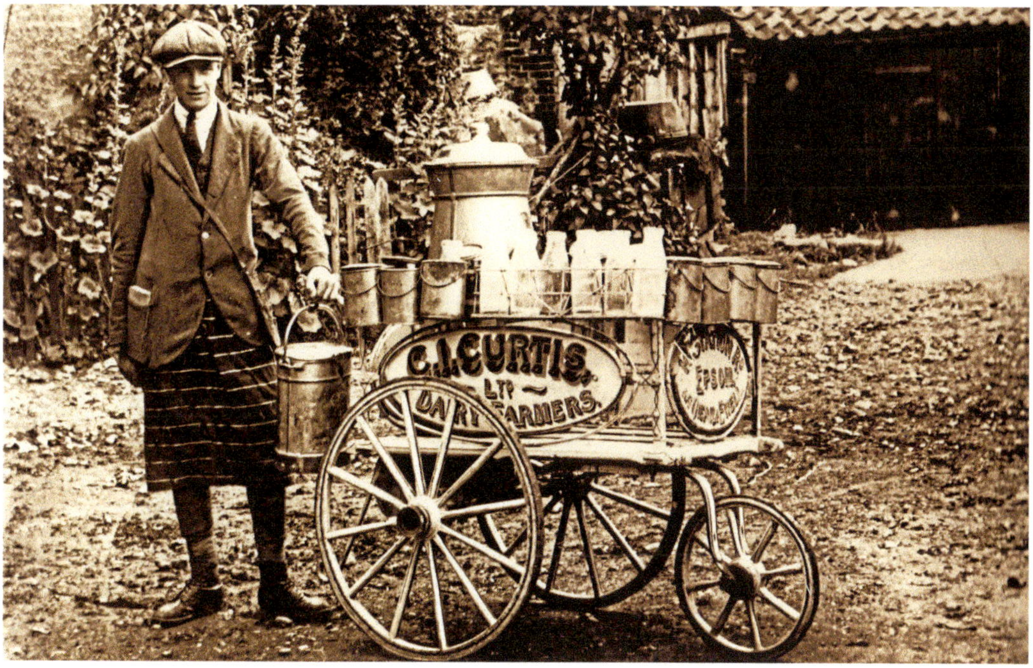

'A glass of Curtis' milk is a meal in itself', said the advertisement. They were based at Fitznells until it was sold in 1925. Next year United Dairies took over the business.

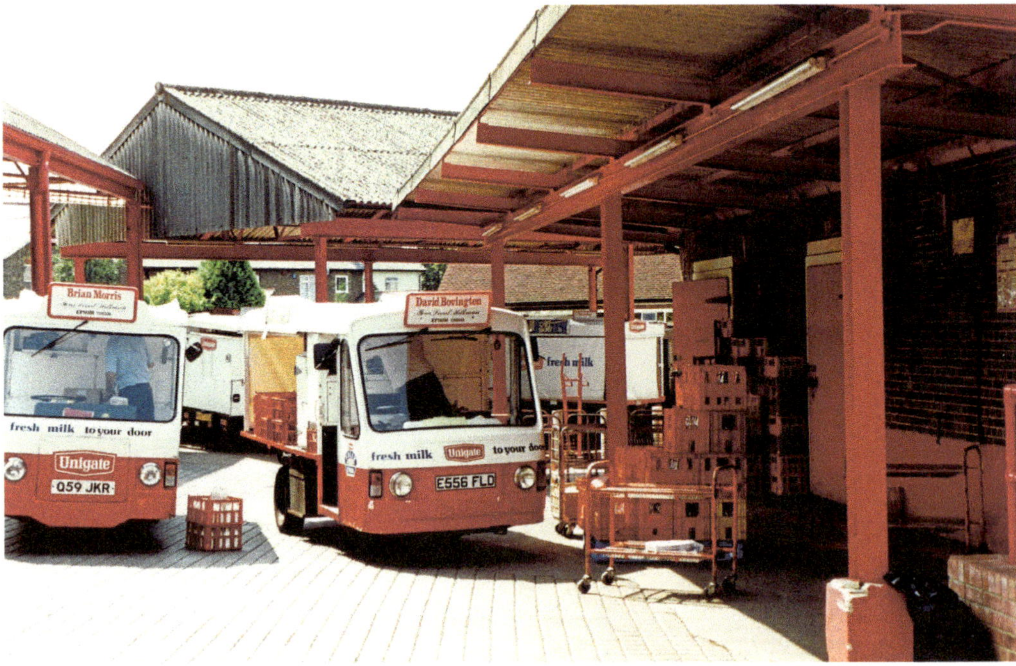

Milk floats at the three Cold Rooms in the Unigate Depot, 1995. This took the place of Skilton's dairy. It closed in 2013, and the business moved to Wimbledon.

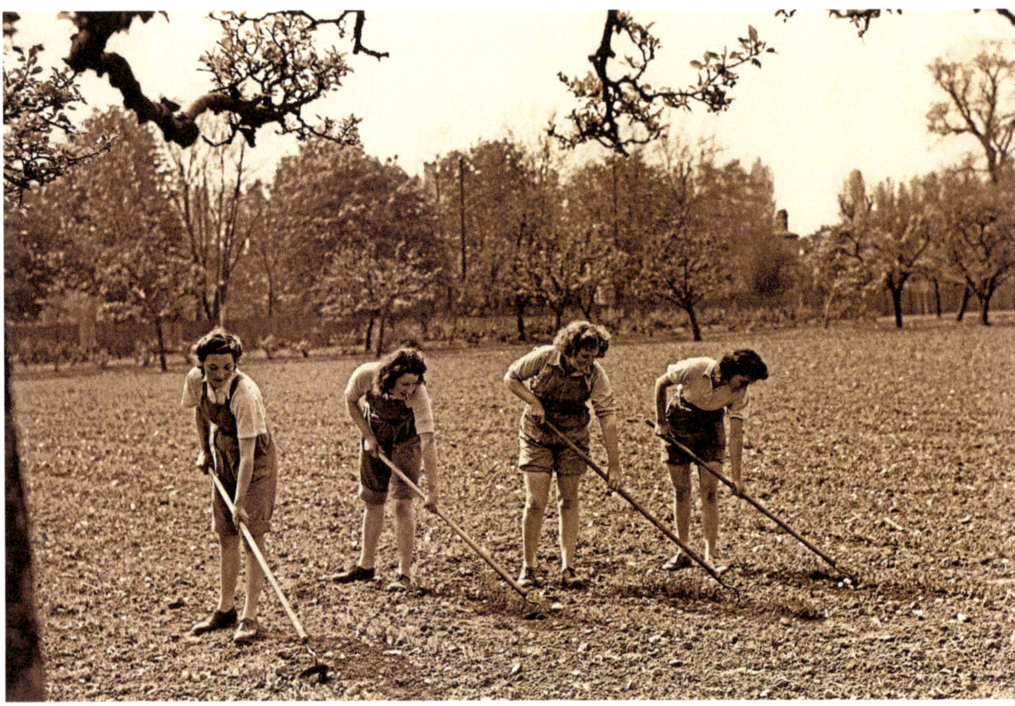

Girls of the Women's Land Army at Horton Farm. From left to right: Paddy Pothill, Hazel Jacobs, Nina Pattison and Pat Dobson. They worked alongside patients from the hospitals.

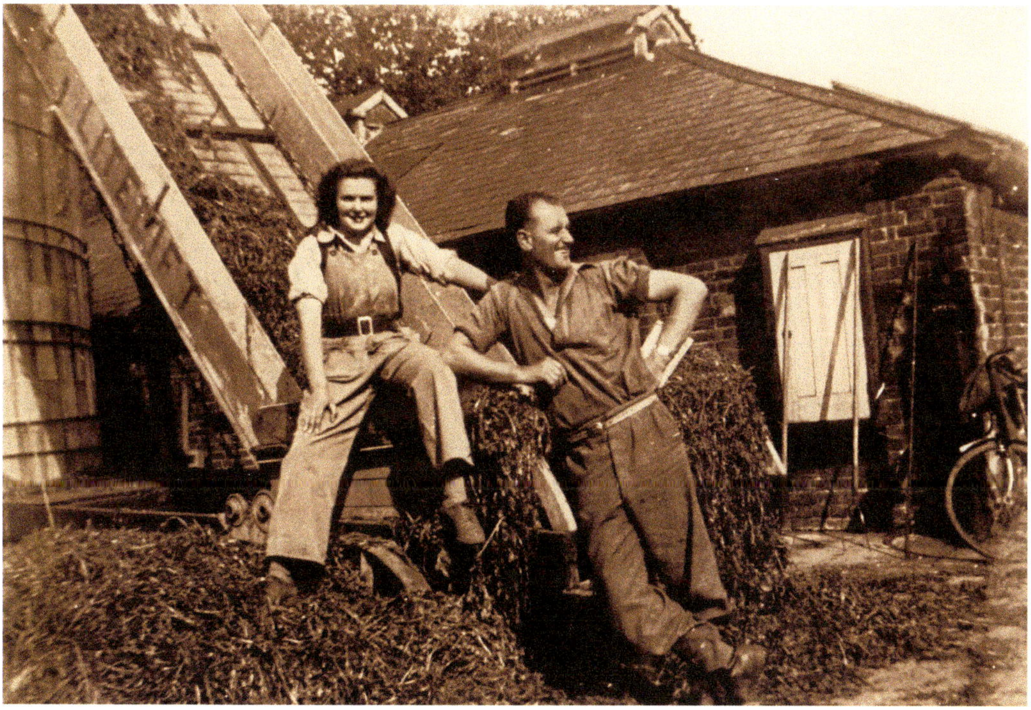

Above: Barbara Knight on the silage heap at Horton Farm, 1946. The Land Girls quickly took to rural life despite backgrounds as an art student, dental nurse and kitchen maid.

Right: Harry and Nobby Wiltshire distributing hay on Epsom Downs – probably to line the crossing at Tattenham Corner, since this was on Nobby's beat as a road sweeper.

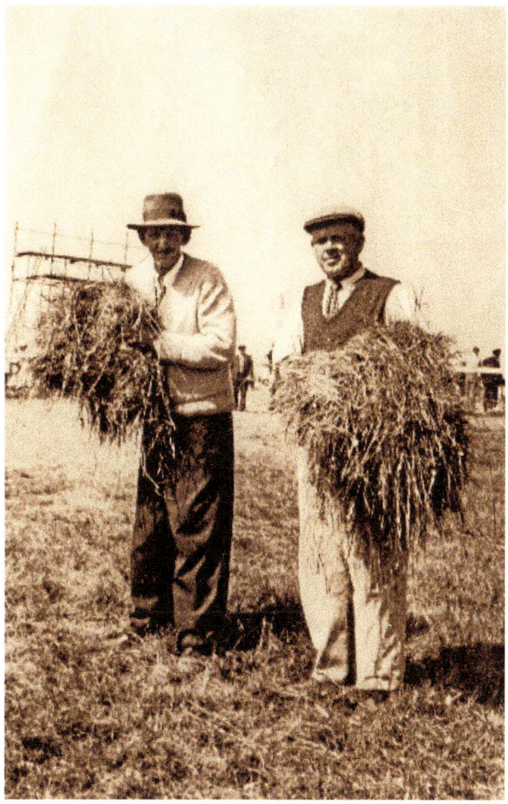

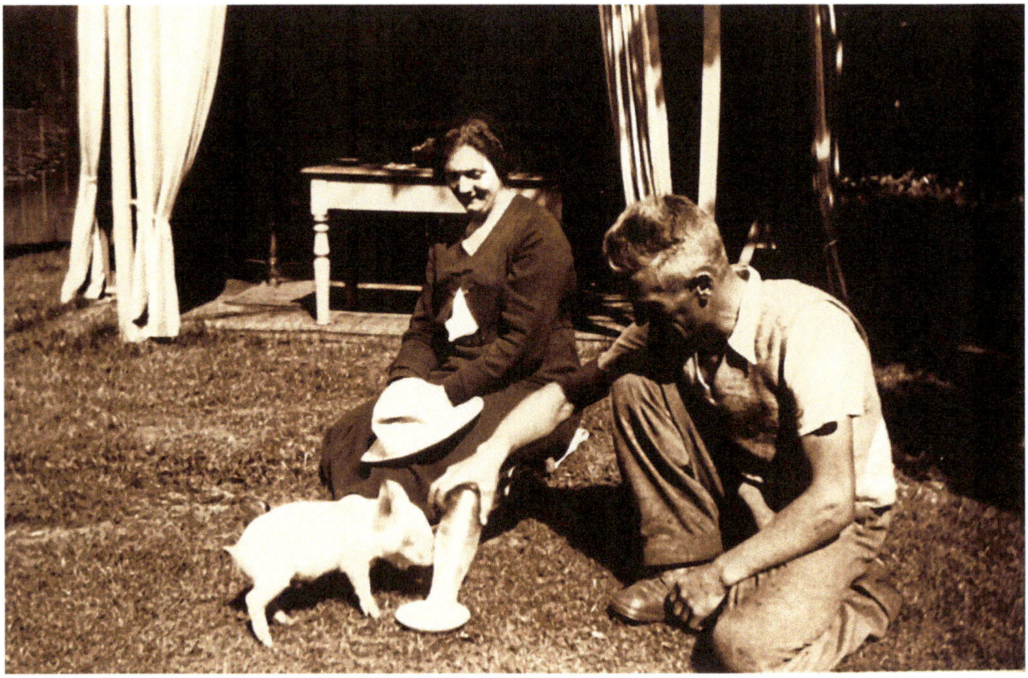

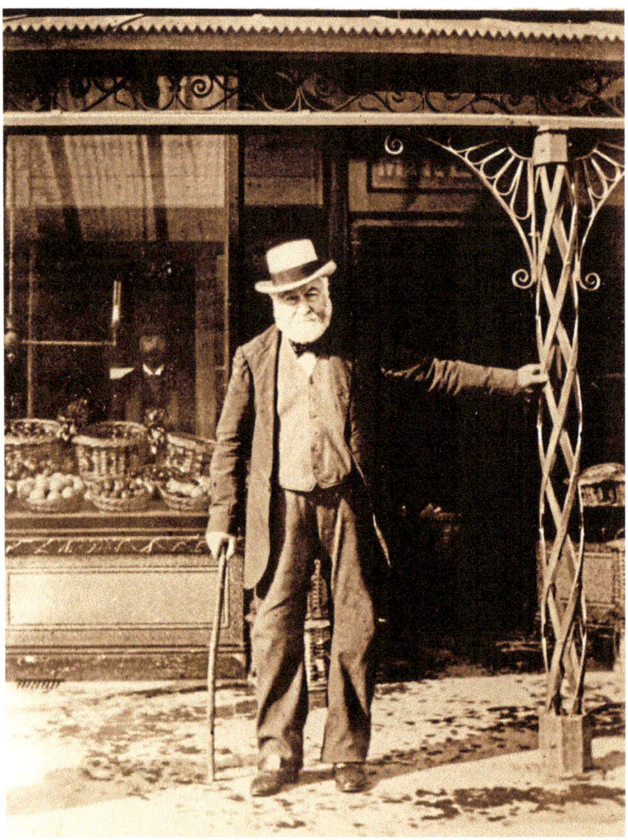

Above: Colin McHardy hand-feeding a piglet at the back of the smallholding at Cefn, off Reigate Road, late 1930s. The piglet came for his daily pinta whenever Colin whistled.

Left: Thomas Miles, the market gardener, outside his shop at No. 84 Epsom High Street. He had a sideline selling large rhubarb leaves to act as sunshades on Derby Day.

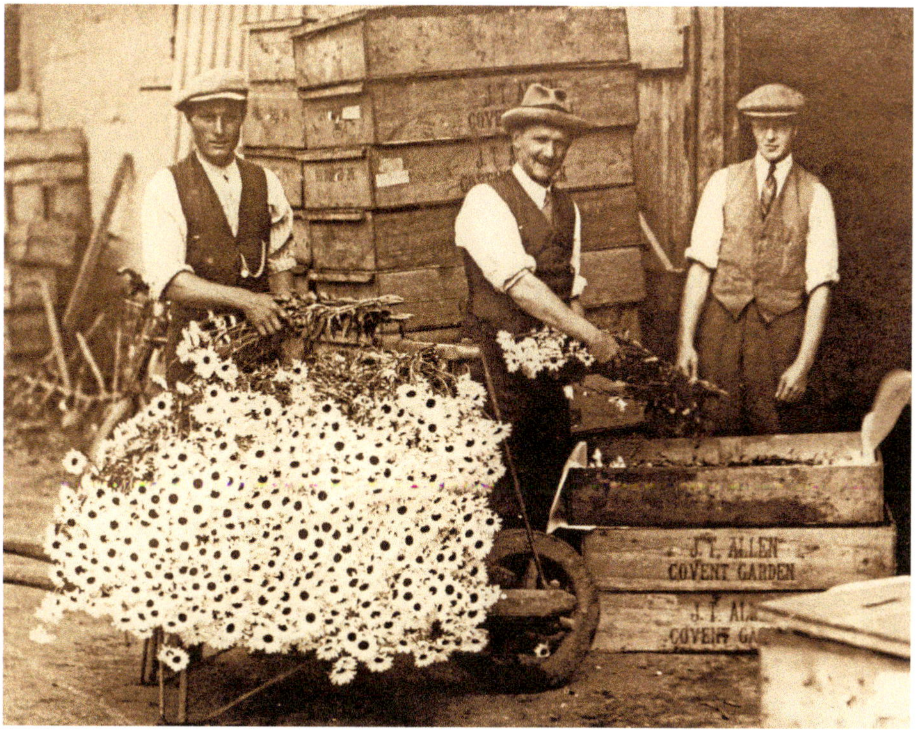

Packing *Argyranthemum* for Covent Garden at the nursery in Ruxley Lane. When business started in 1924, the lane was unsurfaced and a ford ran though the Hogsmill.

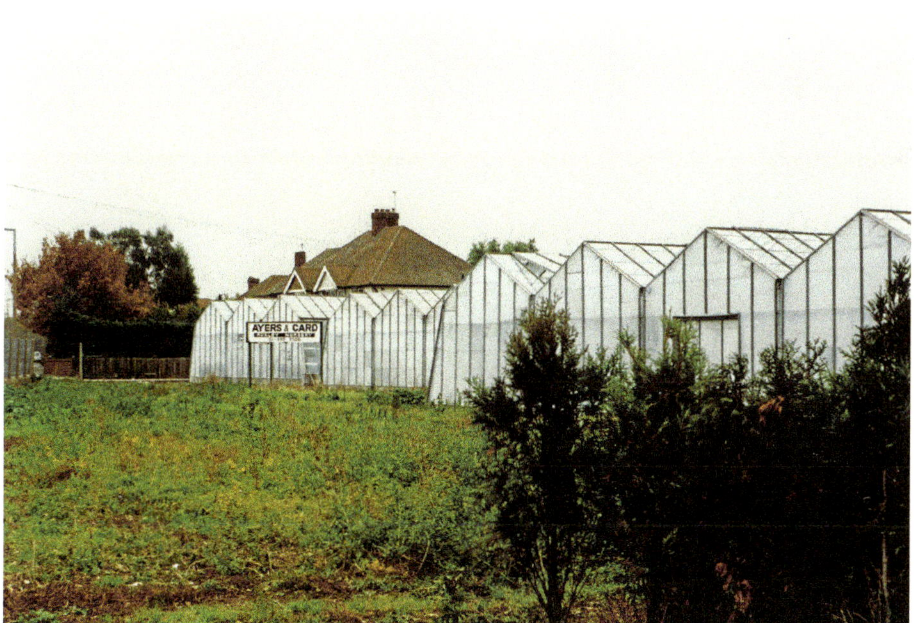

Ayers and Card Nursery in Ruxley Lane closed in 1993, leaving a legacy of street names in a nearby development – Lavender Road, Larkspur Way and Orchard Close.

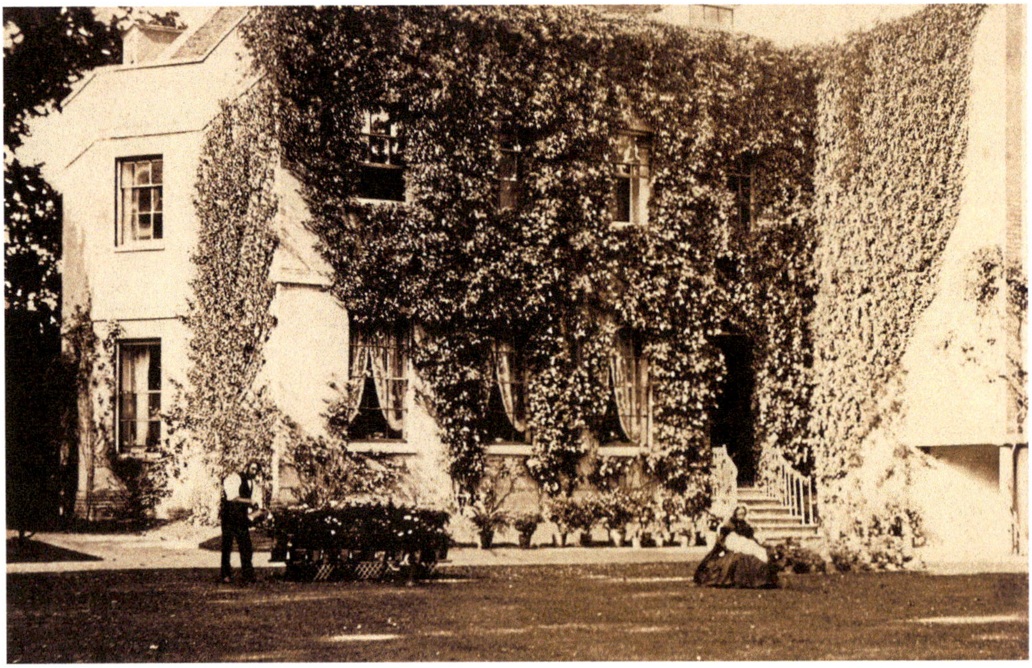

A gardener at Woodcote End House, c.1870. Doctors at this house – Thomas Graham and William Daniel – took in patients with mental disorders. Tranquil gardens were therapeutic.

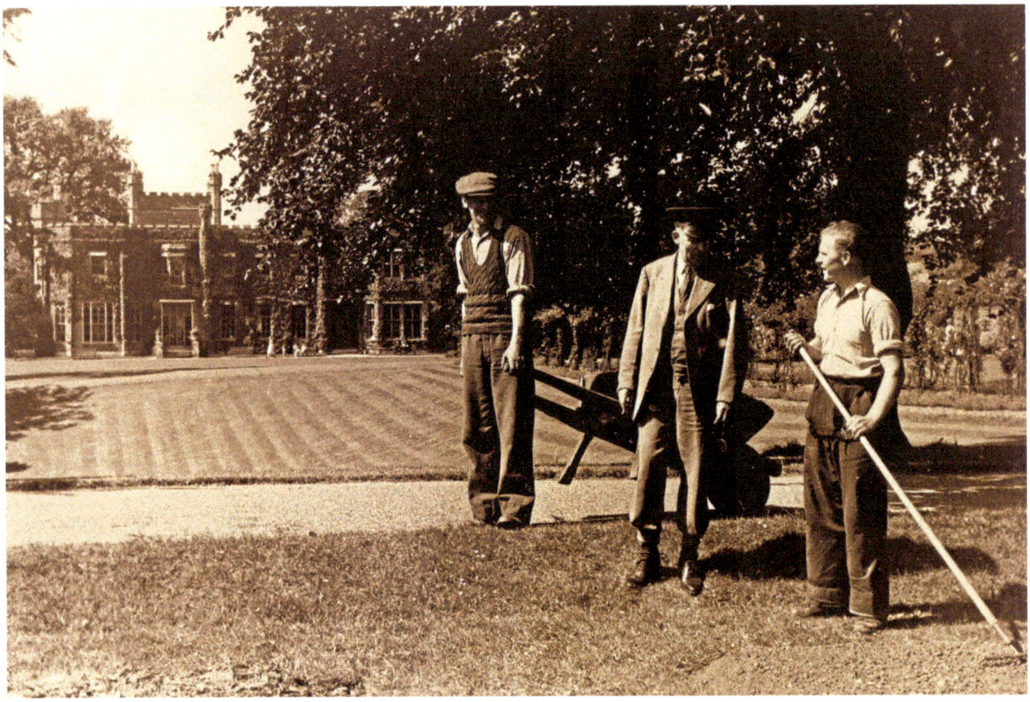

Jim Jones, the superintendent, talking to gardeners at Nonsuch Mansion House. The park, owned for a century by the Farmer family, had been made public in 1937.

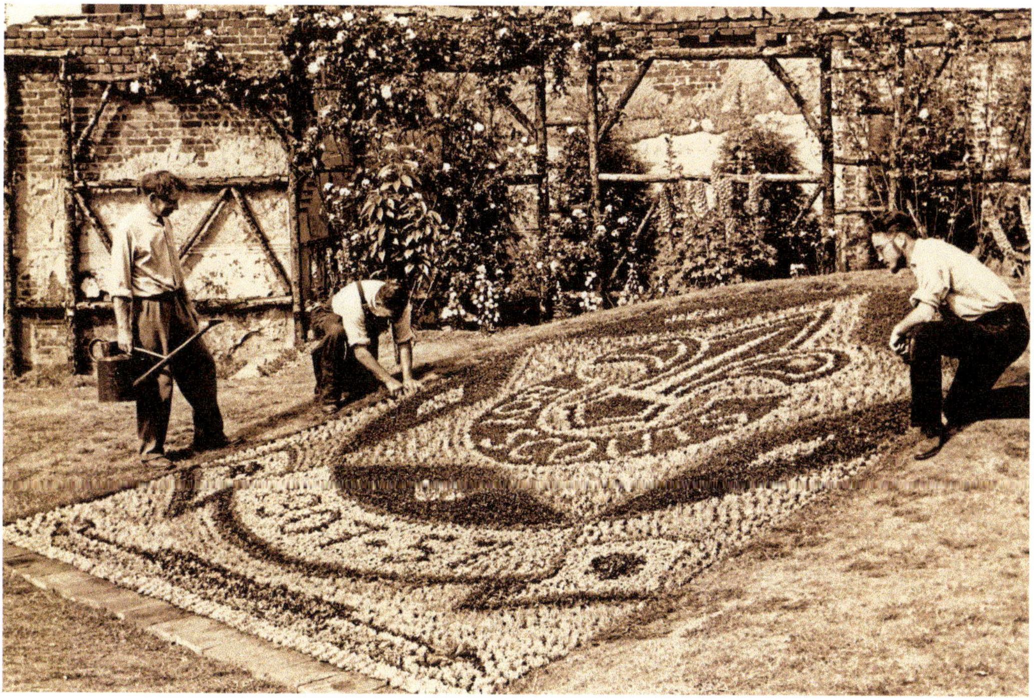

Carpet bedding in 1957 at the Gertrude Longhurst gardens in Ewell High Street, on land presented to the council after the Congregational church moved from the site.

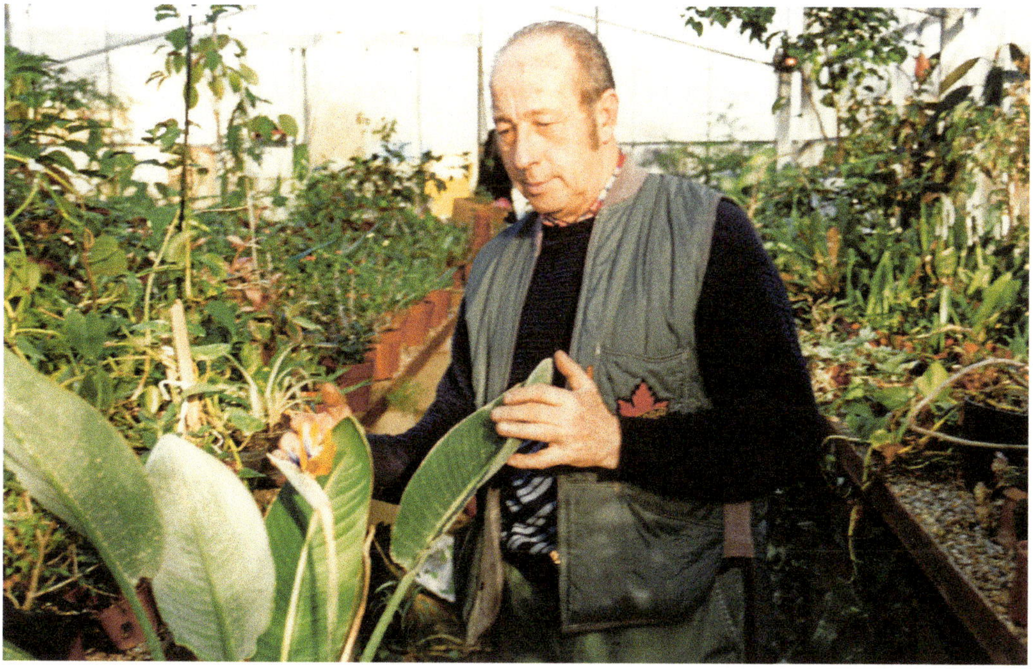

Greenhouses at Horton Hospital in 1989, five years before closure. Once the hospital grew its own food (100,000 cabbages a year), but by the 1960s this had been run down.

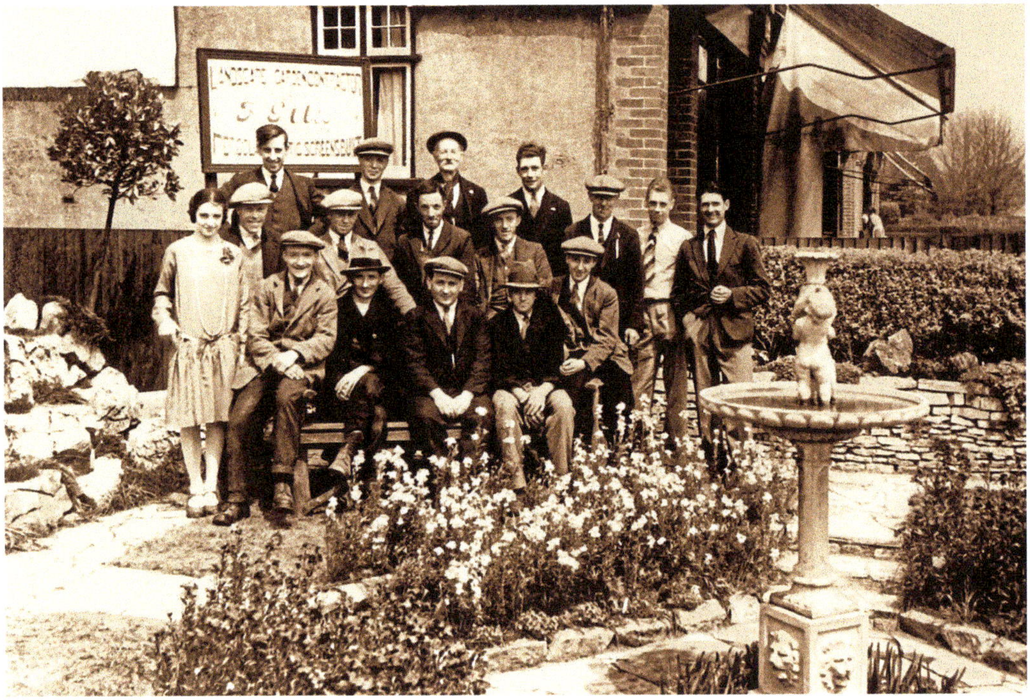

Frank Giles and his staff outside No. 119 East Street, soon after he took over the nursery business in 1934. Wages were 1/3*d* an hour for foremen and 1*s* for other hands.

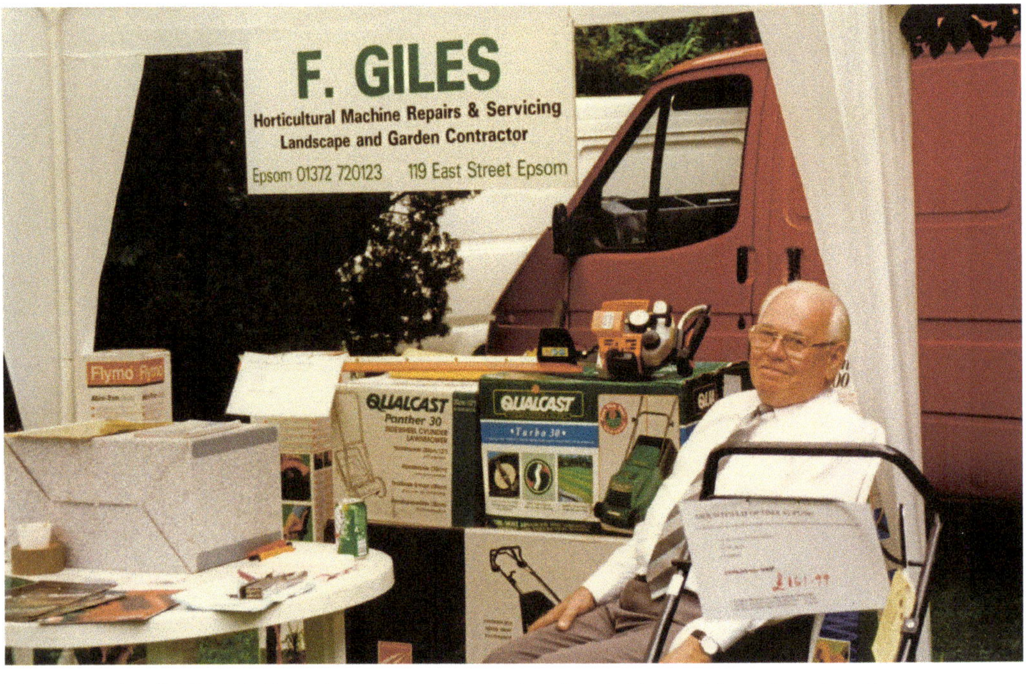

Maurice Giles (1927–2010) took over from his father Frank. He could scythe a bowling green and cut turf by hand all day. 'Lord! They don't know what work is now.'

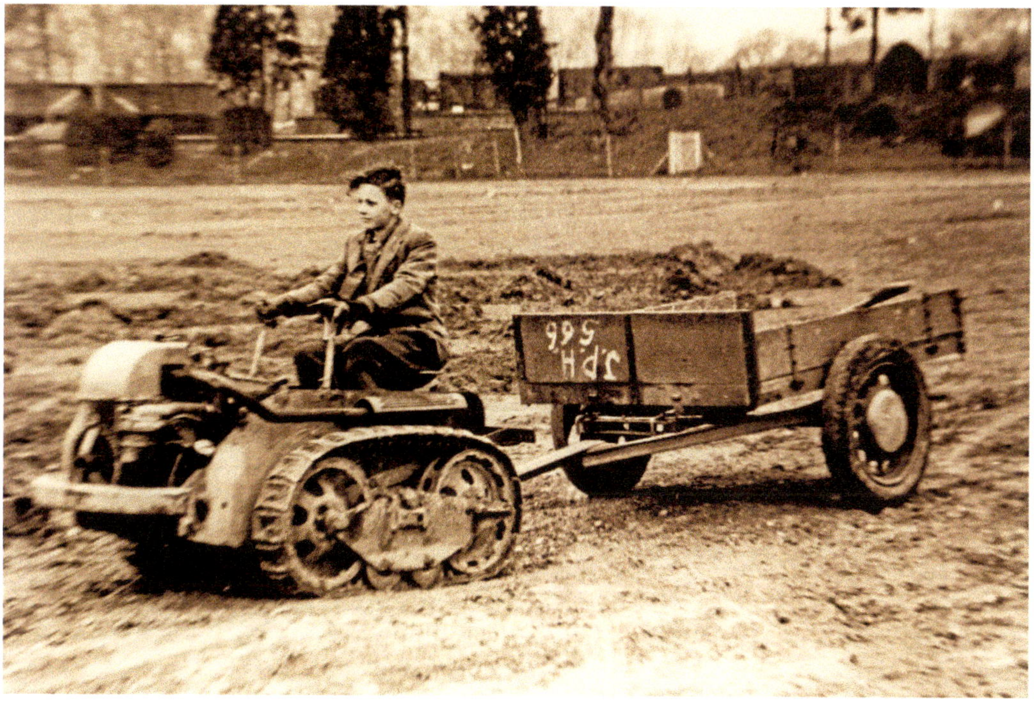

In 1934 Basil Seymour joined his father's market garden at Elmslie Gardens, doing landscape design. The first contract was for sports grounds at Westminster Hospital.

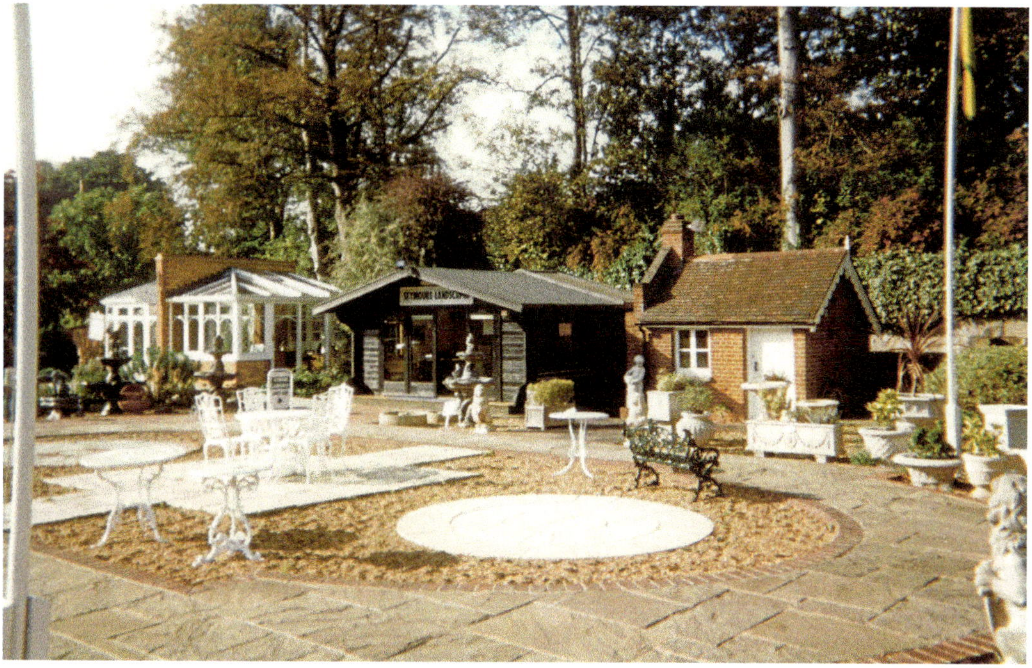

Seymour's Garden Centre at Cheam Road in 1995, when after forty years the business moved from Cheam Road to Cobham. They were regulars at the Chelsea Flower Show.

SAFE AS HOUSES

Until Tudor times all building in Epsom and Ewell was timber-framed, with smaller cottages built in two or three bays and the larger farmhouses laid out in the Wealden style. It was the discovery of Epsom Spa which changed the town, bringing in summer visitors and encouraging City merchants to build their country houses nearby.

From the 1680s, builders worked in the Georgian style to provide these newcomers with mansions, places of entertainment and lodging houses; their banisters, pilasters and architraves were indistinguishable from contemporary work in London. Some of them had moved from the metropolis to take advantages of this boom, like David White who died in 1725 and 'left the Poor his heirs', bequeathing the money he had made from development for the education of children in Epsom, Ewell, Ashtead and Leatherhead.

After the collapse of Spa life in the 1720s, Epsom dwindled back into a village. Though fine properties remained for the gentry, the poor lived in cheap weather-boarded houses, sealed against the rain with black tar. Henry Andrews reported to an enquiry in 1849 that 'a large proportion of the smaller houses in Epsom are badly built, with reference either to comfort or durability. I should think one-third of the houses in Epsom are built of wood'.

After this, a Local Board of Health laid down planning requirements. Until the First World War, most of the development was in the hands of jobbing builders, who would put up one house, sell it on and invest the profits in the next. For a regular income, they relied on repairs and services. The Chuter Brothers, if their advertisements of the 1860s are to be trusted, could build a house, paint it, paper the walls, make or retail the furniture, and then fix the roof as well. George Goodship and Robert Saunders established themselves in some old cottages off Ewell High Street in 1903, rebuilding the adjoining property as a long workroom. Here they soldered plumbing, cut up wallpaper and made coffins, as opportunity arose.

With trade practices like this, technical innovation was rare, although in the 1870s Thomas Furniss used reinforced concrete to build some shops at No. 26/8 West Street in Epsom. He had lived in America as a young man, and brought back a can-do attitude – finding that there was no supply of reinforcing rods in England, he threw in old bicycles and abandoned bedsteads instead. The boundaries between business, public and family life were negotiable. When trade was slack in 1900, James Cropley of Church Road built Dean Estate in Ashtead and then moved several of his men in as tenants, so that he wouldn't lose them. The rent was set at 7/6*d*, which was uneconomic, but he saw the buildings as an asset for the family rather than invested capital.

The first large-scale development came in 1898 after the estate at Horton had been purchased by the London County Council as a site for mental hospitals. First the old manor house was converted, then new asylums were built at Horton, the Epileptic Colony (afterwards St Ebba's) and Long Grove. At the peak of activity in 1905 around 1,100 men were at work, some 900 of them recruited from the London unemployed and brought down from Waterloo daily in special trains. To discourage them from hanging about in local pubs, their wages (7*d* an hour) were withheld until they were on the railway platform ready for home. At West Park, the final hospital, ground surfaces were levelled with spoil from digging out the London Underground. Work was held up by the First World War and did not finish until 1924.

After the electrification of the newly formed Southern Railway in 1925, the building of large housing estates became financially profitable. Ten years later the development of Worcester Park, Sparrow and Coldharbour Farms created the new suburb of Stoneleigh and brought Ewell into the outer London belt of urbanised land. The rising tide of middle-class housing persuaded owners of the large mansions to sell their properties and move deeper into leafy Surrey – the grounds of Hookfield were developed by the Roll brothers in 1932, and in 1935 Woodcote House was bought by Earnest G. Harwood, who had previously developed the Ewell Downs estate. 'All the natural beauties of the original park are being preserved', he claimed, and certainly something of its exclusivity, since the standard cost of a house here was £1,100 to £1,400. Care was taken to mix and match the architectural elements so that every house looked different. Jack Gleeson, the son of a Sheffield builder, had come south to expand the family business and developed the Nonsuch Court Estate in 1937 for similar prices, although with a more limited range of house types. On the smaller estates, consisting of only one or two streets – Chase Road, Hazon Way, Parklawn Avenue – prices were around half as much, but houses shared the same half-timbered style. Only a few properties in Stoneleigh flirted with concrete modernism.

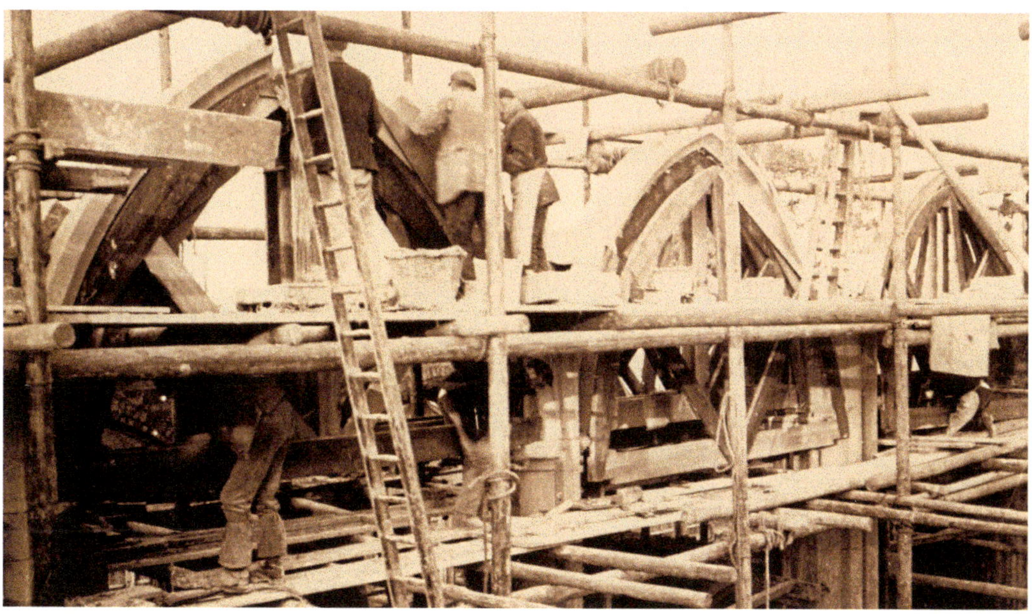

St Barnabas' Church was originally a tin chapel but in 1908 it was rebuilt to a grander design by A. E. Williams using bricks from the Nonsuch Brick Co.

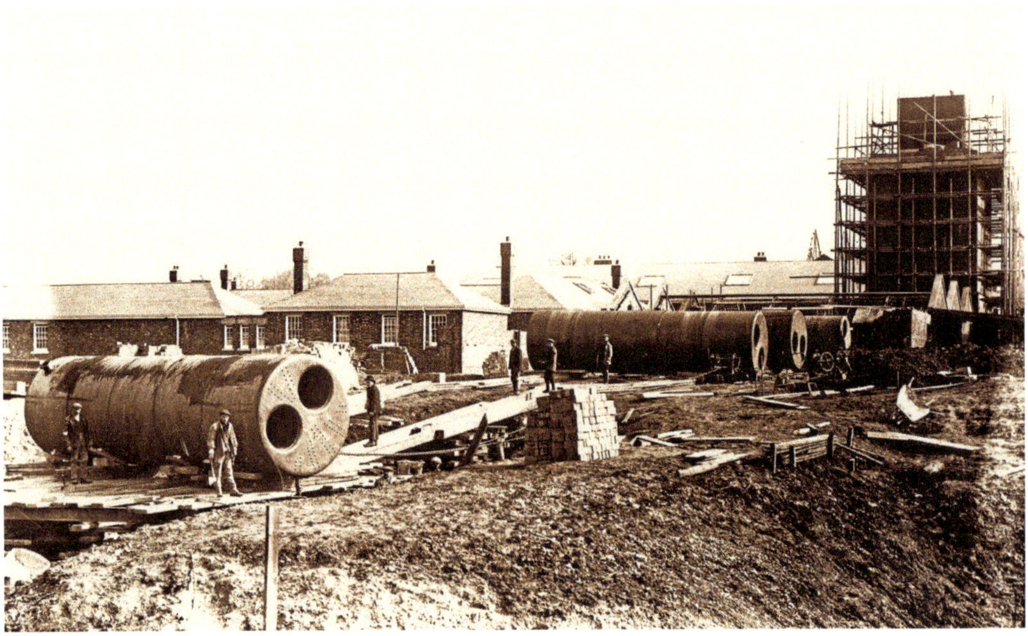

West Park Hospital was the last to be built in the Horton cluster. The 120-foot tower, on a base of blue engineering bricks, was built to accommodate three large water tanks.

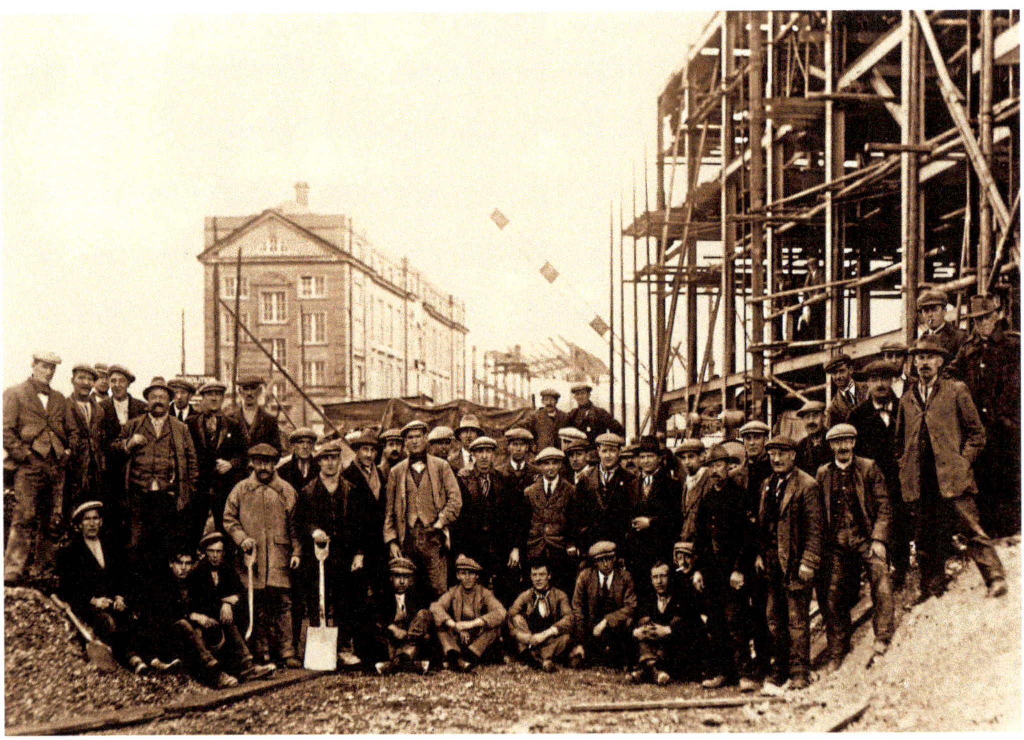

The original 1830 Grandstand was demolished and rebuilt by 400 men between the 1926 and 1927 Derbies, although the General Strike cut off vital supplies of girders.

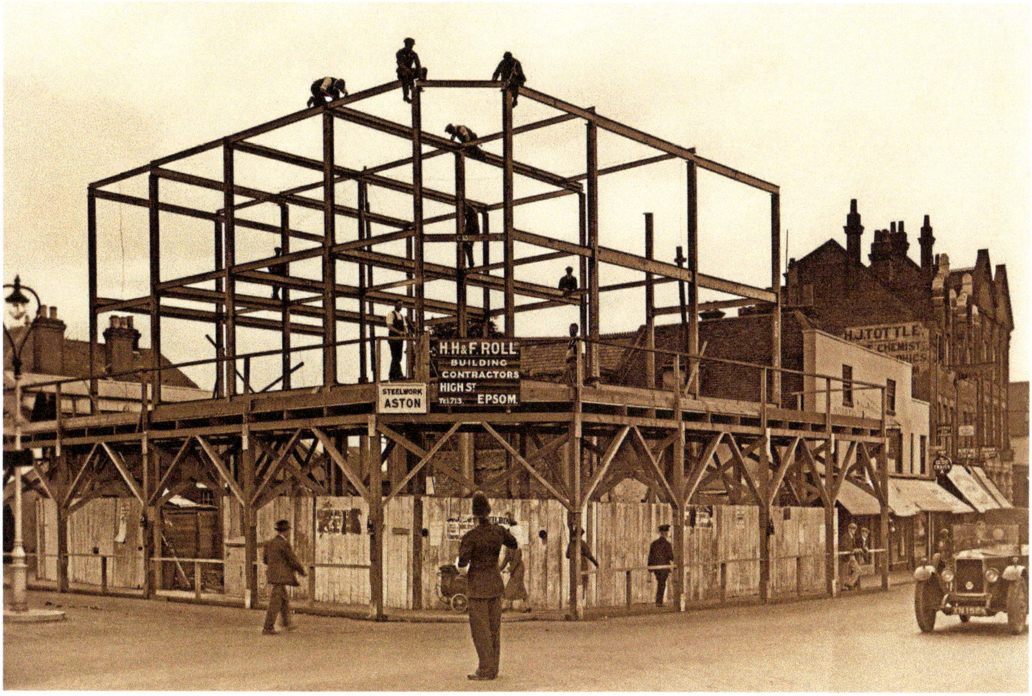

In 1935 Lloyds Bank rebuilt premises on High Street and Waterloo Road. In 1936 Surrey County Council decided to widen the road, and the bank that went up came down.

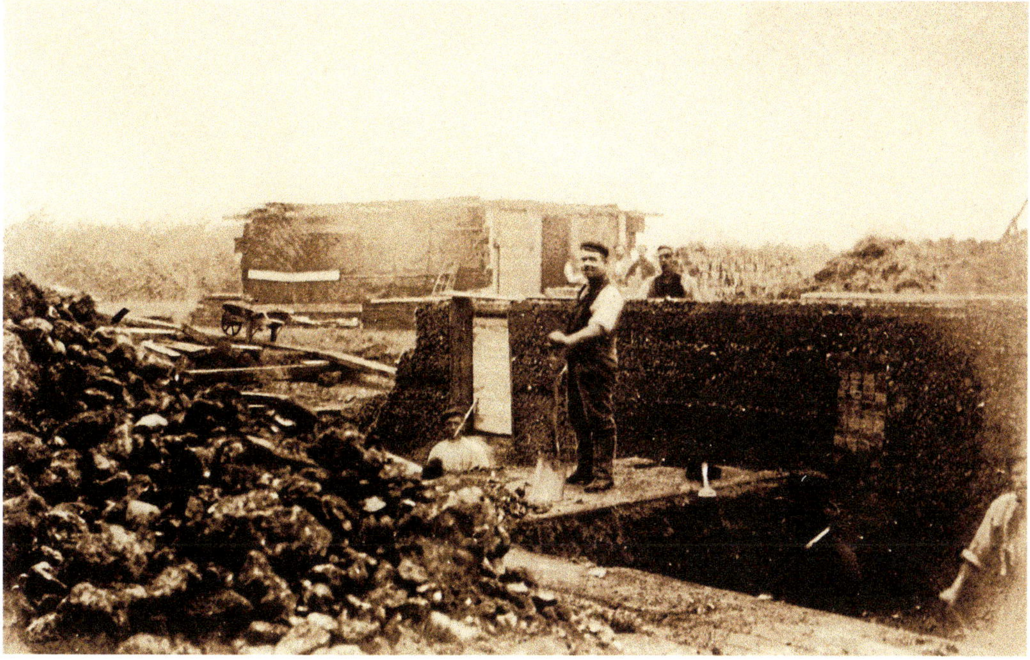

No. 21 Temple Road was the second concrete house to be built in Epsom, in 1899, after the Furniss shop in West Street. It was part of the development of the Chase Estate.

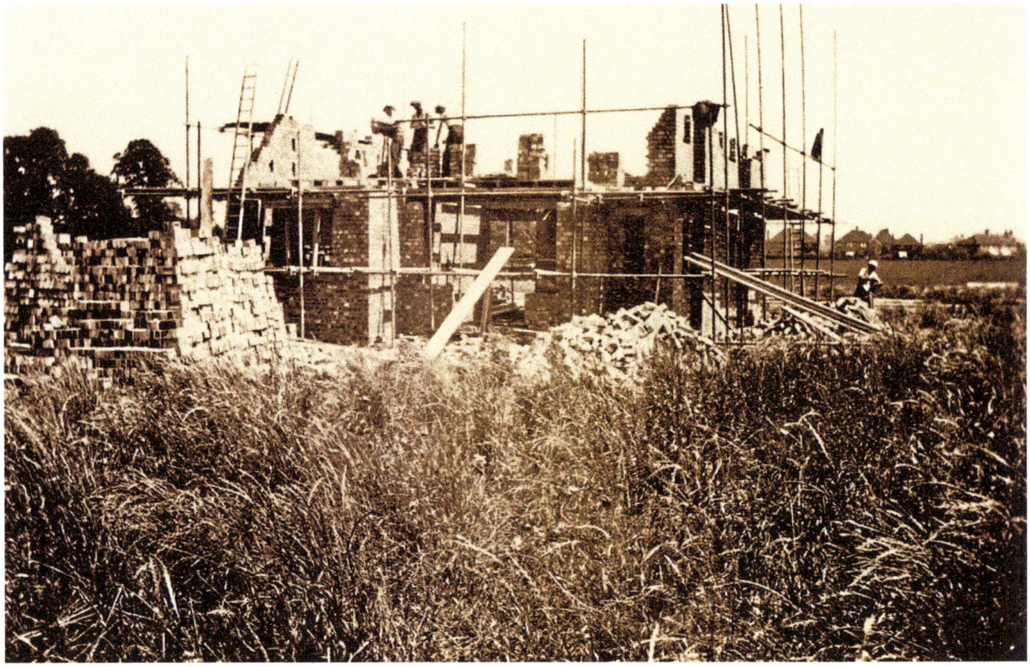

A view of No. 10 Hays Walk in the summer of 1935, three weeks into development. The house was built with a loan from the Temperance and General Provident Institution.

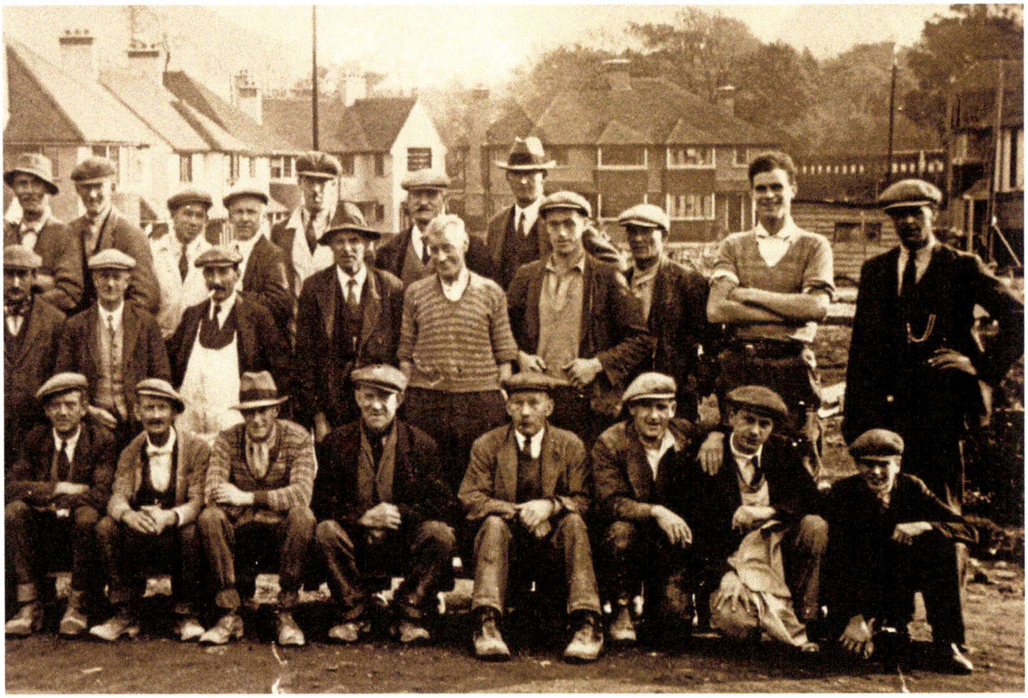

Roll's staff pose on the new Hookfield estate. Harry and Frank Roll took over from their father (of Roll & Taylor), building the Ebbisham Hall and short-lived Lloyds Bank.

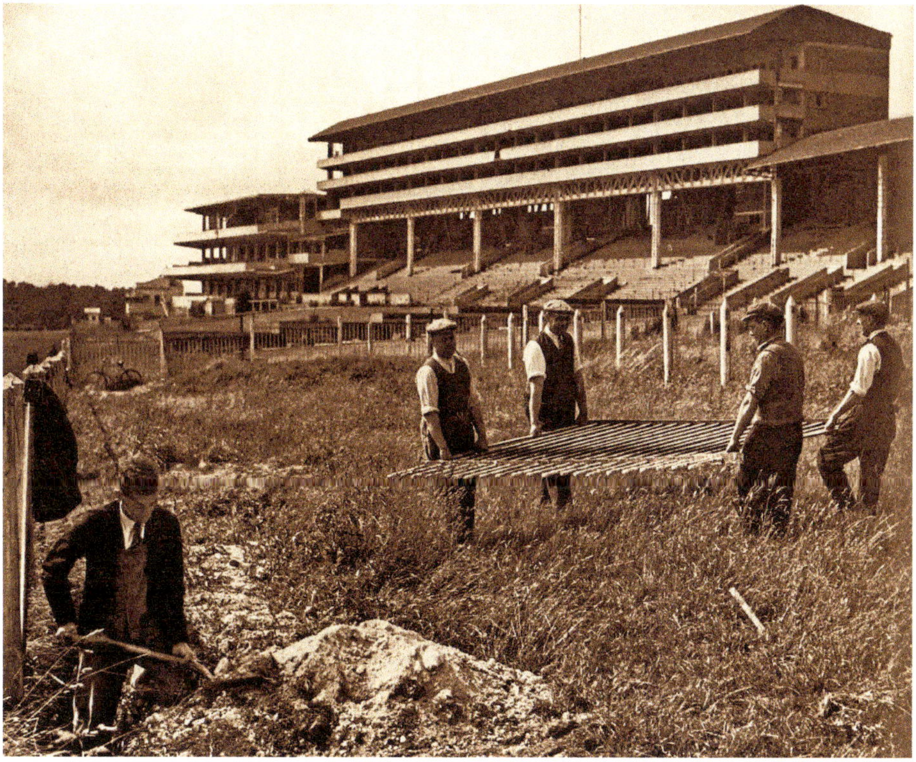

Wartime needs for scrap metal led the council to take 21½ tons of fencing from its parks, and in July 1942, despite protests, railings were removed from the Grandstand.

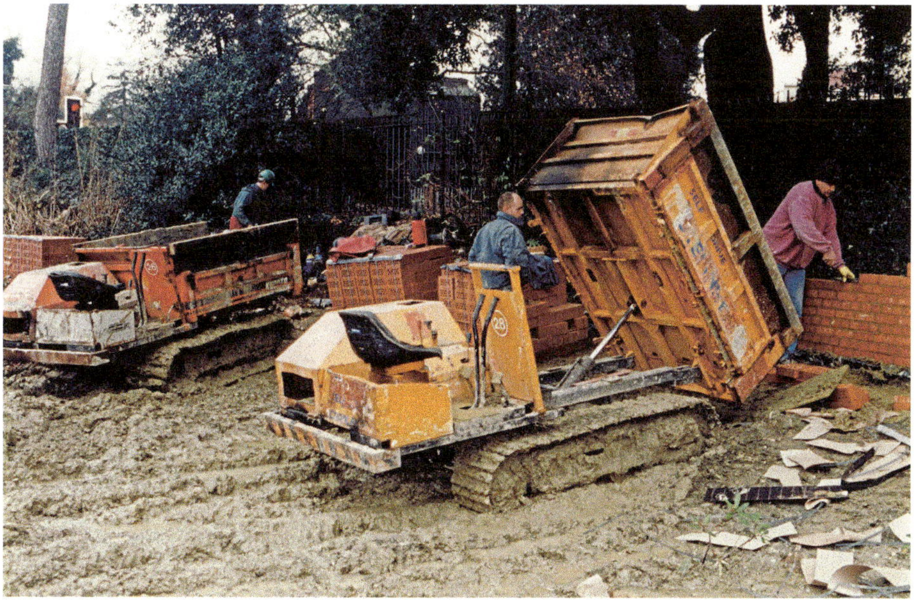

In 1996 the lake at Bourne Hall ran dry. Ecco Construction laid pipes in the subsoil to let the water rise, with a watertight membrane above to prevent it from sinking again.

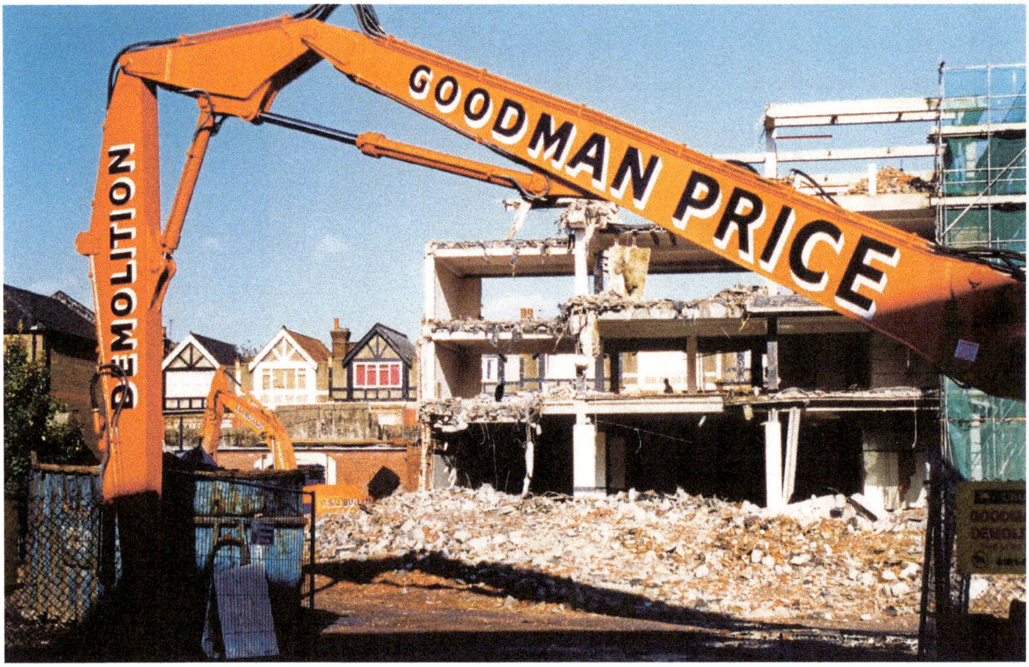

The demolition of Epsom's first supermarket, the 1960s Gateway in Upper High Street. It was replaced by an eight-screen, 2,000-seat Odeon, which opened in 1999.

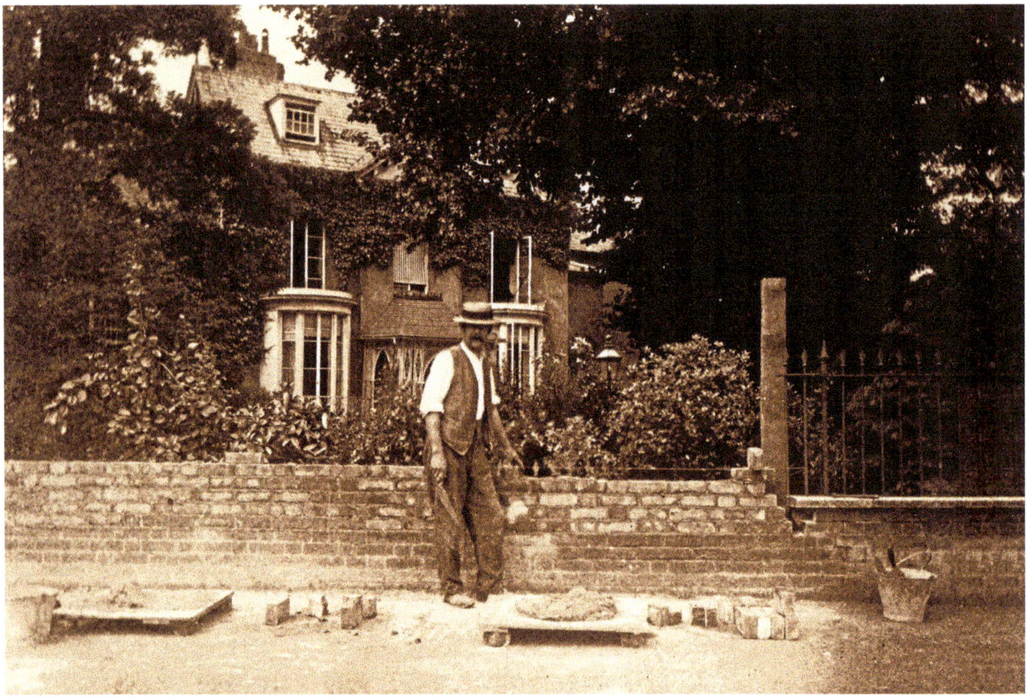

Fred Palmer, the bricklayer of North Looe Villas walling The Grange (formerly The Elms) in London Road. Demolished after the war, this site is now St Mary's Close.

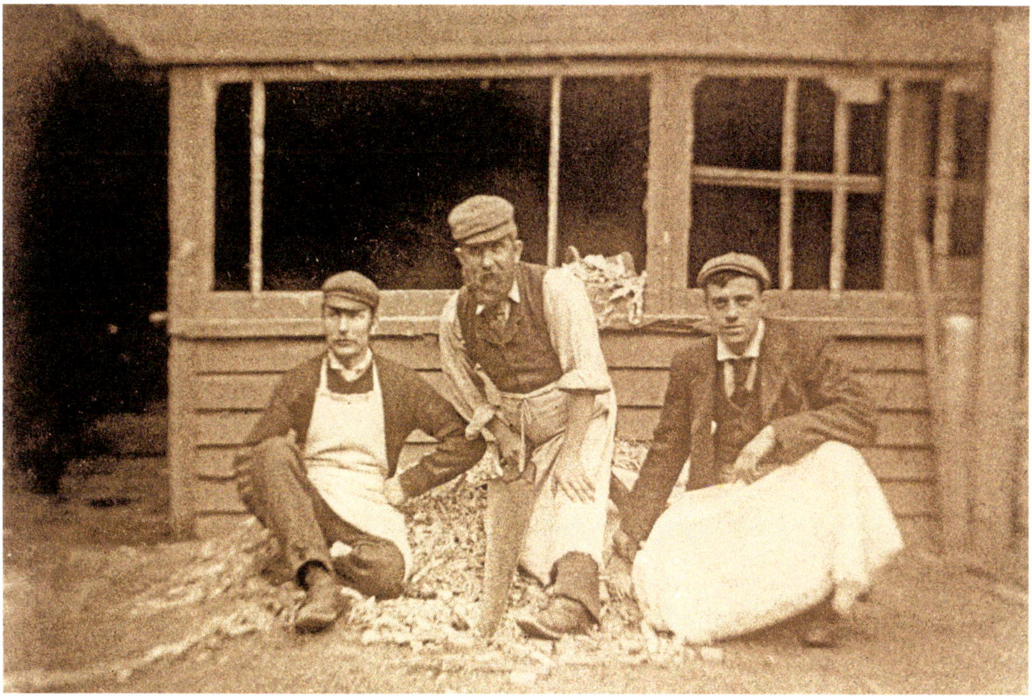

Carpenters at No. 26–28 West Street working for Thomas William Furniss. He was a coal and corn merchant as well as a builder, and ran a chalk pit near Reigate.

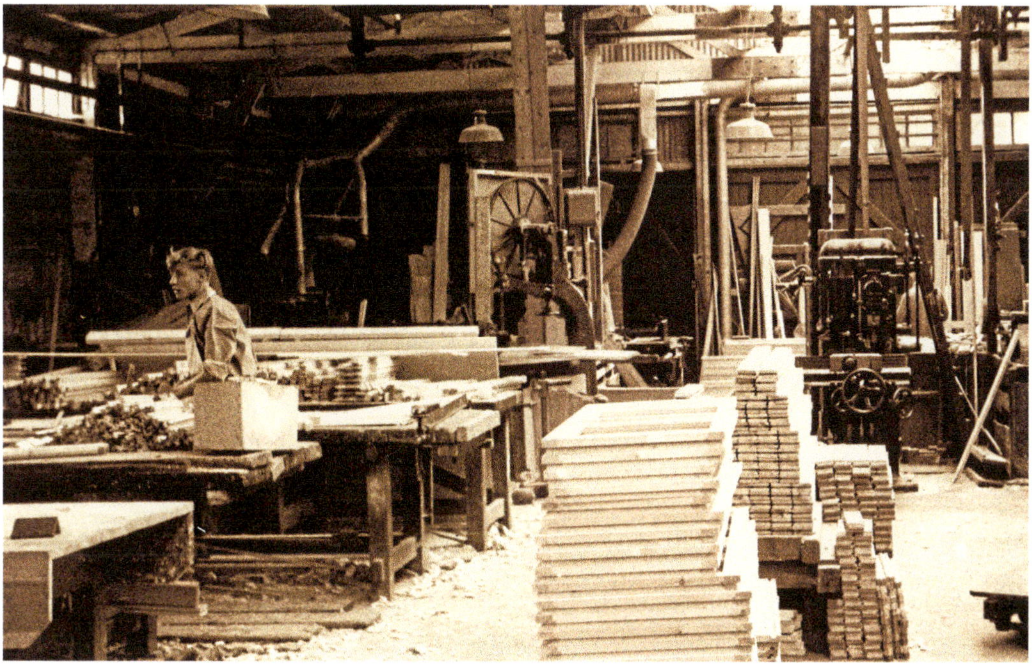

The joinery workshop at Roll's in Ashley Avenue. The Roll brothers bought Ashley House and sold it to the Rural District Council in 1926, keeping land at the back.

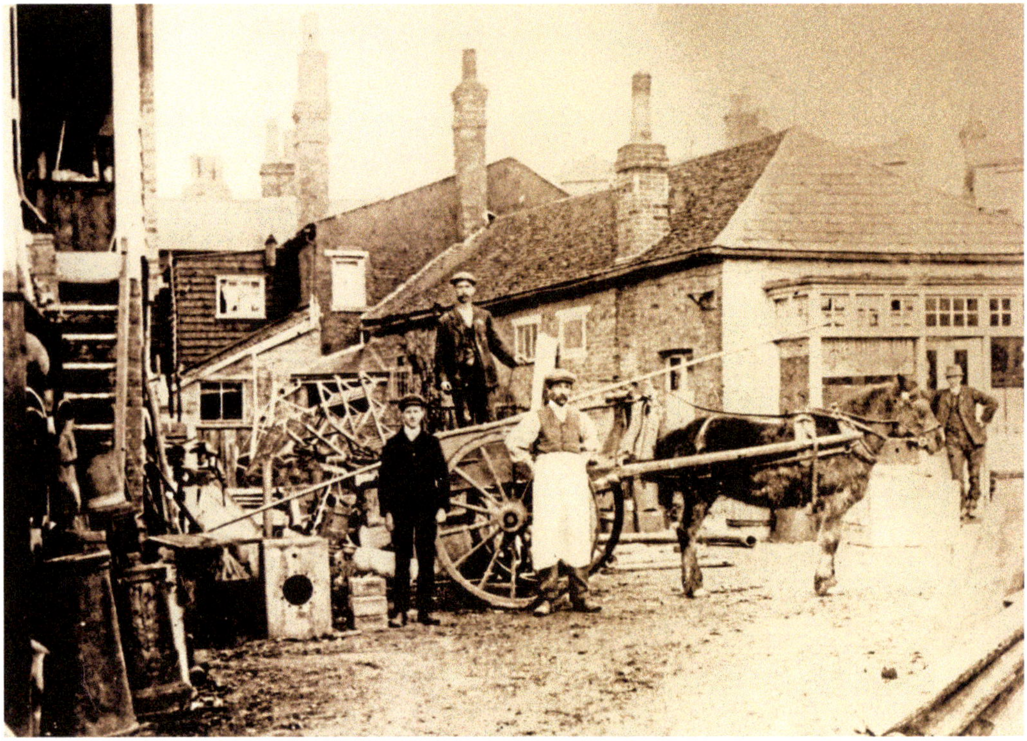

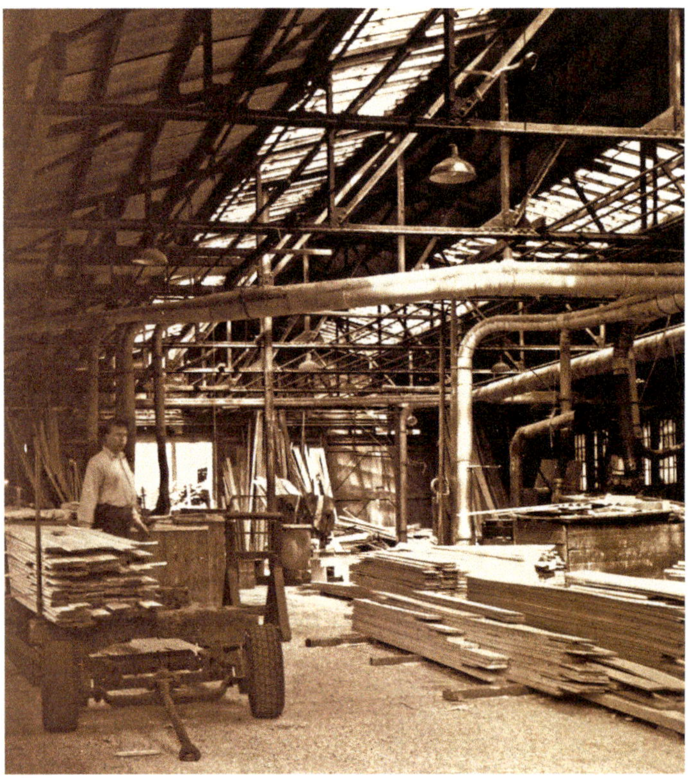

Above: Goodship and Saunders set up their builders' yard in Ewell at Nos 46–50 High Street. After a fire in 1912, the black-tarred weather-boarded workshops were rebuilt in brick.

Left: Longhurst's timber yard stood between Upper High Street and the railway. An apprentice carpenter in the 1850s, Edwin Longhurst became a builder and councillor.

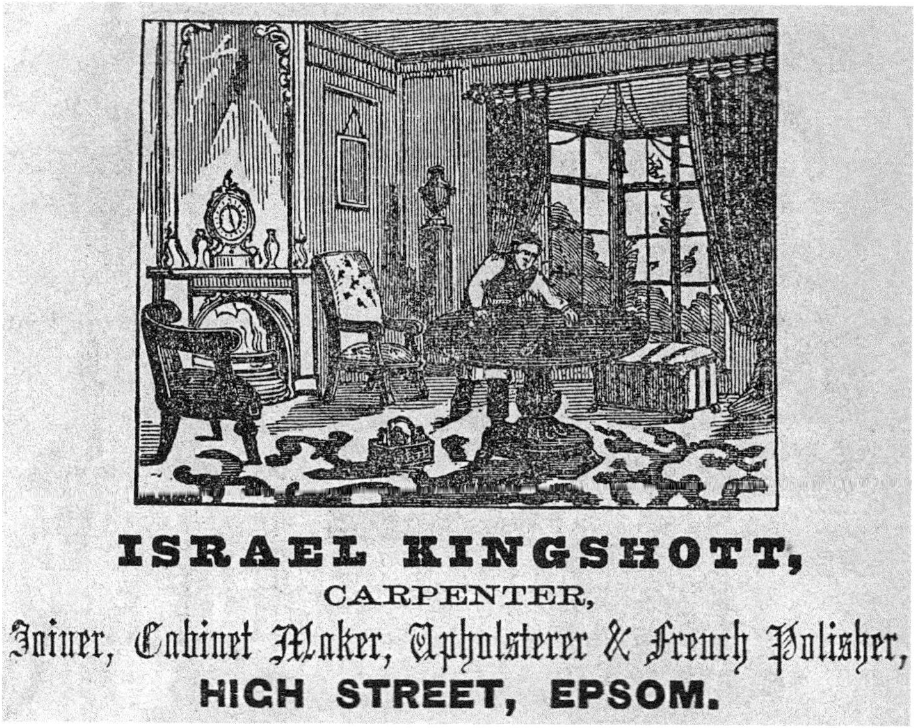

In 1860 the Kingshotts were trading in Epsom at No. 28 High Street. Israel did carpentry and Frances the embroideries and fabrics: 'Carpet, Damask, Chintz, Dimity'.

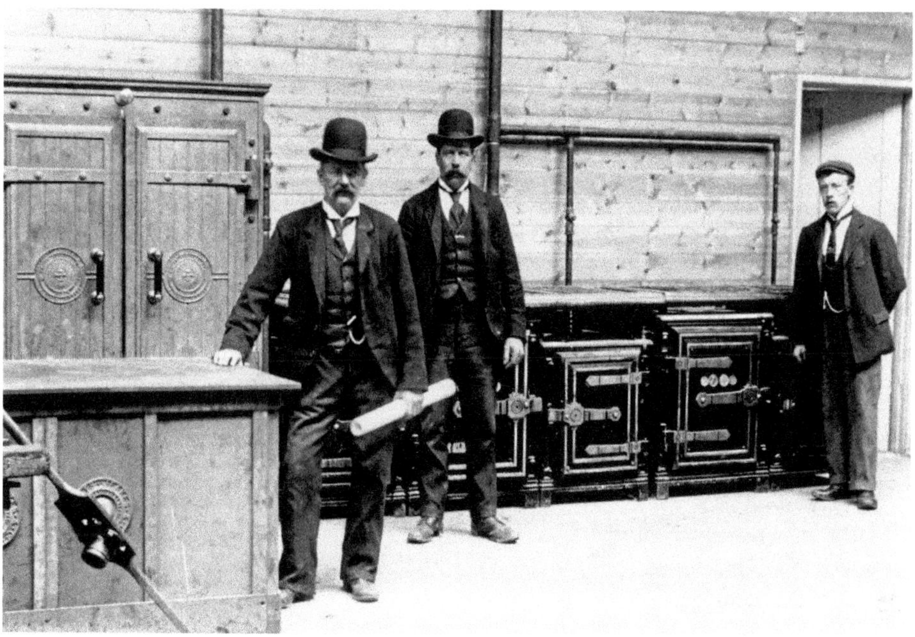

William James Baker of West Ewell served his apprenticeship at Dorset's the ironmongers in Epsom. Here he is putting in a kitchen boiler at a Leamington hospital.

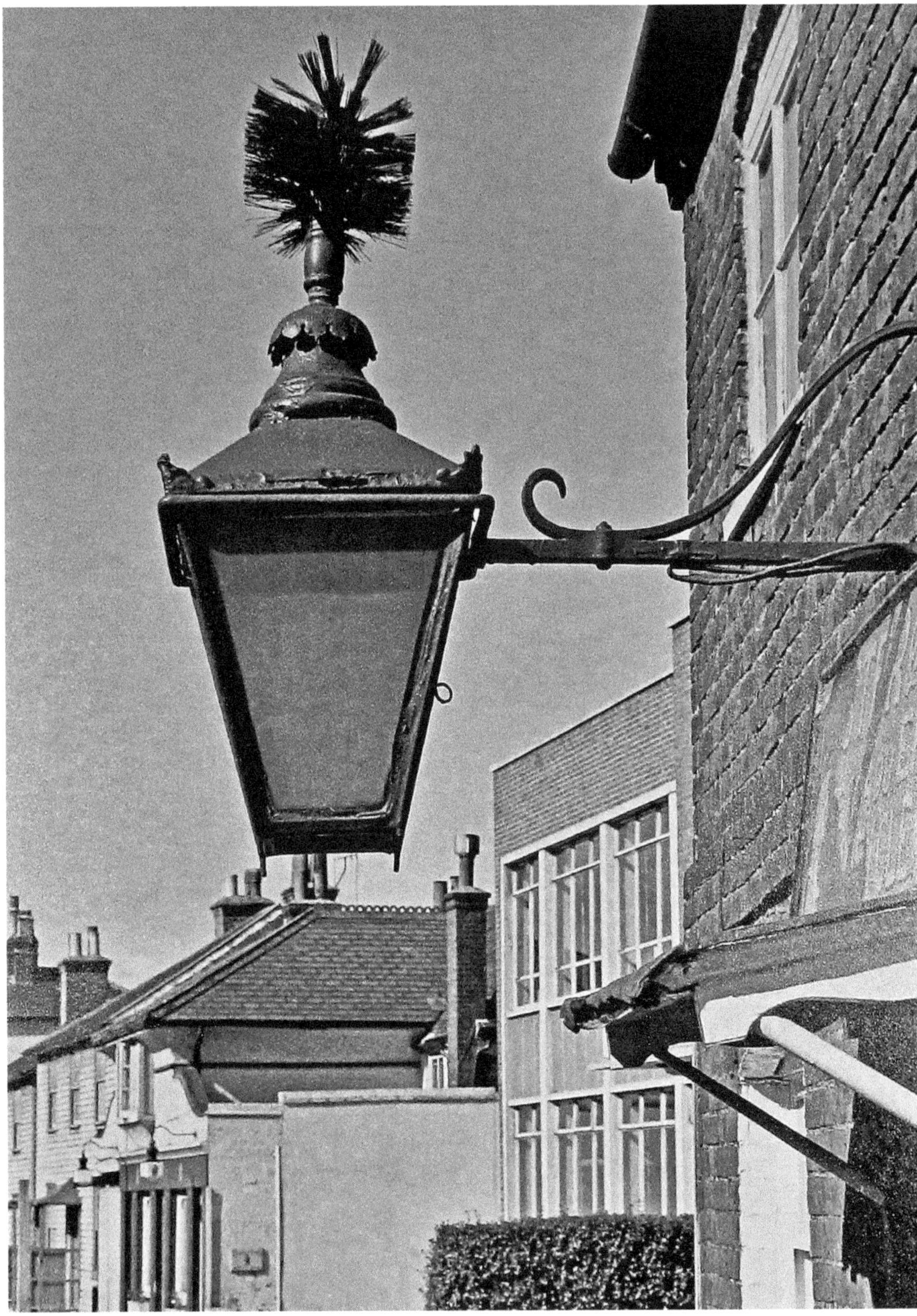

George Richard Ratcliff was a master chimney sweep in 1861, employing two men. His house at No. 33 East Street was marked for many years by a brush over the door.

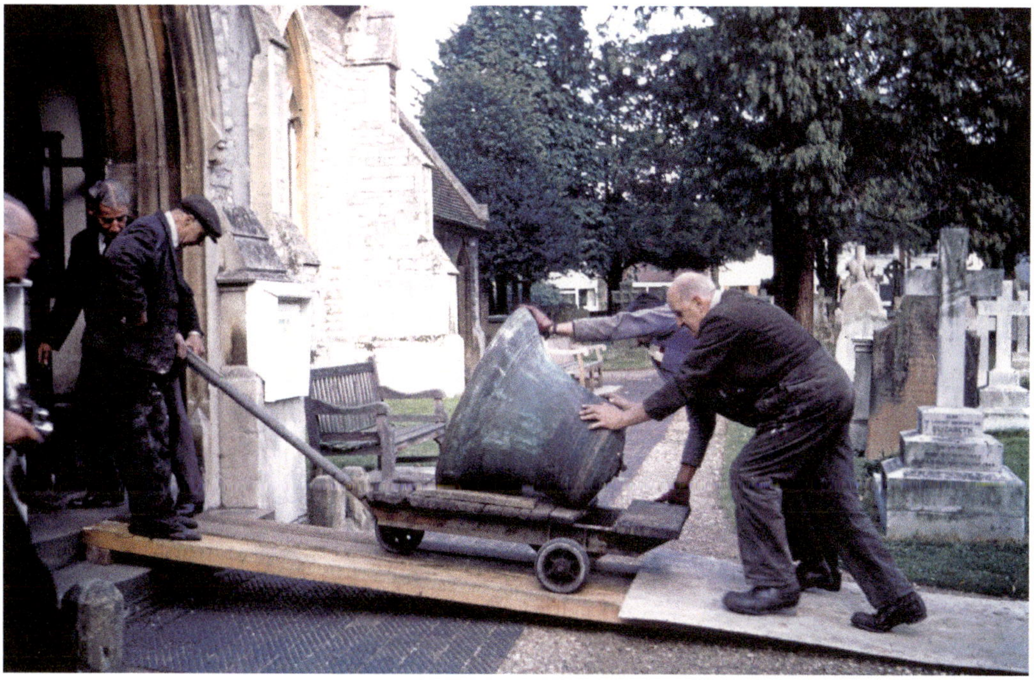

Above: In 1970 the bells of St Mary's were restored and hung on a new iron frame. There had been previous restorations in 1848 (with the move to a new church), 1890 and 1925.

Right: A nest of 700 wasps destroyed by A. E. Read at Chestnut Avenue in 1949. In the big houses, this was a regular job for gardeners – with forty nests at Ewell Court in 1893 alone.

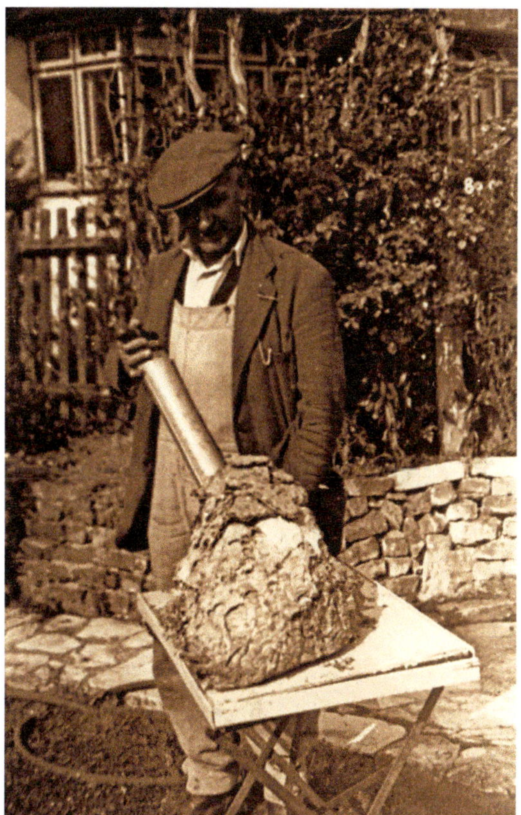

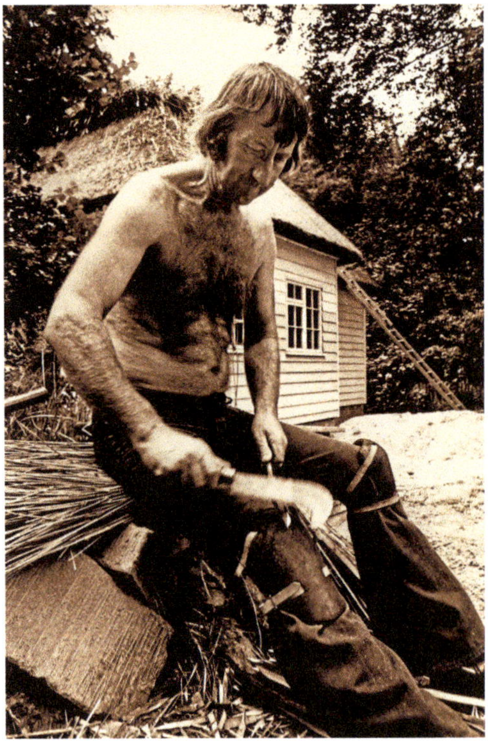

Mr Anderson the thatcher at work on Epsom Downs in 1977. He is using a spar hook to give a point to the spars or broaches that will peg down the thatch.

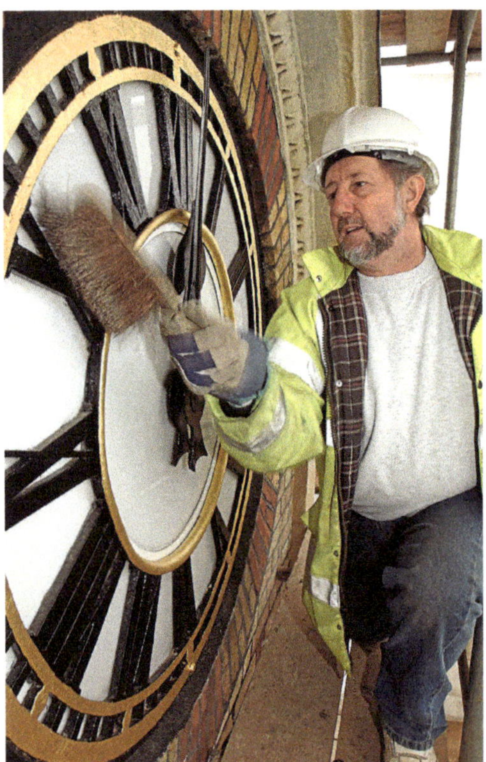

Putting the final touches to the dial on Epsom Clock Tower in 2004. When first installed in 1848, the clock was maintained by William Charman of Nos 75–77 High Street.

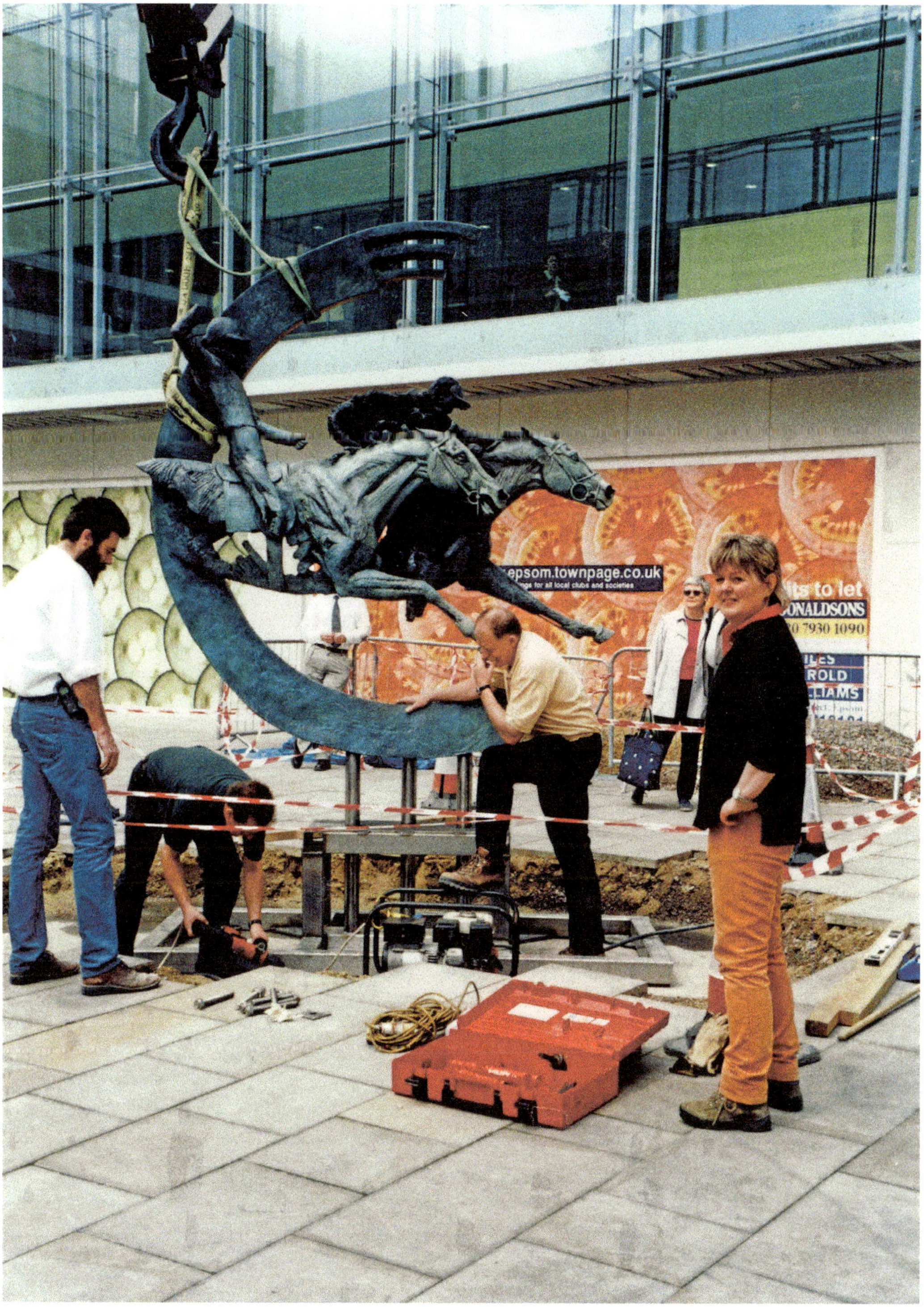

Judy Boyt the sculptor overseeing installation of her *Evocation of Speed* in the Derby Square. It shows Diomed, the first Derby winner, racing the 2001 winner, Galileo.

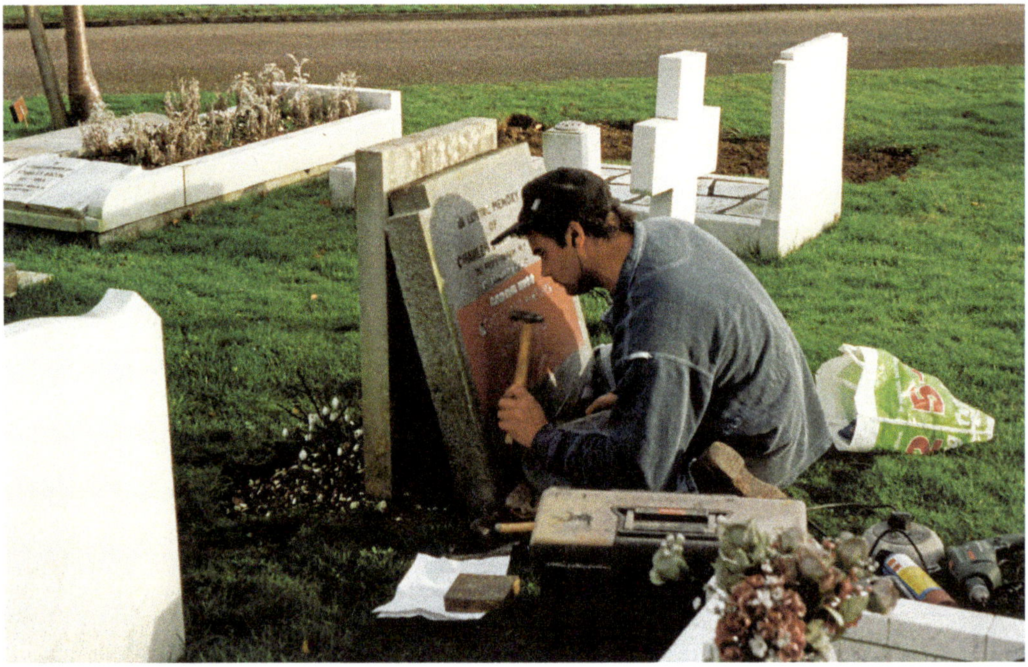

Updating a headstone in Epsom Cemetery, 1999. The cemetery was laid out in 1871, landscaped by Joseph Rawnsley of Epsom Nurseries and was expanded in 1923.

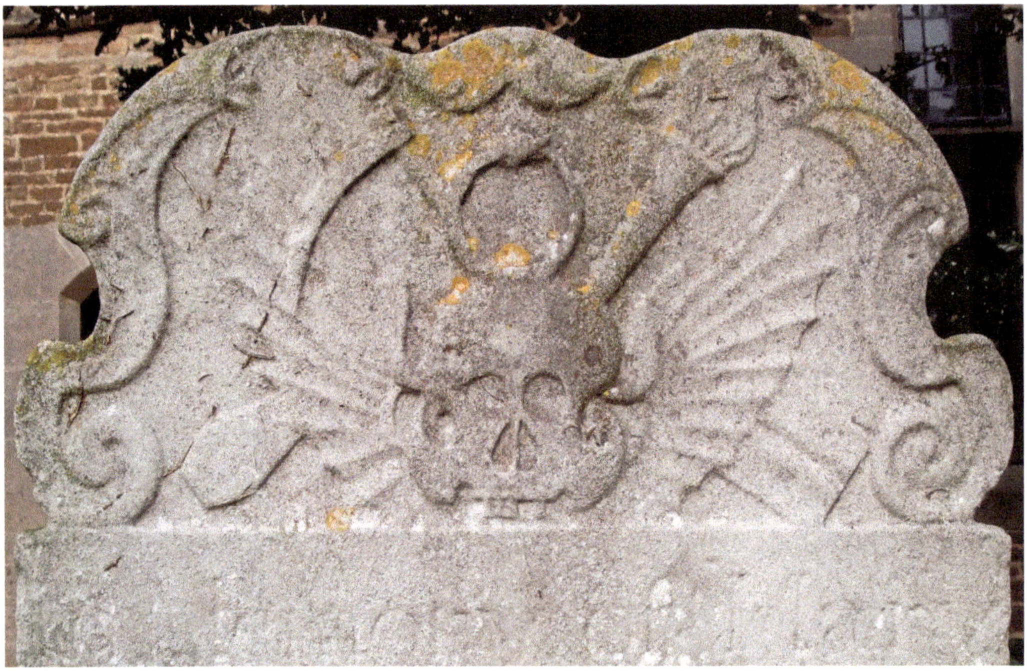

The final home of Mary Lane in St Martin's churchyard. Her tombstone, dated 1750, is one of many carved by a local craftsman who liked skulls and emblems of eternity.

HOME COMFORTS

Trade in food and domestic goods began with Epsom Market, set up in the 1680s by the Evelyn family when they were lords of the manor. It fell into disuse as the Spa declined, although it revived in the 1820s with the new growth of the town. Then it lapsed once more and was finally brought to life at the end of the century by Thomas Hersey, the cycle-maker of South Street who put out stalls in the High Street and refused to take no for an answer. In 1914 the council took over. It didn't matter that the market was held in the middle of the road since there was little or no motor traffic, but with the passage of time this became more dangerous and in 1991 the southern half of the road was diverted away from the High Street.

Until well into the nineteenth century, manufacture and retail of food were in the same hands: bakers made the bread that they sold and butchers killed their own animals. The need for specialised equipment meant that premises stayed in the same trade for generations. William Lemon's bakery gave its name to a street, Lemon's Lane (now Church Road), and was remembered for its large oven, heated by furze faggots and visible to bystanders through the front door – it was in the poor quarter of town, and people who could not afford fuel of their own used to take their Sunday roast to be baked there. John Sheath, who ran a bakery in the High Street in the 1850s, was the eldest of seven boys; three of his brothers became bakers elsewhere in Surrey, and the rest went into other branches of the food business. His eldest son, Leonard, followed at the Epsom shop, and the other two sons again went into baking, at Ashtead and Leatherhead.

Butchers also tended to keep to the same premises; they needed a yard in which the livestock could be penned, and a slaughterhouse. Cracknells stood on the corner of the High Street and Spring Street in Ewell – the slaughterhouse window, barred with latticework, was set high so children could not see though it, but they climbed up to look all the same. At Christmas the shop would display two pigs' carcases lying in straw, each with a lemon in its mouth. Behind this were the stables, for all the butchers had carts for delivery to the big houses. The cottage folk would come in for sixpence of beef pieces and the local roadman would buy a piece of steak and fry it on his shovel.

Health standards at these small businesses were rough and ready. When John Cooper took the fish shop at No. 51 High Street in Ewell, the fish came by train from Billingsgate, packed in ice. The frying shed was at the bottom of the garden, and all the fish and chips had to be carried along the garden path, across a covered yard, and through the family's living room to the back of the shop. Cooper went bankrupt in the First World War, but a more successful fish business was created not long after when Alfred Charles Marshall took over the shop at No. 59 High Street on his father's death in 1924. Before then the family's business model had been to buy, sell, and then go to the races and spend the money. Marshall was more organised and over the next ten years he set up three new Epsom branches and others in Leatherhead and Dorking, holding office in the Borough Council and the National Federation of Fishmongers. At its peak he employed 100 people, from the boys kept for bike deliveries to the waitresses at the fish restaurant next to the Odeon. But after his death in 1958 it slowly wound down.

George and James Randall moved to Epsom in the 1880s and set up a factory for soft drinks in Clayton Road, selling from premises in South Street. They began by taking five gross of mineral waters up to the Derby, and that established a market. Competition was stiff and after the First World War the business was about to pass out of the family when Percy, who had been learning the business in New Zealand, came back and changed the marketing strategy, specialising in real fruit squashes. Built in 1935, his new factory was almost immediately requisitioned for making munitions in the war, but returned to the business afterwards and was still operating during the 1950s.

Family businesses tended to build up and then break down again – except for pubs, which were slowly concentrated in the hands of the brewers. Epsom had two breweries of its own. Pagdens, incongruously sited just outside St Martin's Church, had a portfolio originally put together by William Cobbold in the eighteenth century and including the Amato, Eclipse, Old Kings Head, and Queens Head, with the George and Lord Nelson in Ewell. Bradley's brewery had the Ladas and Wellington, along with Ewell's Eight Bells and Glyn Arms. It was taken over bv Page & Overton of Croydon in 1903, while in 1931 Pagdens became part of Mellersh & Neale of Reigate, the beginning of a process of acquisitions and mergers that would leave all brewing in a few hands.

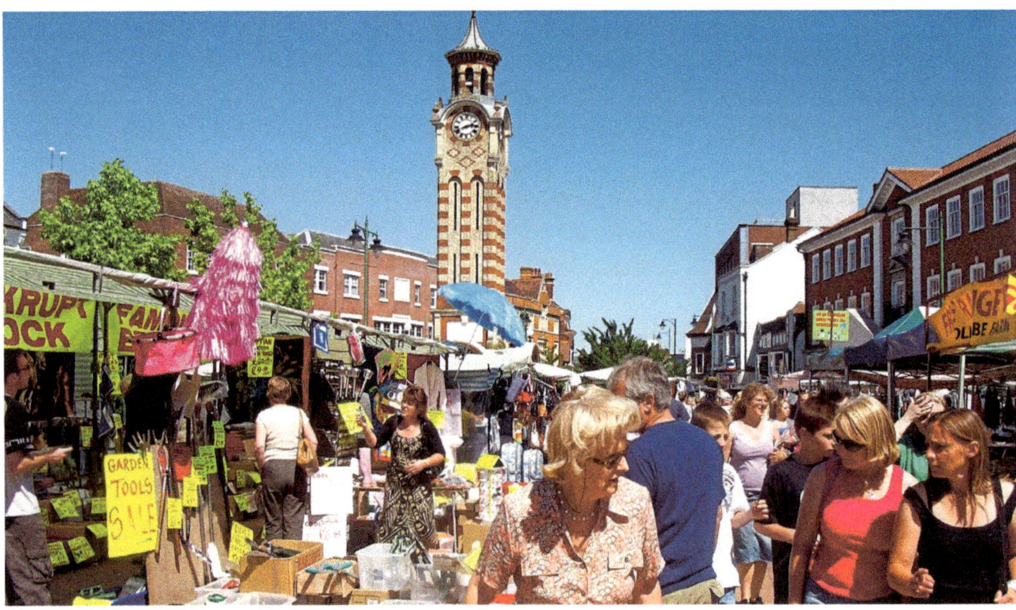

Originally run by the Lord of the Manor, Epsom Market was taken over by the council after its revival in 1914; the council acquired manorial rights in 1955.

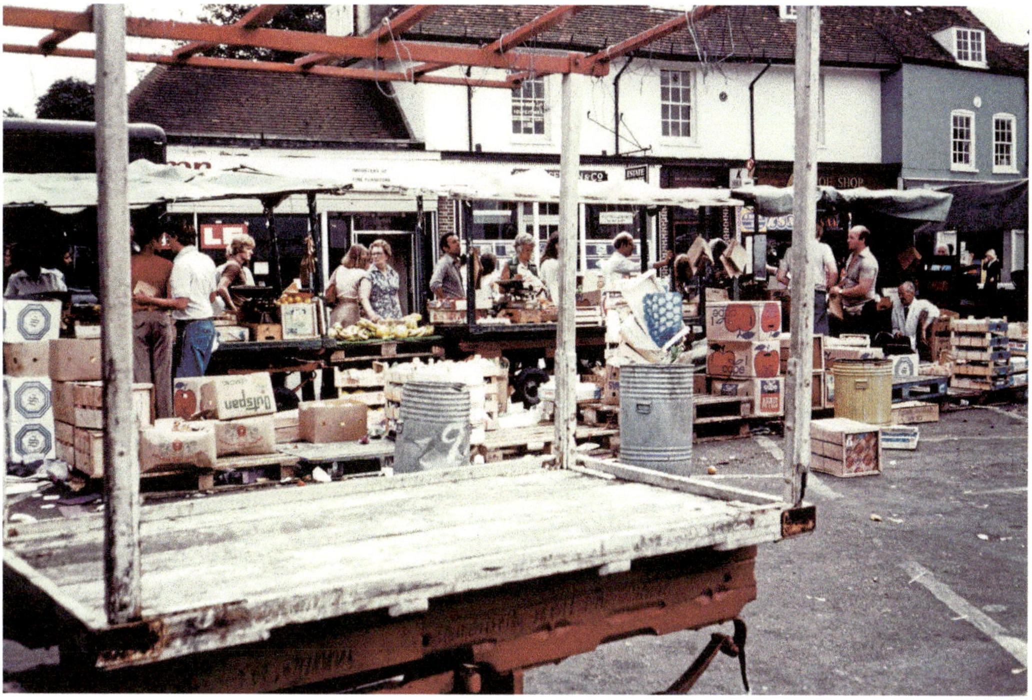

In the 1940s, when the future playwright John Osborne used to work Saturdays in the market, it was sandwiched between two lanes of traffic. A safer layout came in 1993.

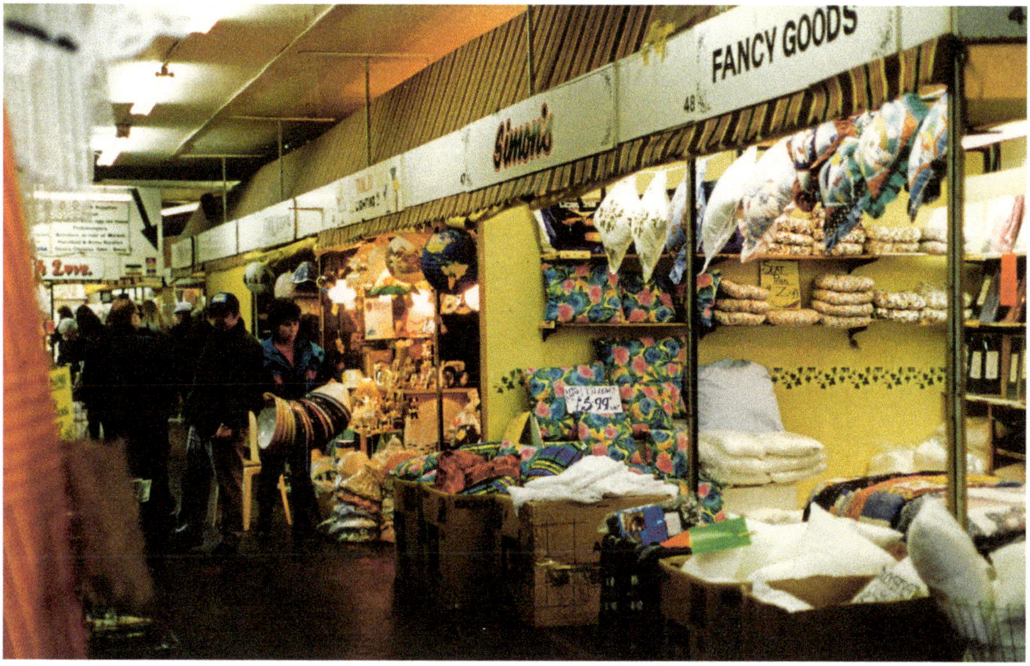

In 1980 the Indoor Market was set up at No. 78 High Street, formerly Pages Motors. Sixty small traders took advantage of the site until 1998, when it was sold to Morrisons.

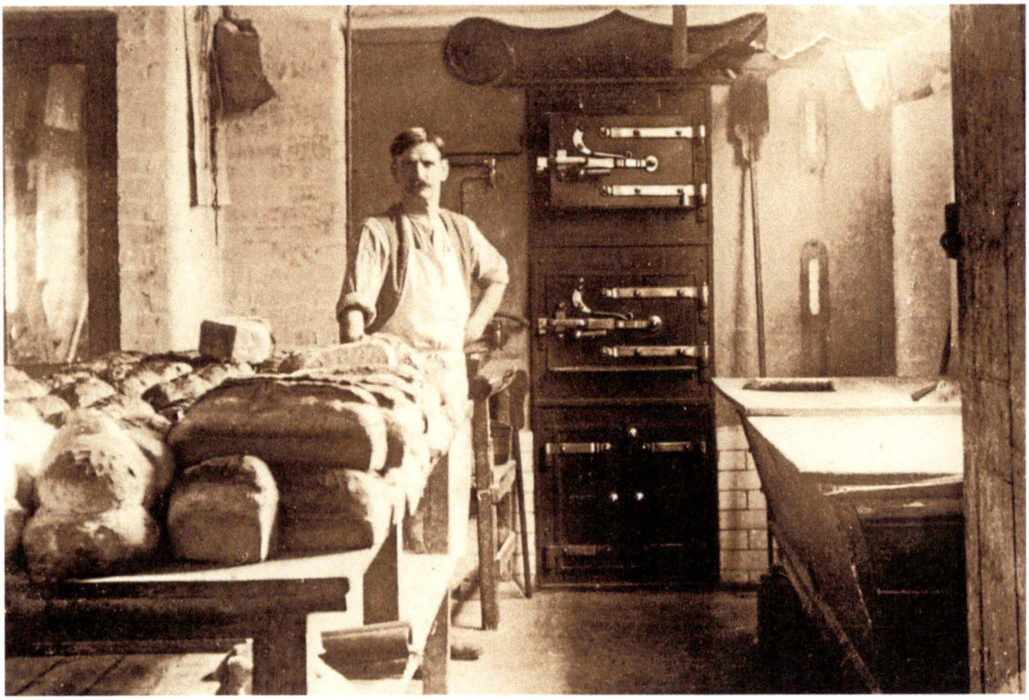

Edward Turner took over the bakery at No. 72 (afterwards No. 92) East Street from Esther Lemon after the First World War and expanded into Ewell, Cheam and Sutton.

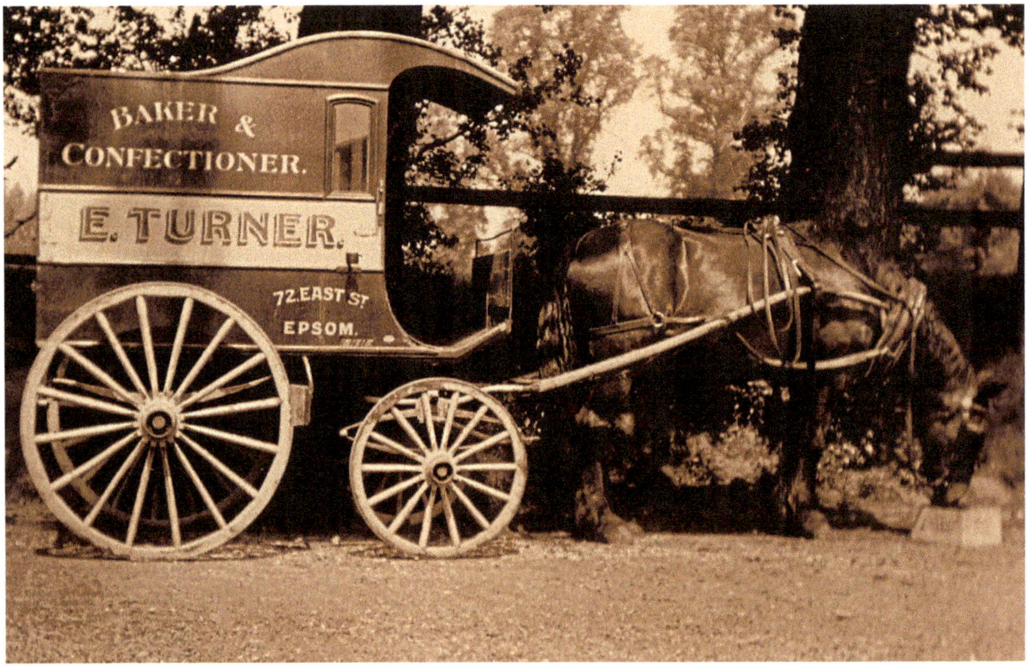

This horse and cart, stopping outside Gibraltar Rec, was standard transport for bakeries. In the 1930s, Turner's had five as well as two handcarts and three motor vans.

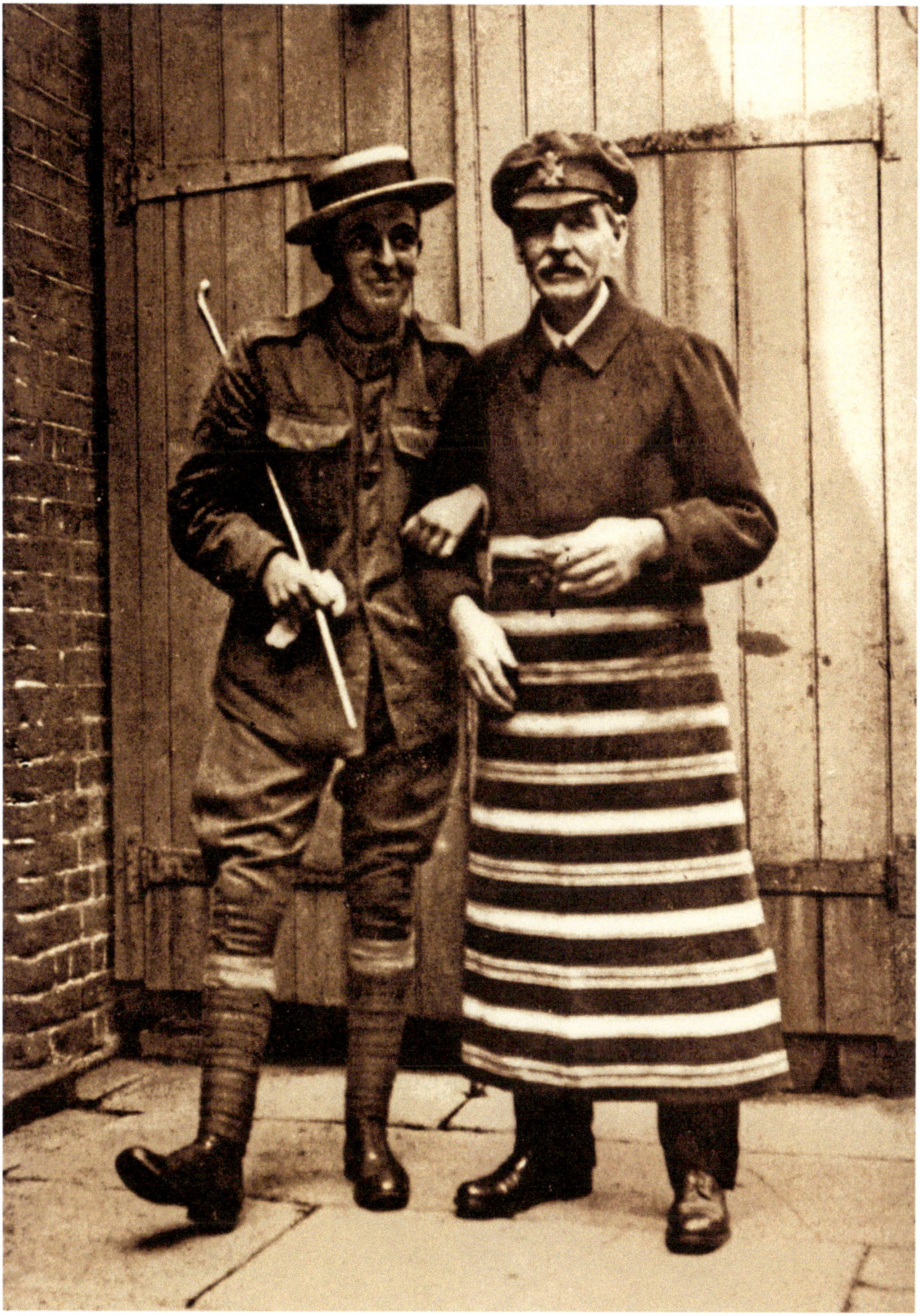

Edward Norrington was a family butcher at No. 22 High Street in Epsom. Here his son Raymond swaps caps before resuming duty at the Front in 1916. Raymond did not return.

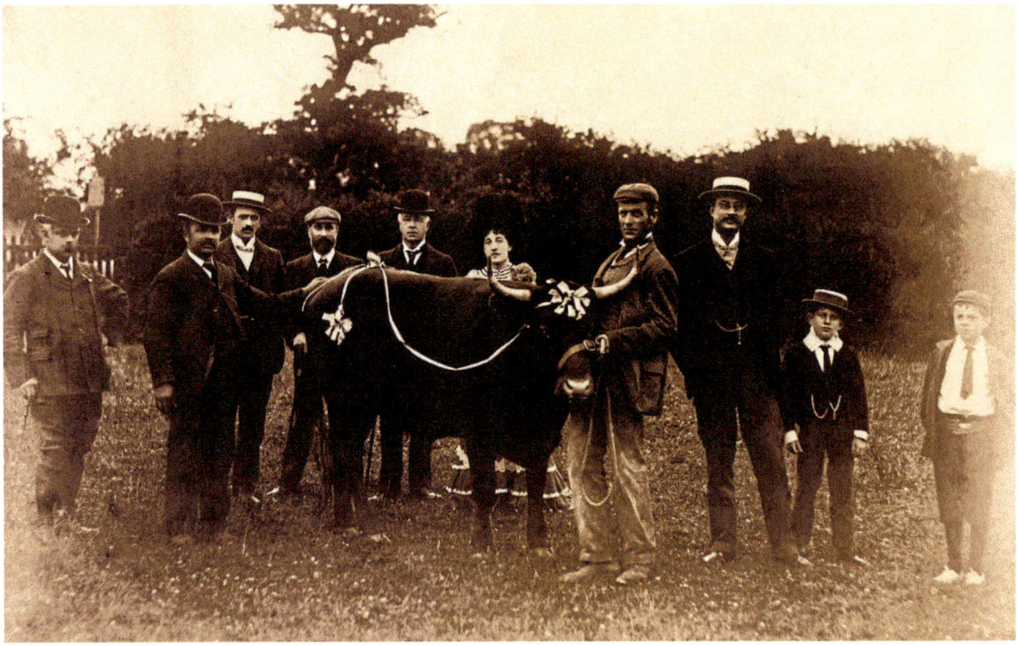

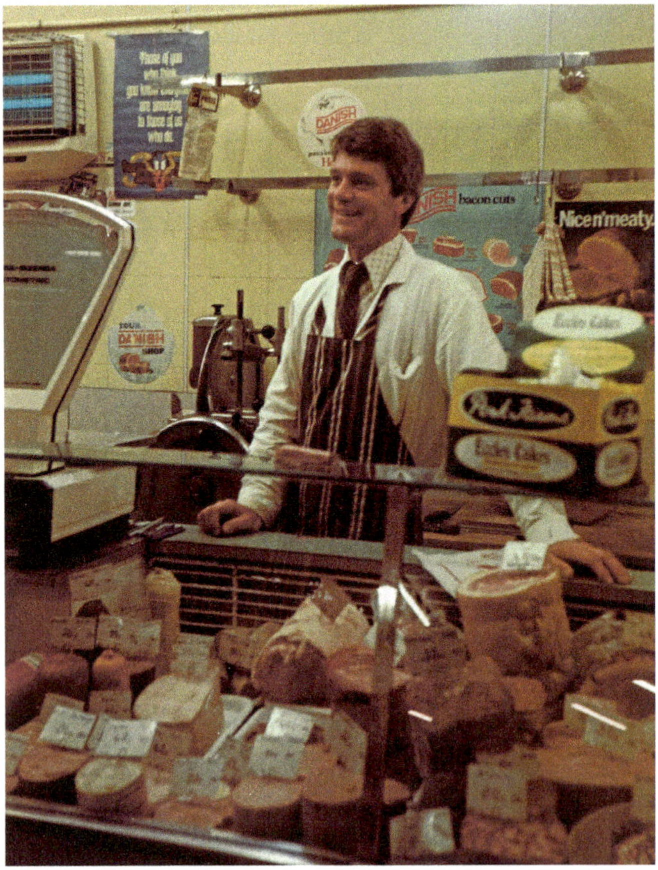

Above: Charles Polhill the butcher pats a Devon ox. Ribboned in red, white and blue, it was led through Epsom and roasted in front of the Clock Tower for the 1902 coronation.

Left: 'Lovely Bernard' in the 1970s at Norman's butchers, No. 9 Corner House Parade. The shop was later taken over by Kenneth Eve until it became an online business in 2015.

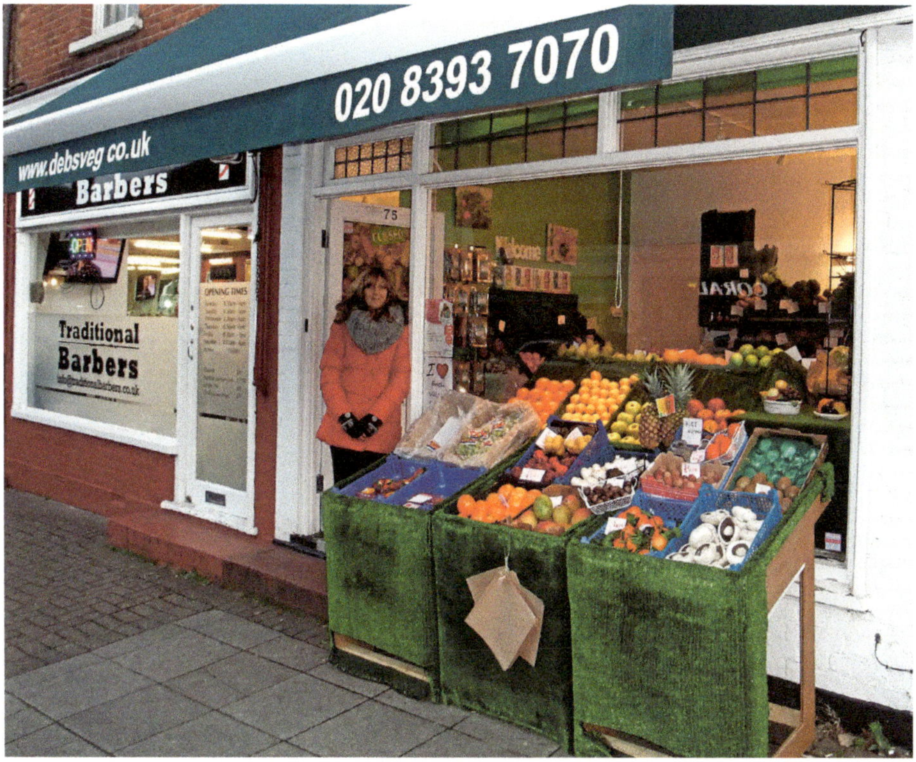

Deb's Veg in Ewell High Street flourished briefly in 2012 before competition from the newly opened Sainsbury's Local became too much. Fastfix Your PC took over.

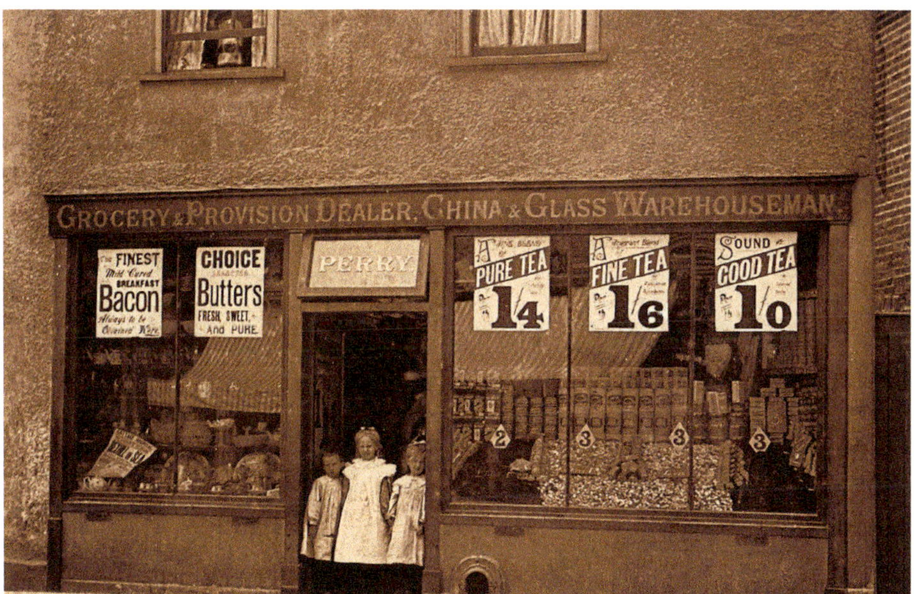

George Perry's children in the 1890s at the family grocery at No. 40 High Street, Ewell. After a family tragedy in 1905 they moved to Exmouth, and Alf Spencer moved in.

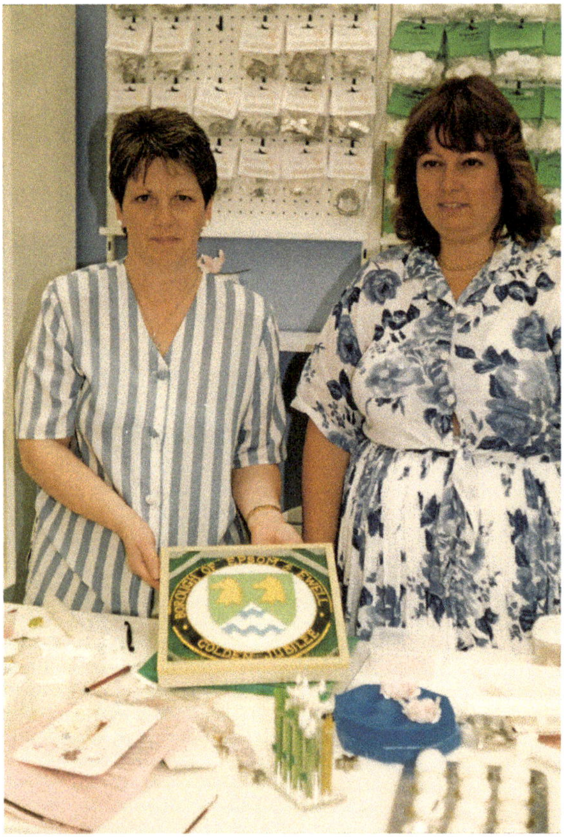

Left: No. 40 High Street later became Corteil & Barrett's cake shop. Here staff show off an armorial cake, restored in 1993 and believed to be the only cake kept in Borough regalia.

Below: Matilda Westgate with Smut the dog at No. 70 Kingston Road. Her husband Spencer had been a bricklayer but started a grocery, tobacconists and newsagents in 1906.

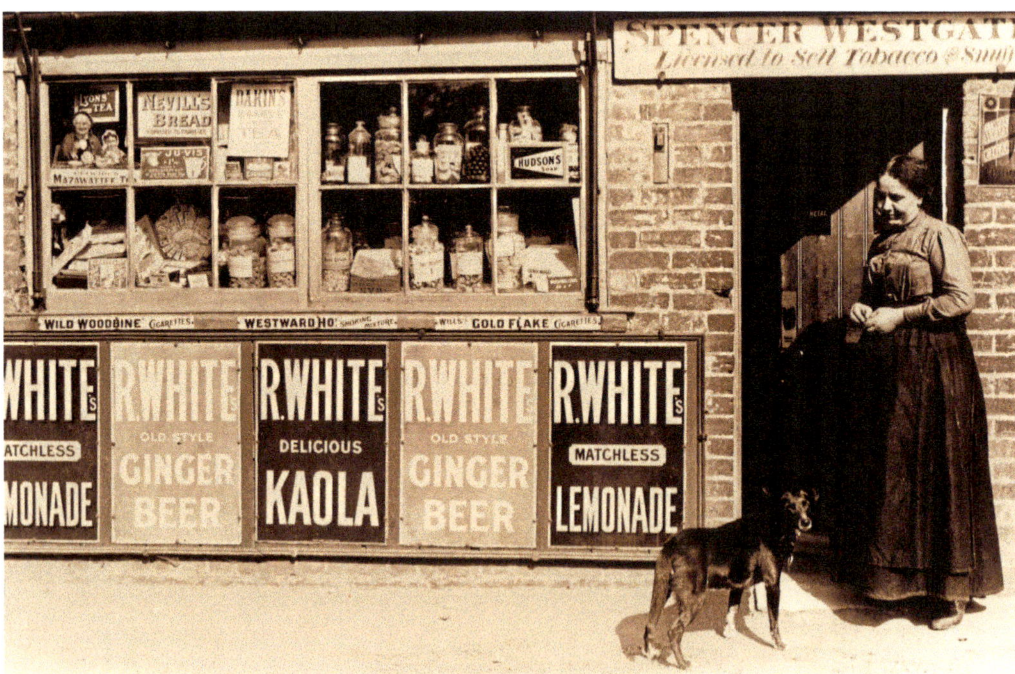

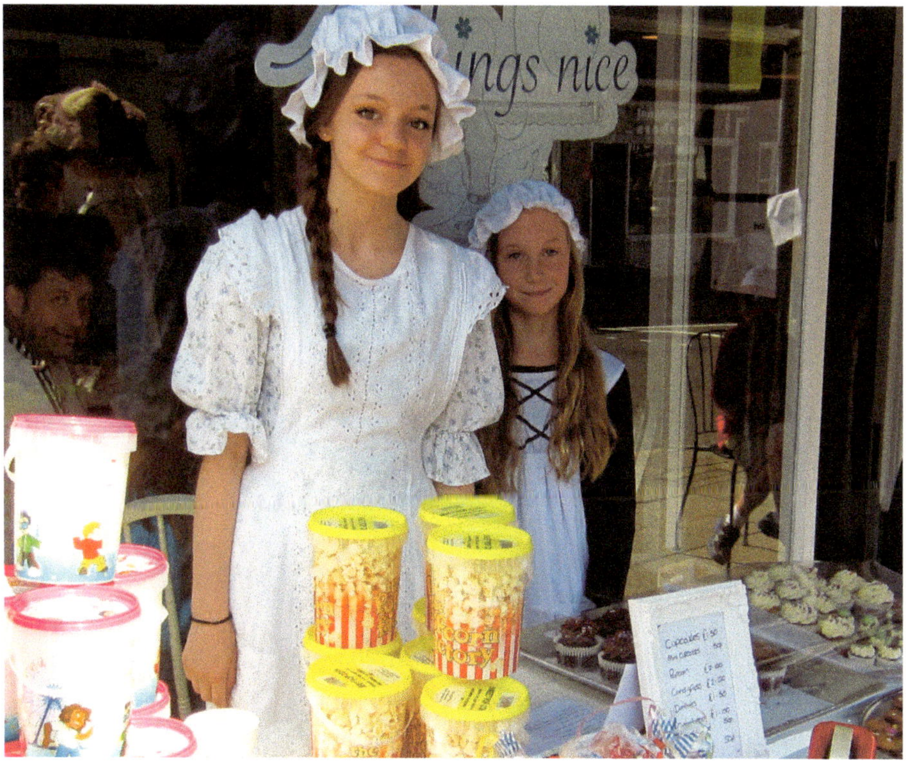

Girls at All Things Nice dress up for the Ewell Village Fair of 2014. The café's premises at No. 90 High Street had previously been the shop for Curtis Dairies.

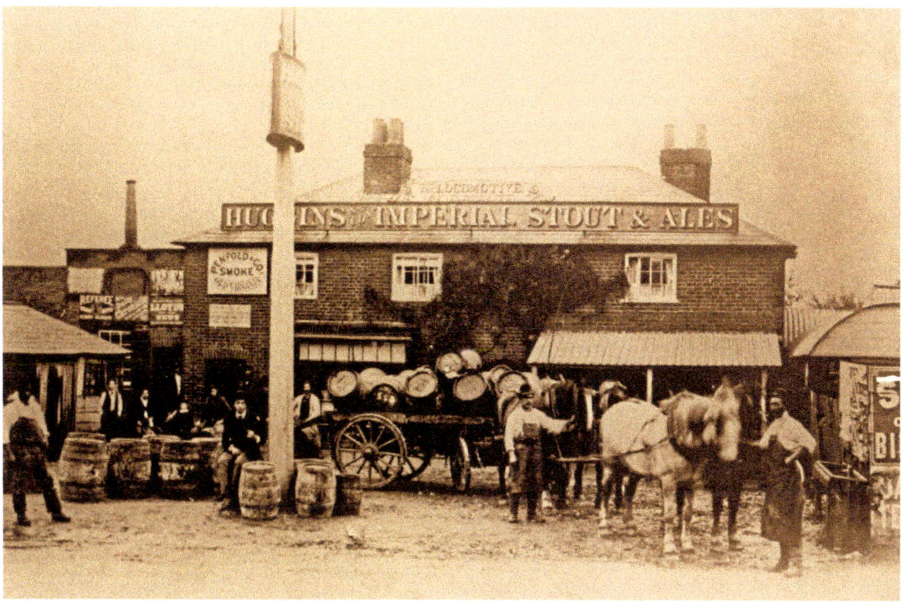

Brewer's drays deliver Huggins Stout to the Locomotive, a free house until 1929 when it was bought by Watney's. After they sold it in the 1980s it became a wine bar.

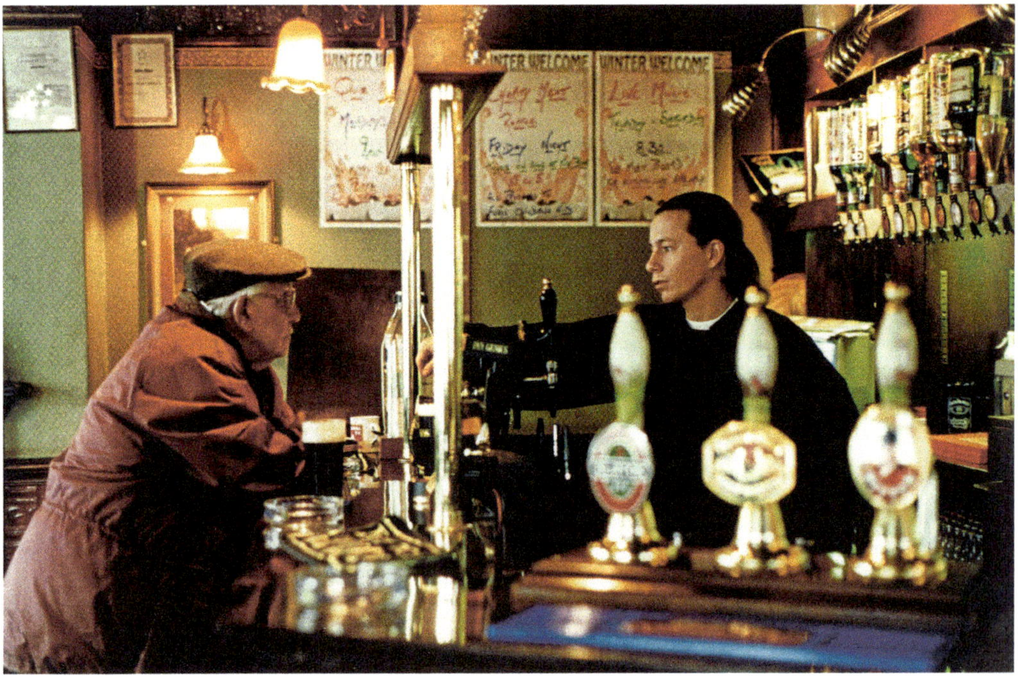

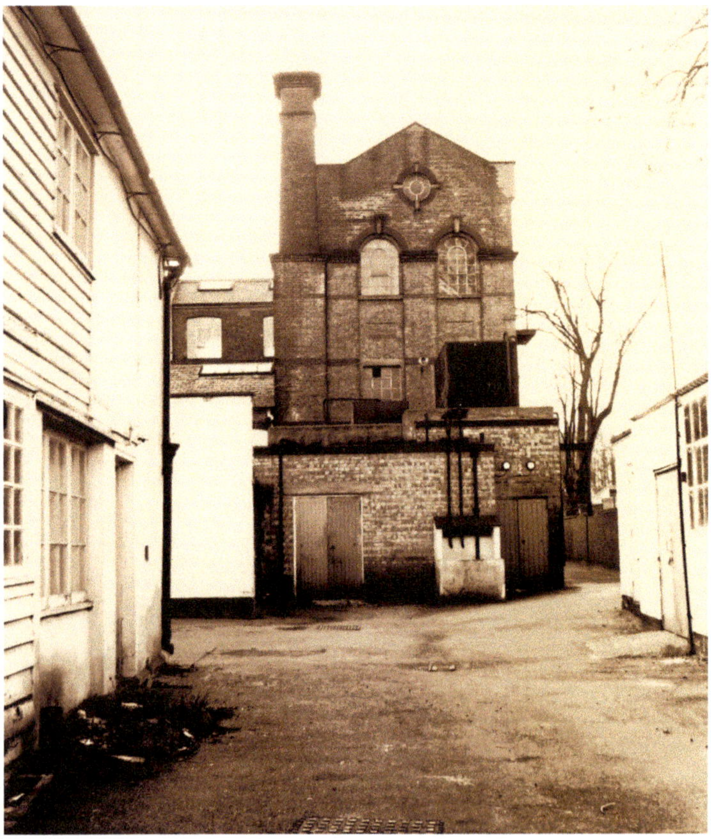

Above: A quiet moment at the King William IV in Ewell, 1996. Home of the King Bill Folk Club, the pub was briefly a Firkin outlet, then converted to an Italian restaurant in 2008.

Left: William George Bradley built his brewery in 1870 at the back of the High Street. It was closed by Page & Overton on the merger of 1903, but remained standing until 1985.

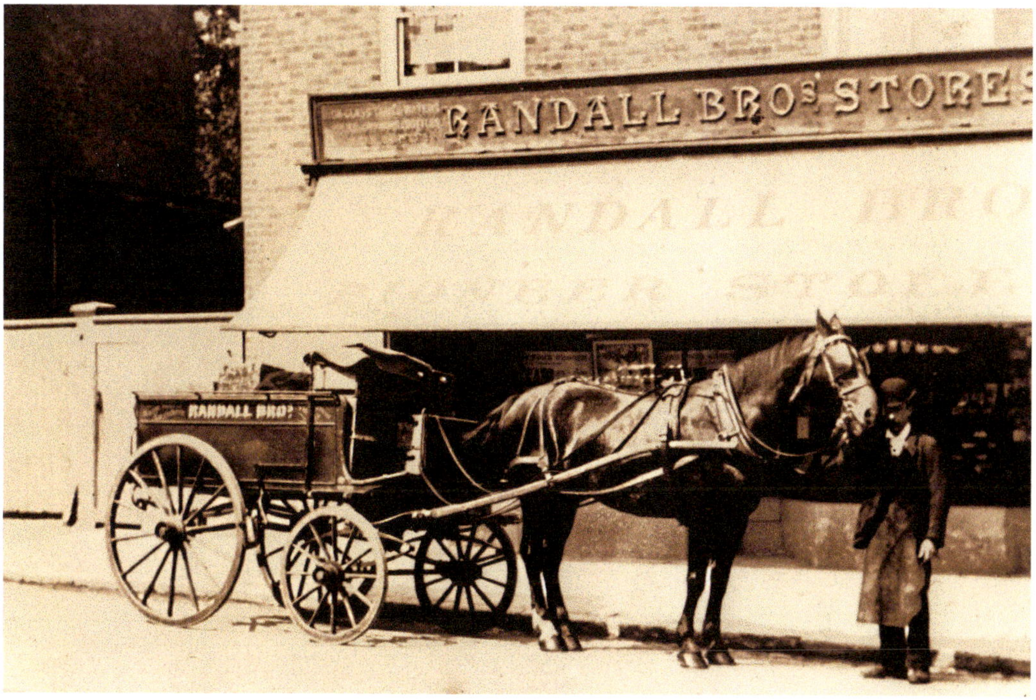

Charles Measures went into partnership selling mineral waters with George and James Randall from No. 18 South Street. In 1916 they experimented with a car hire business.

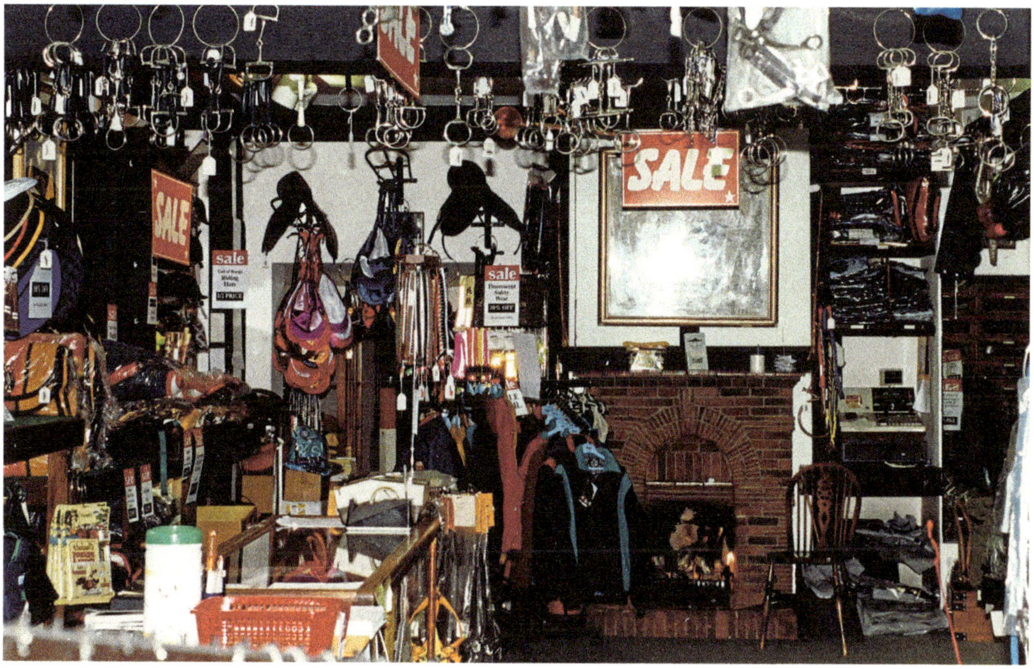

Lester Bowdens in the January sales of 1994 before the move from No. 113 High Street to the old Spread Eagle. They had made silks for Derby winners and the royal family.

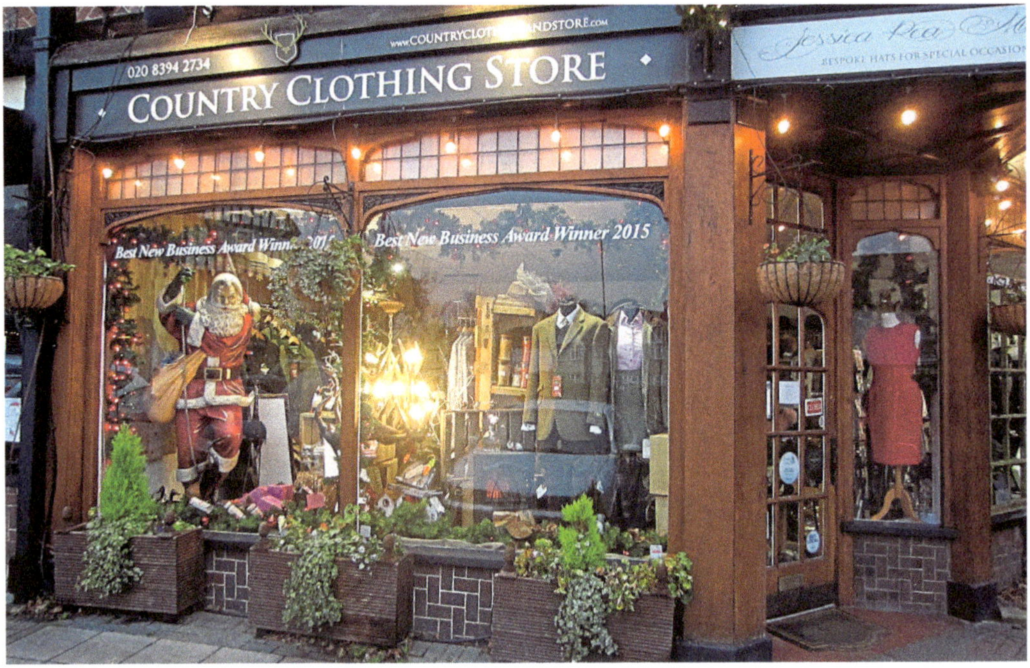

Country Clothing Store, seen here in the run-up to Christmas 2016, was opened by John The Fence Matthews of Tadworth, also in charge of the Equestrian Store at the Derby Arms.

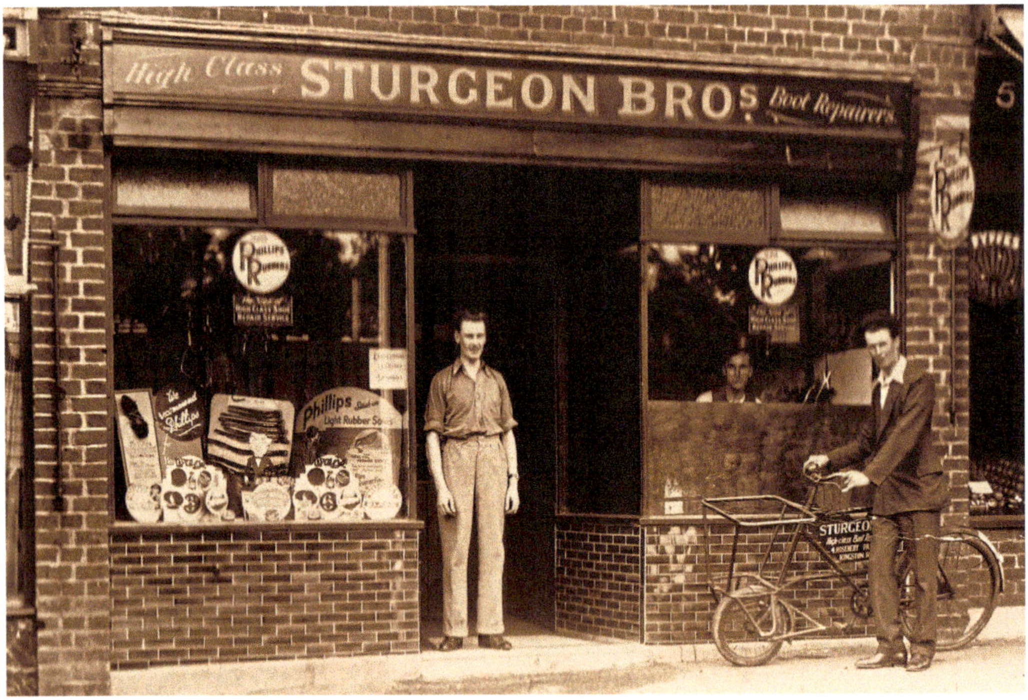

Brothers John and Arthur Sturgeon in front of the boot repair shop opened in 1934 at No. 4 Rosebery Parade in Kingston Road. They soon moved to larger premises.

Right: The shoemaker's workshop at Horton Hospital, with sole and heel knives for cutting leather. Established in 1904, it was run by John Beams from 1950 until closure.

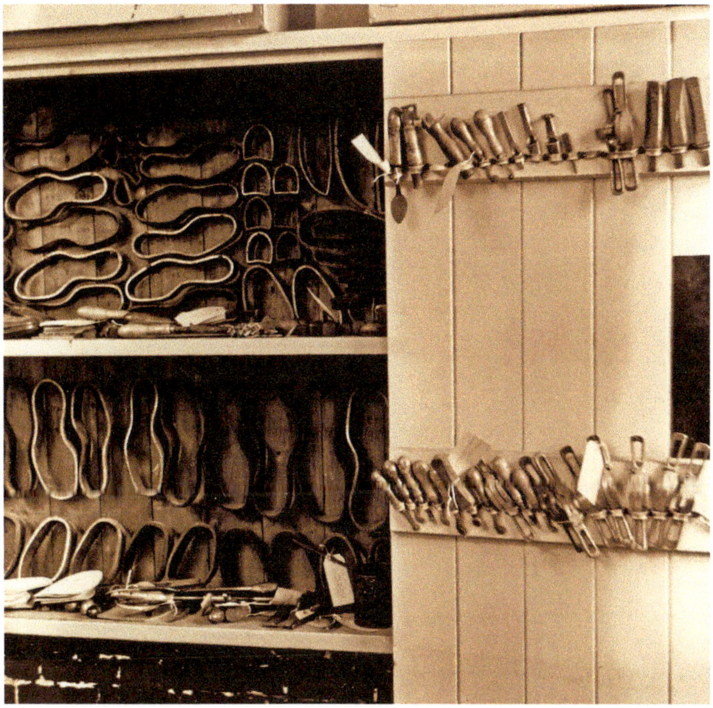

Below: Robert Dearle the tallow chandler in later life, when the smelly process of candle-making had given way to mass manufacture. He died in 1908, having seen eighty Derbies.

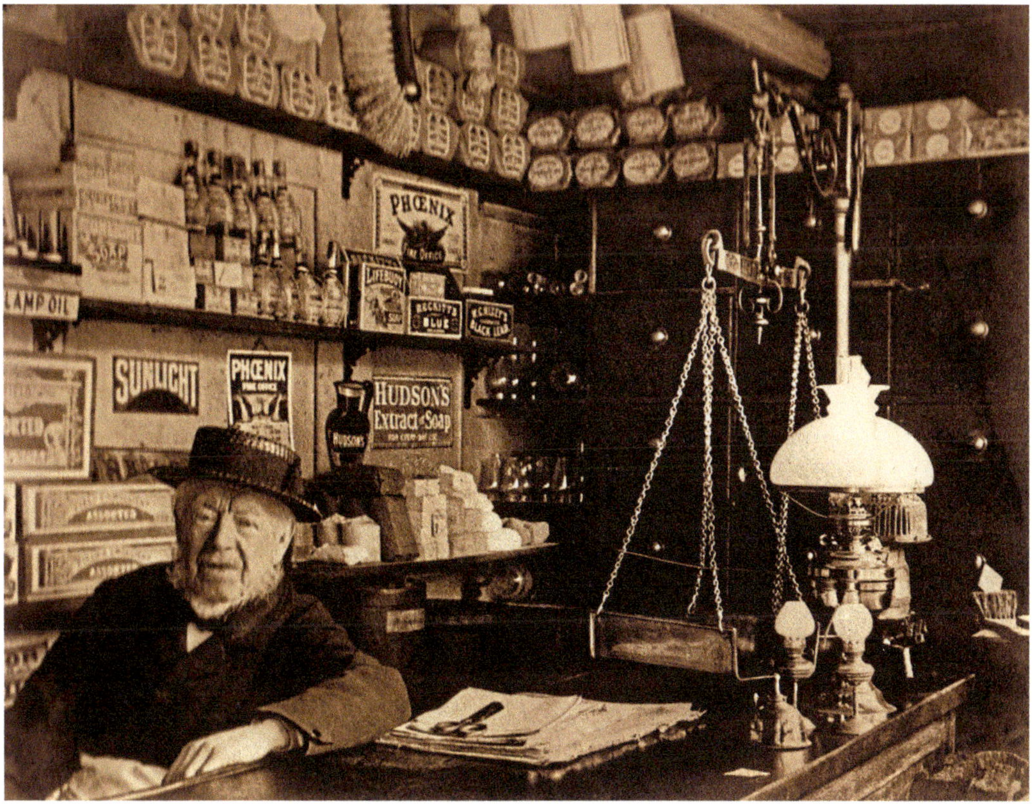

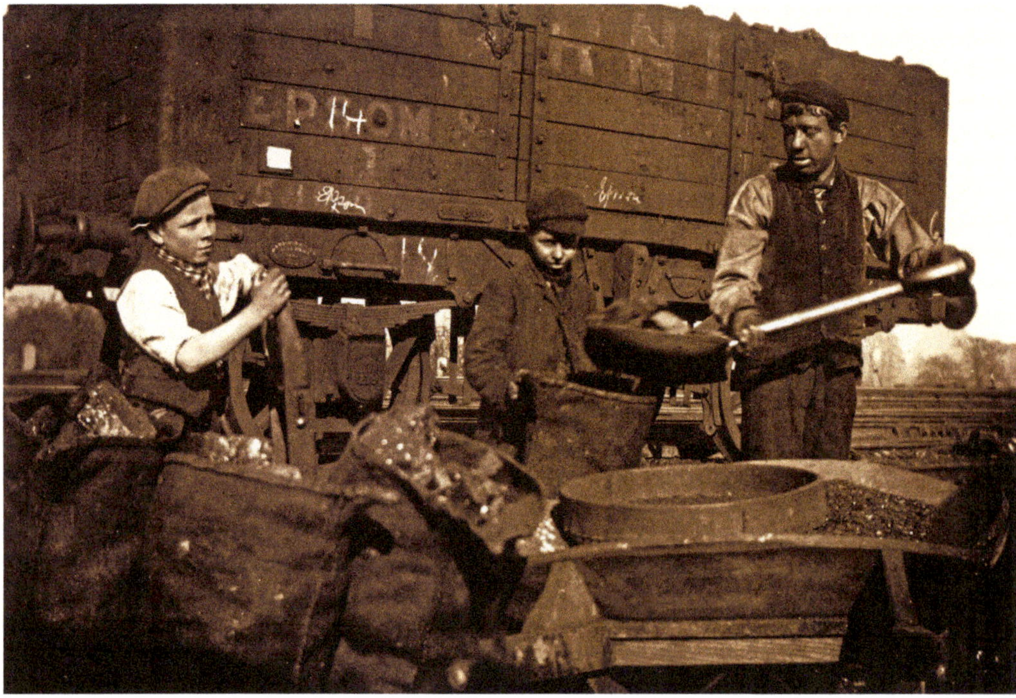

Unloading coal at Furniss' wharf in West Street. In the 1920s a 1-ton Ford lorry replaced the old horses and carts; the growth of suburbia had provided more customers.

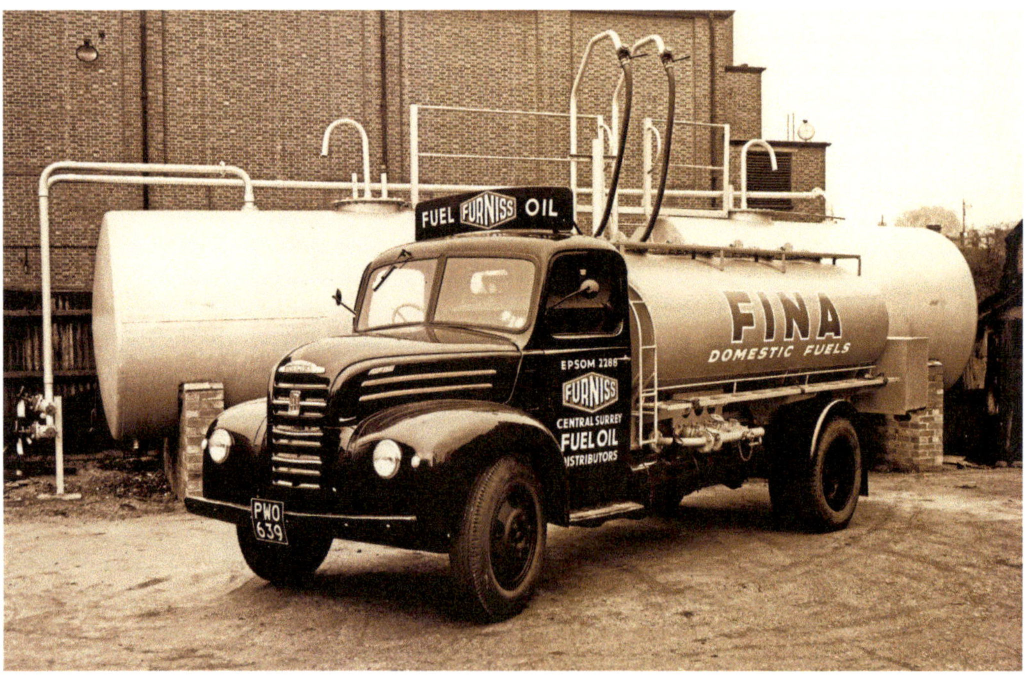

Furniss stored their oil in a yard backing onto the Odeon Cinema at Nos 114–6 High Street. The business closed in 1983 as the public converted to gas for central heating.

ON THE ROAD

Communications mattered in seventeenth-century England – the establishment of a daily post from Epsom to London during the Spa season was particularly newsworthy – but little was done to support them. Ratepayers were supposed to send men and carts to mend the highways, but this could be evaded, and in 1678 Humphrey Beane of Dorking Road led the Epsom gentry in a campaign of non-compliance. Since road maintenance was charged to the parish, any quagmire on the border was likely to be ignored by both sides: the Kingston route down Cox Lane was neglected from 1671 to 1685 despite repeated instructions from the magistrates.

The solution lay in turnpike roads, like that established by an Act of Parliament, which put a private company incharge of what is now the A24 from Dorking through Epsom and past Nonsuch towards London, and the A240 towards Kingston. The money collected at toll gates, like the one that gave its name to Woodgate at the top of Kingston Road, paid for good working roads. The great James McAdam saw to the surfacing of the wet patch between Bourne Hall and Glyn House in 1849, staying at the Spring Hotel while he invited tenders.

Better roads meant faster travel. The ostlers of the Spread Eagle and the Kings Head groomed and despatched Hunt's stagecoach, the first of the day, as it left for London at 8 a.m., and throughout the day a further seven coaches ran to the City, the last one leaving at 4.30 p.m. The 17-mile trip took two and a half hours, and there were a similar number making the return trip, some continuing as far as Brighton. Numbers were small, since each coach accommodated only fifteen passengers, most of them on the outside enduring the weather, which could be cruel. One coachman, William Furniss, died of exposure on the road between Ashtead and Half Mile Bush.

Stagecoaches were driven out of business by the railways, but freight transport from the railheads continued to rely on horses well into the twentieth century. Shoeing forges, wheelwrights and waggon-makers were a living tradition; the blacksmith's forge at No. 9 High Street was 'black with the smoke of score of years; the interior was full of strong lights and deep shadows, pleasant to see on a winter's day; and the rhythmic *ting* of the small hammer answering the sledge hammer was a pleasant thing to hear'. These men took pride in their work. Long after he had finished and sold one of his carts, James Wyatt of Ashtead was seen following it all the way up London Road just to see that the wheels ran true. The carters themselves were as committed to high standards. Tom Pocock of Ewell specialised in removals, even though some of the larger houses could take upwards of a week to pack and unpack. For deliveries to other parts of the country, he would secure the van and load it onto the train, knowing that it would be treated with equal care by the removal firm at the other end. His son William looked after the heavy horses, winning prizes at Crewe Annual Horse Show and Hampton Court Royal Horse Show.

At first a motor car, like a smartly turned-out carriage, was the preserve of the upper middle classes. When John Swift became Works Manager of the Woodcote Motor Co., he got the job because he had travelled on the Continent, and made contacts with the pre-Revolutionary Russian aristocracy. In 1928 he decided to branch out on his own, and learnt that Curtis Dairies were willing to sell off an acre on Reigate Road, with easy access to customers on the prestigious Ewell Downs estate. The gamble paid off five years later when the newly built Ewell Bypass brought a stream of traffic past his garage. By 1936 the premises had been rebuilt, and there were seventy people working there. After the war the business was squeezed by shortage of materials and customers, but it kept going through providing factory space for electro-plating and the assembly of lightbulbs.

The demand for new and improved roads spurred Surrey County Council into action. In 1921 they had bought the land between the railway and Chessington Road for their main highways depot, turning out around 250 tons of asphalt and tarmac each day. Stone road kerbs were made here, and so were the concrete decks of the bridges that replaced fords at Bonesgate and Ruxley Splash. Also based at the depot were the large tar-spraying machines, the first in the area. They were pulled by a 12-ton steamroller, and with steam heated by the roller's boiler, they could spray 2 miles of road in an hour or so, with up to 100 men on hand to cover the tar with grit.

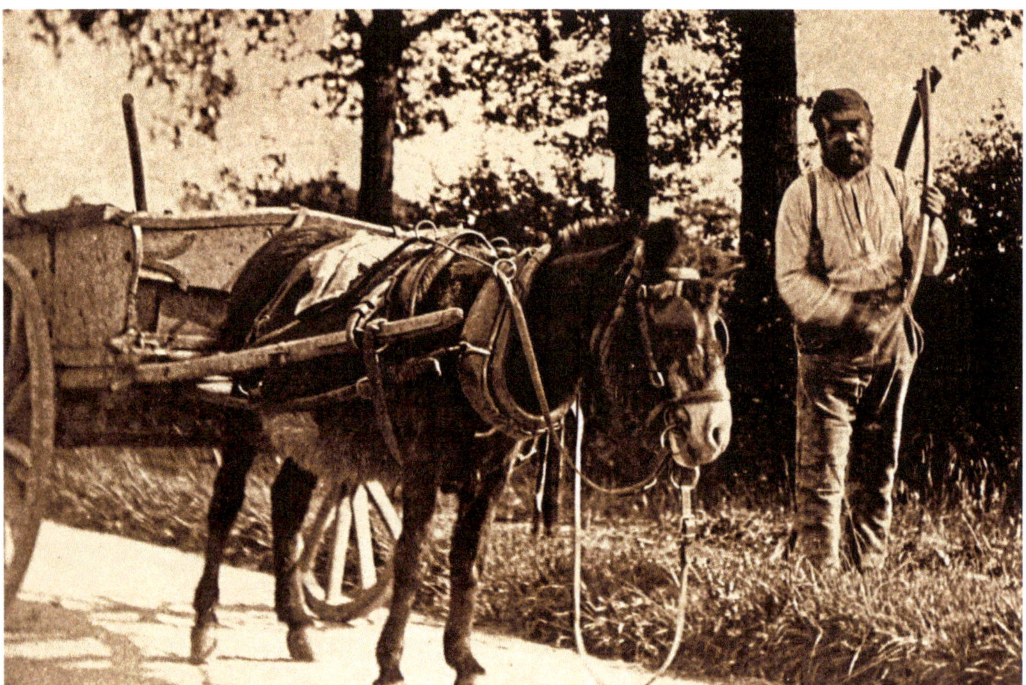

A roadman – possibly Joseph Penfold – in Chessington Road *c.*1890, with the scythe he used for cutting back the verges. He worked for the Urban District Council.

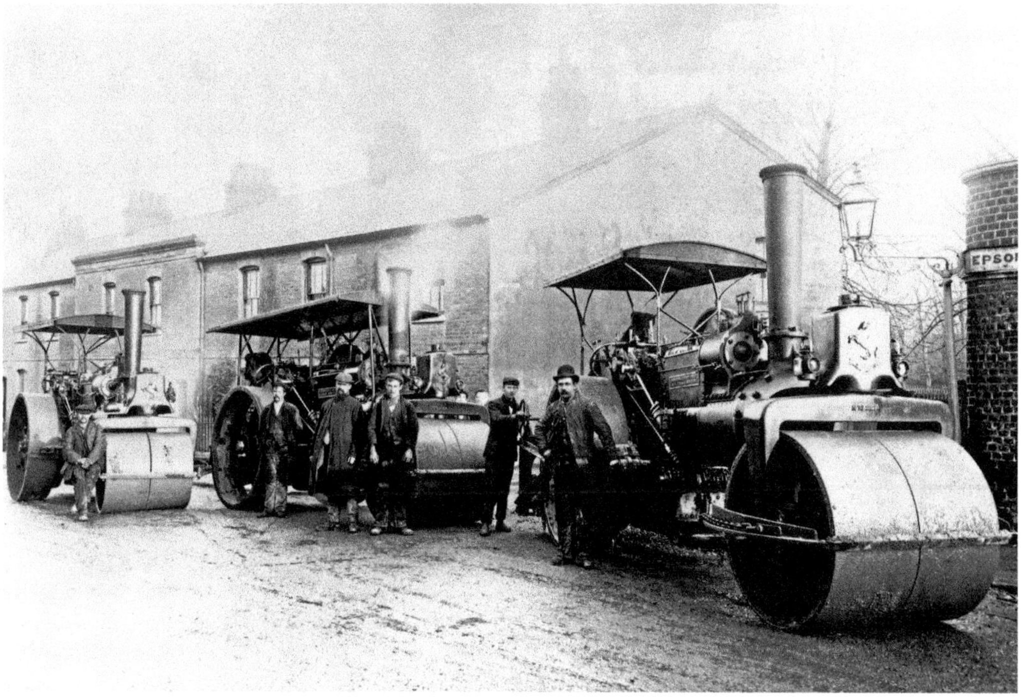

Three Aveling & Porter steamrollers outside No. 87 Ewell High Street. The council bought one from this firm; it got out of control in fog and caused £33 worth of damage.

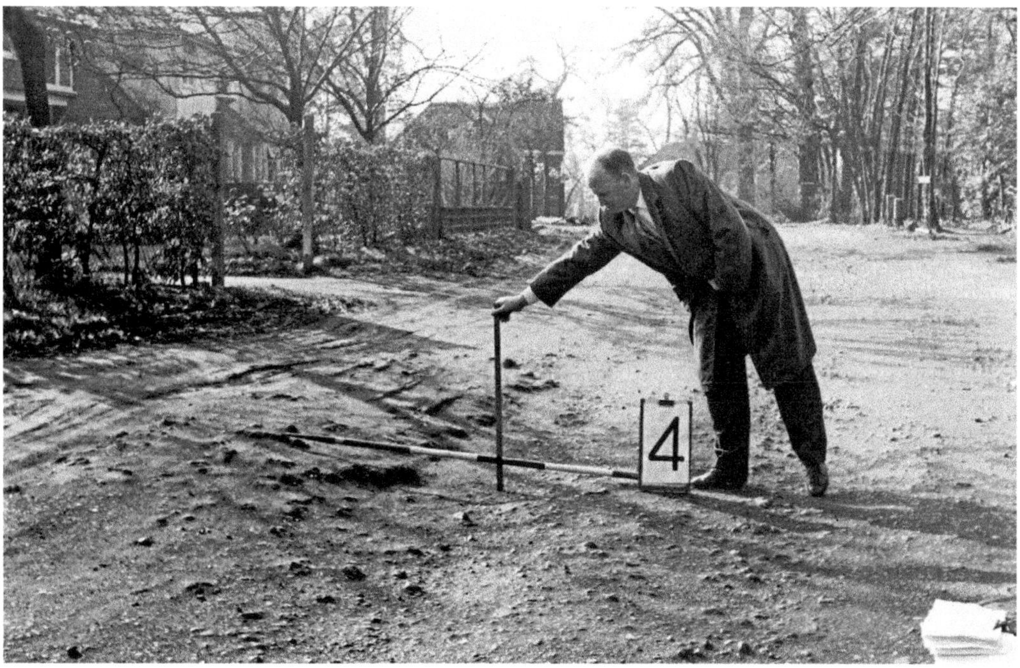

Measuring potholes in The Avenue with 1960s technology. Ninety miles of road fell to the responsibility of the Borough Council, either directly or as agent for the county.

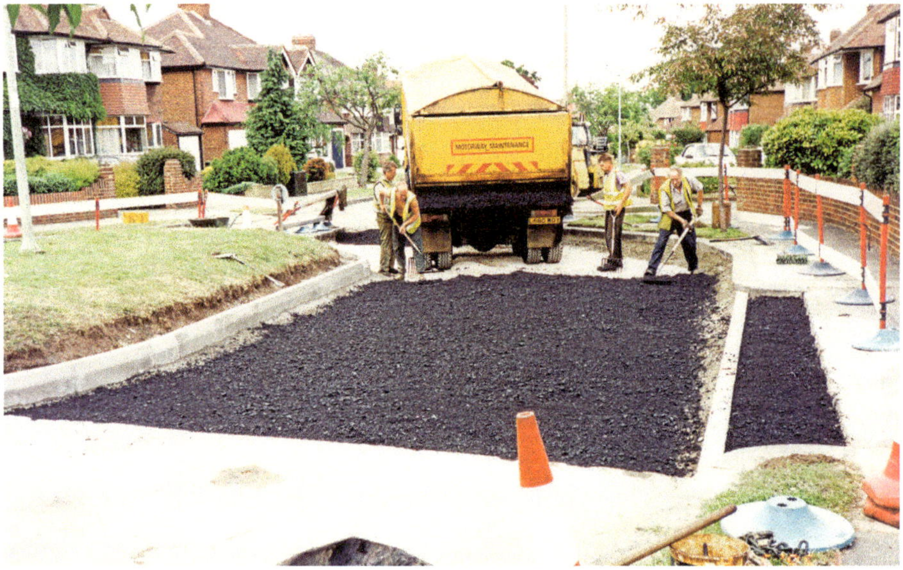

Resurfacing Stoneleigh Avenue in 1995. From the start of the twentieth century, the council had a plant for manufacturing at Highways House beside Ewell West station.

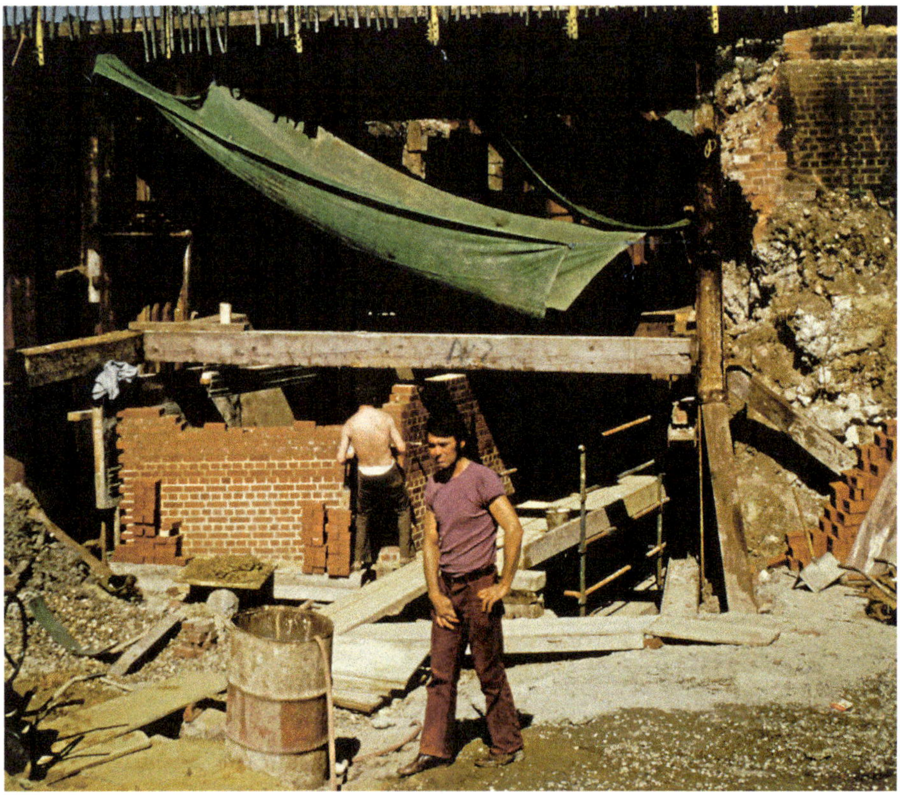

Building a new embankment beside Kingston Road, which was sunk deeper under the railway bridge in 1972. The bus stop here keeps the traditional name of Beggars Hill.

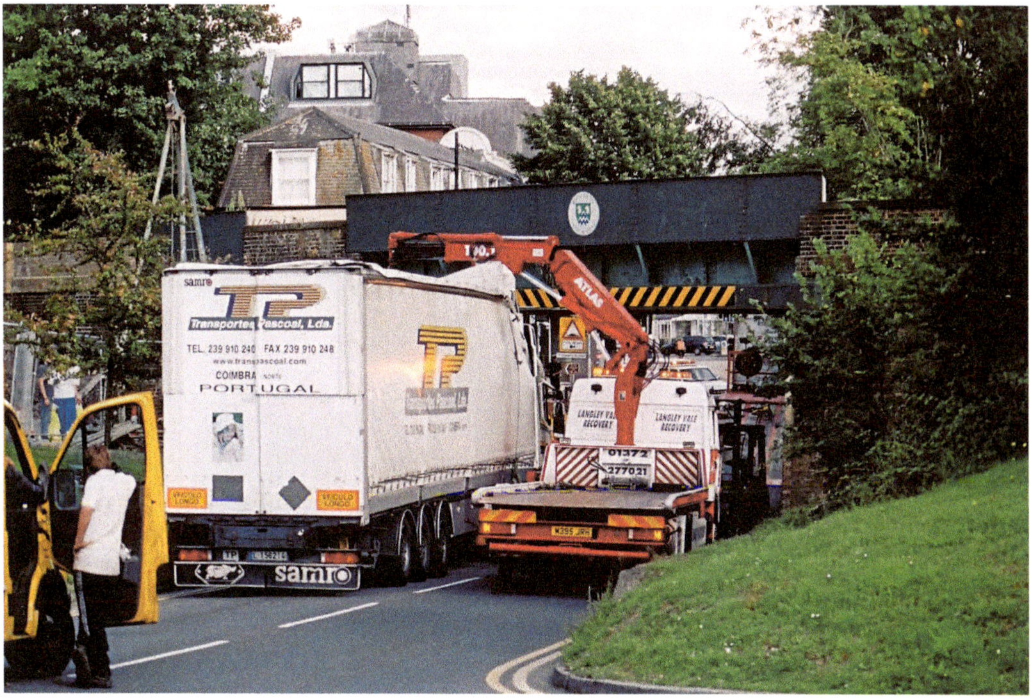

Problems at the West Hill railway bridge in 2007. Langley Vale Vehicle Recovery of No. 69 Grosvenor Road will save the day. Beyond the bridge is the Furniss house, Nos 26–28.

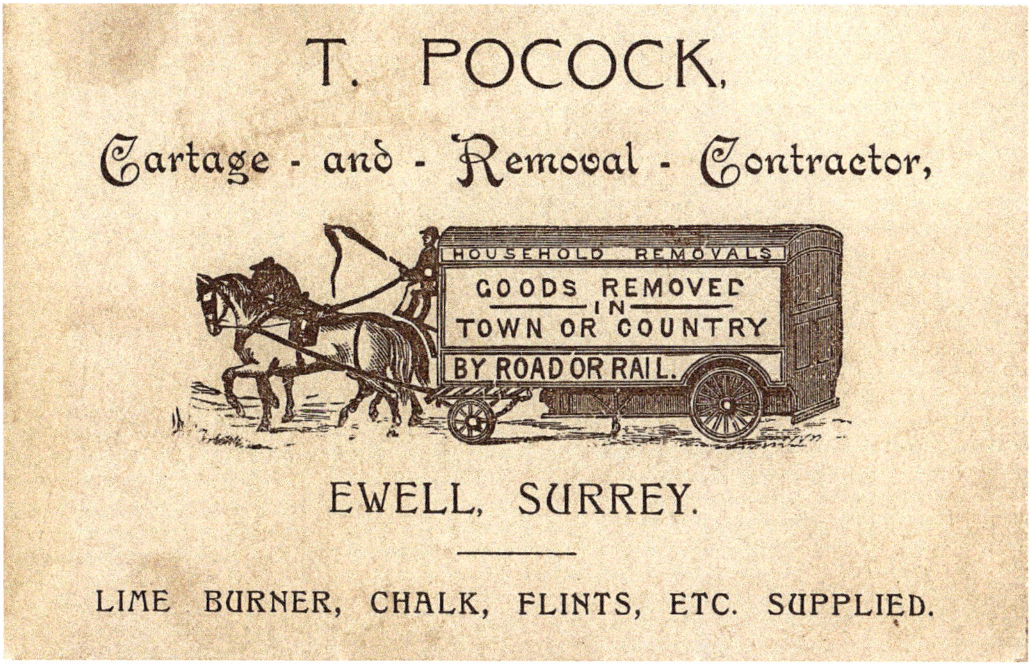

In the 1890s Thomas Pocock began operating his own haulage company. He also owned a chalk pit off Longdown Road, where Podgy Edwards ran the limekiln.

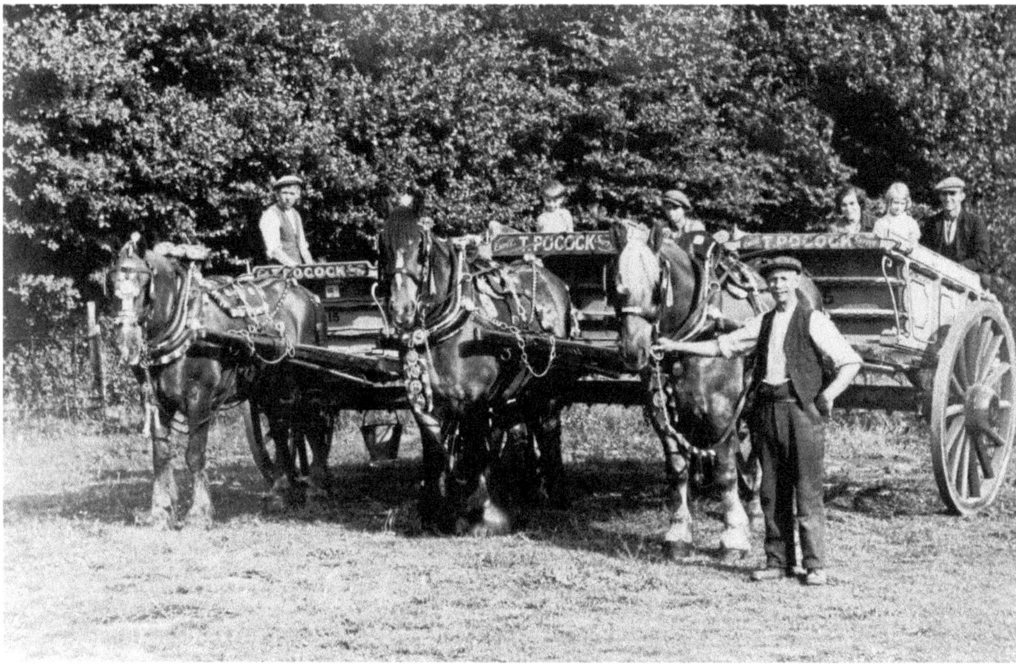

William Pocock, son of Thomas and father of young Tom, had a dozen heavy horses at his yard in Chessington Road. They didn't go over to lorries until the 1970s.

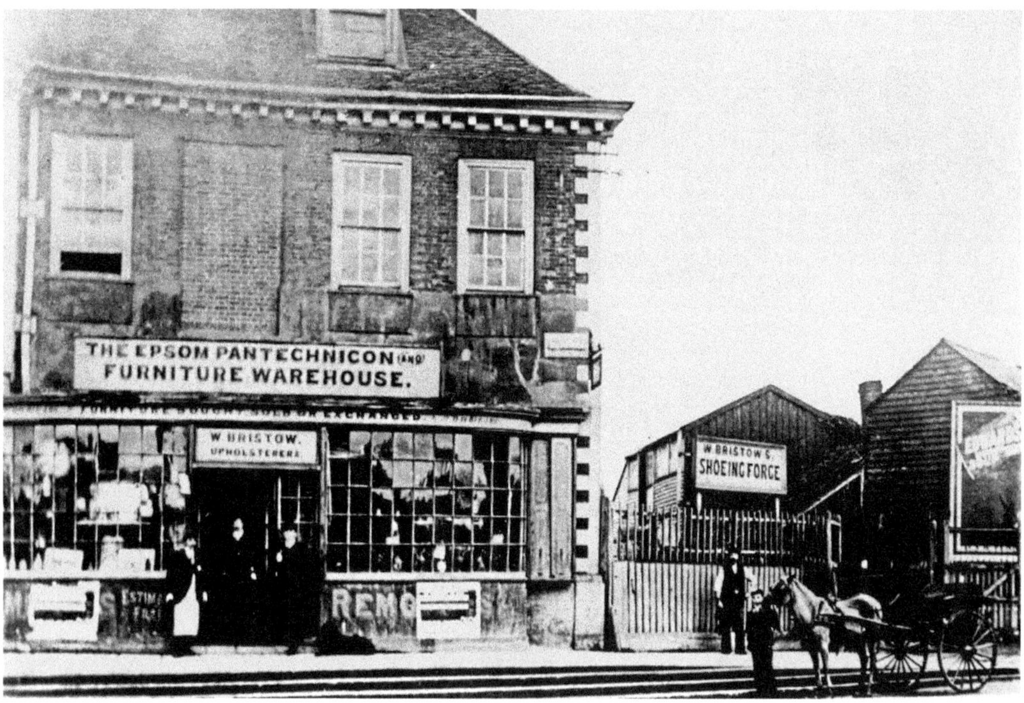

William Bristow ran livery stables at the Spread Eagle and a warehouse in the old Assembly Rooms. He always wore a fine silk frock coat, with smoking cap and monocle.

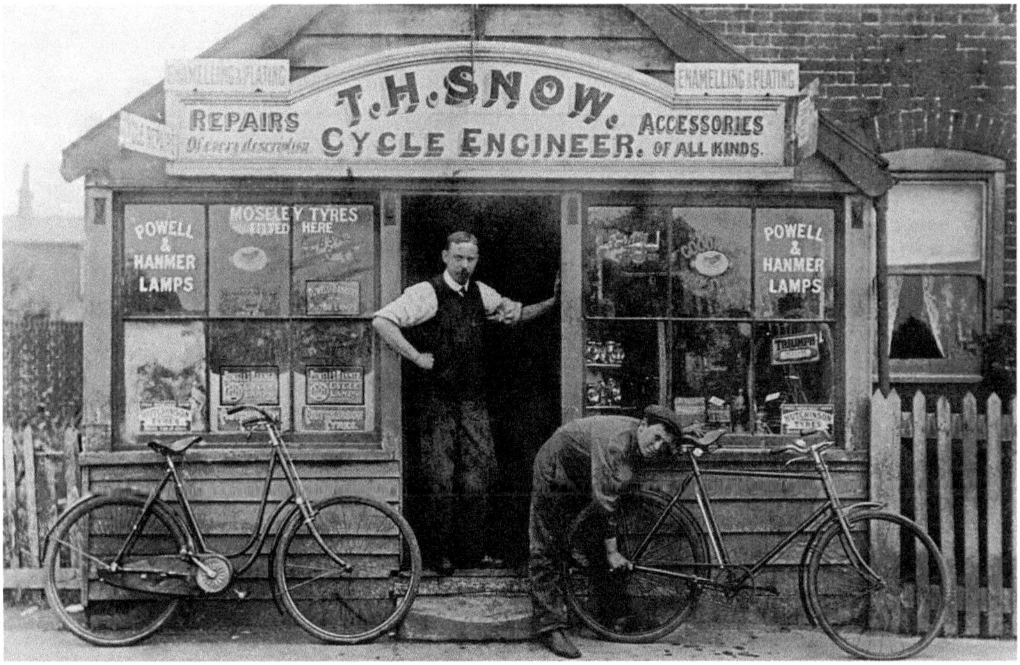

Tom Snow and his son Frederick at No. 60 East Street. Theirs was a growing business: the Wellington advertised as a Cyclist's Hotel and No. 2 South Street as a Cycle Store.

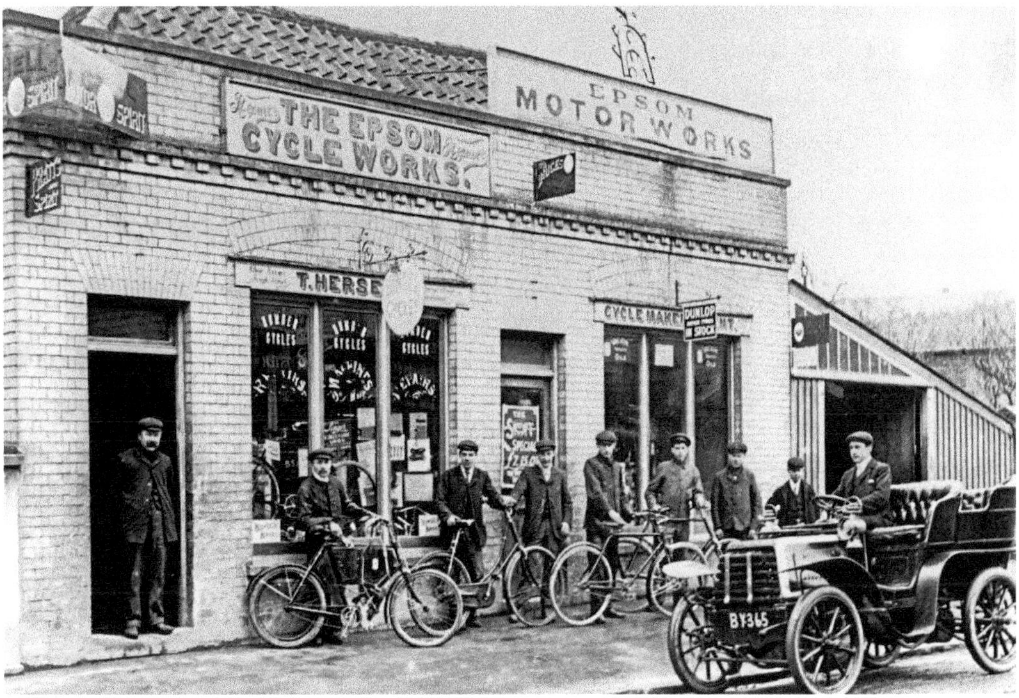

Thomas Hersey's cycle works, at the top of South Street, later became a garage. In 1916, after he had rebuilt it, he was appointed dealer for Studebaker cars from America.

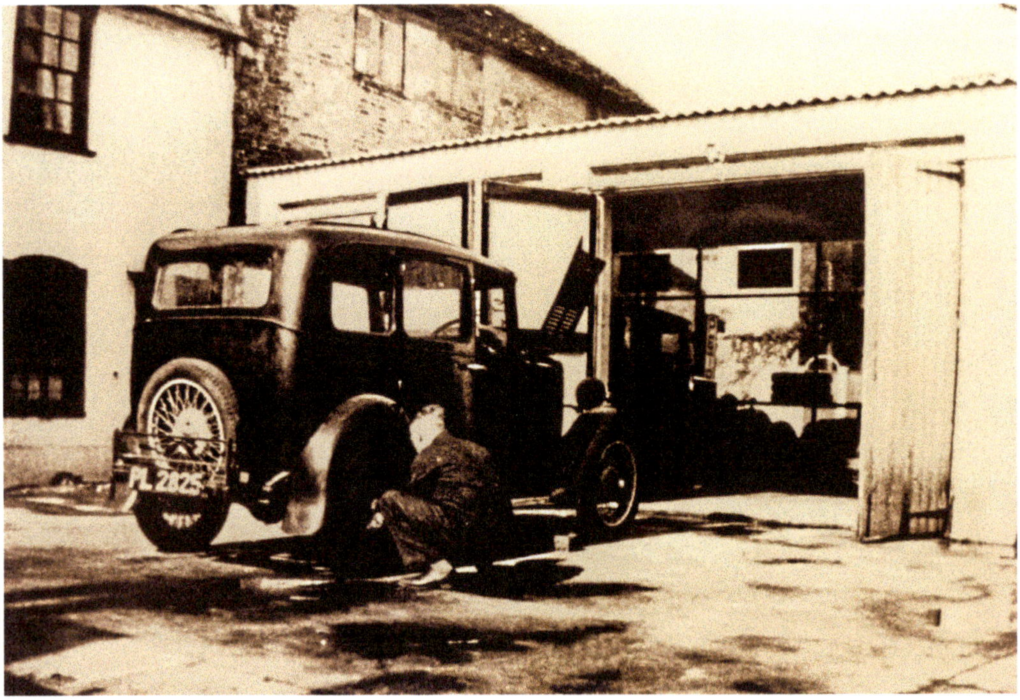

The old racing stables at No. 28 Church Street can be seen behind the shed, although they have given way to the motor business incorporated as the Farm Garage in 1927.

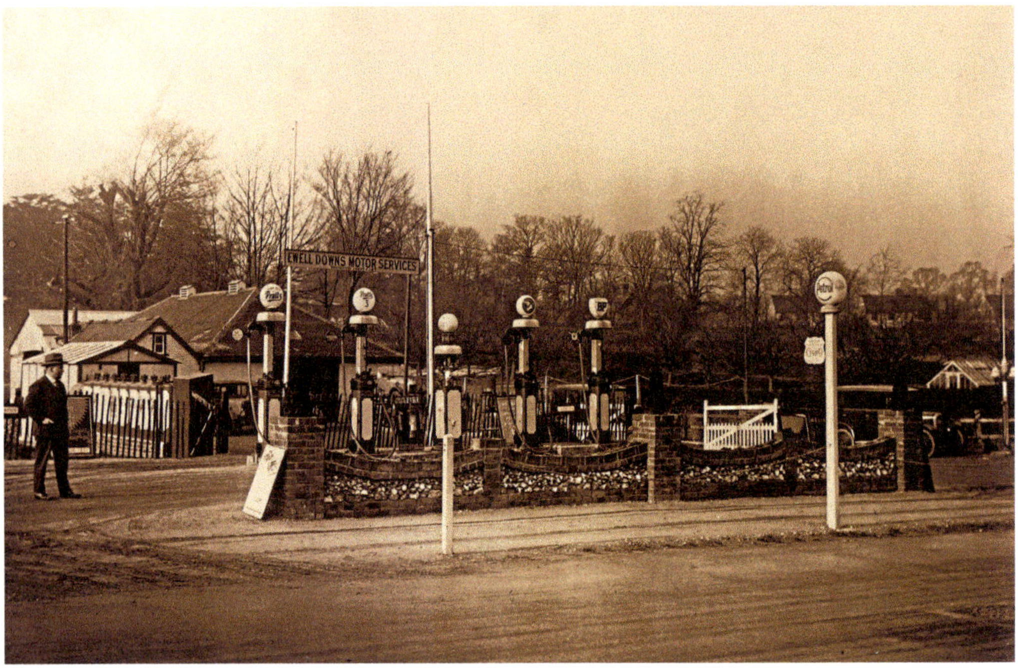

John Swift trained at the Woodcote Motor Co., successor to Thomas Hersey's business, then started out on his own in 1928 with a converted cowshed by Reigate Road.

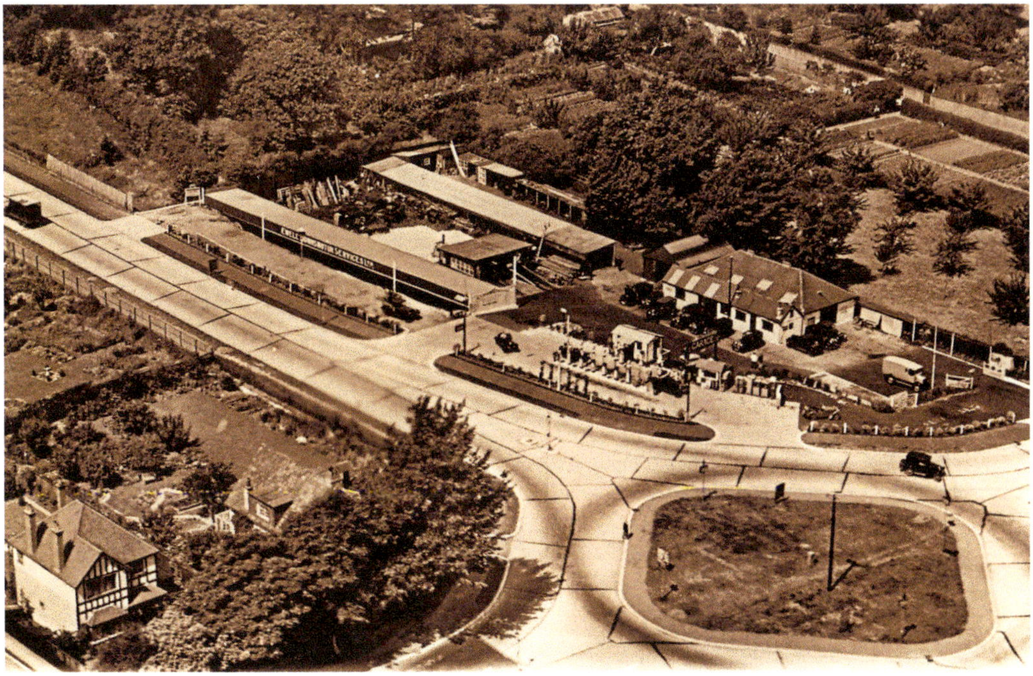

Above: Ewell Downs Motors flourished after 1933, when the new bypass brought traffic to its door. Petrol pumps were fitted and a steel-framed workshop replaced the cowshed.

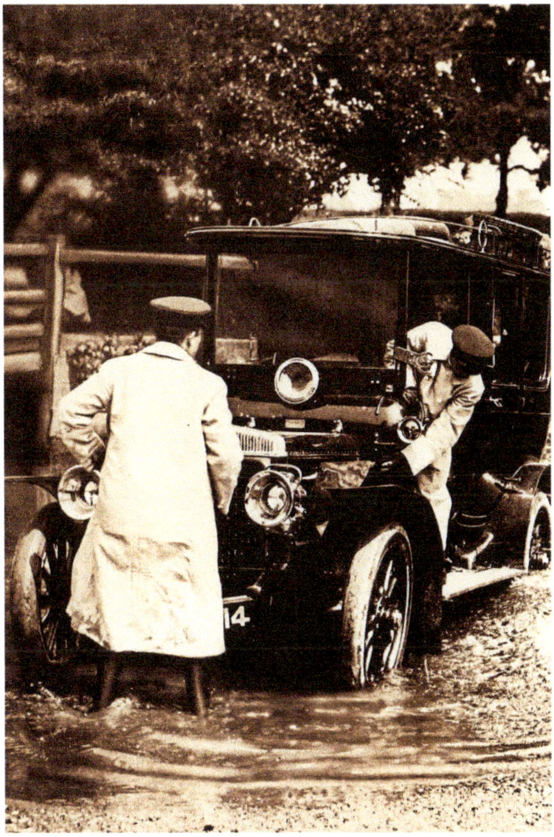

Right: At the Ruxley Lane splash, the Hogsmill could flood the road for 50 yards. Lord Lonsdale, who always went to the Derby in his trademark yellow car, got stuck here.

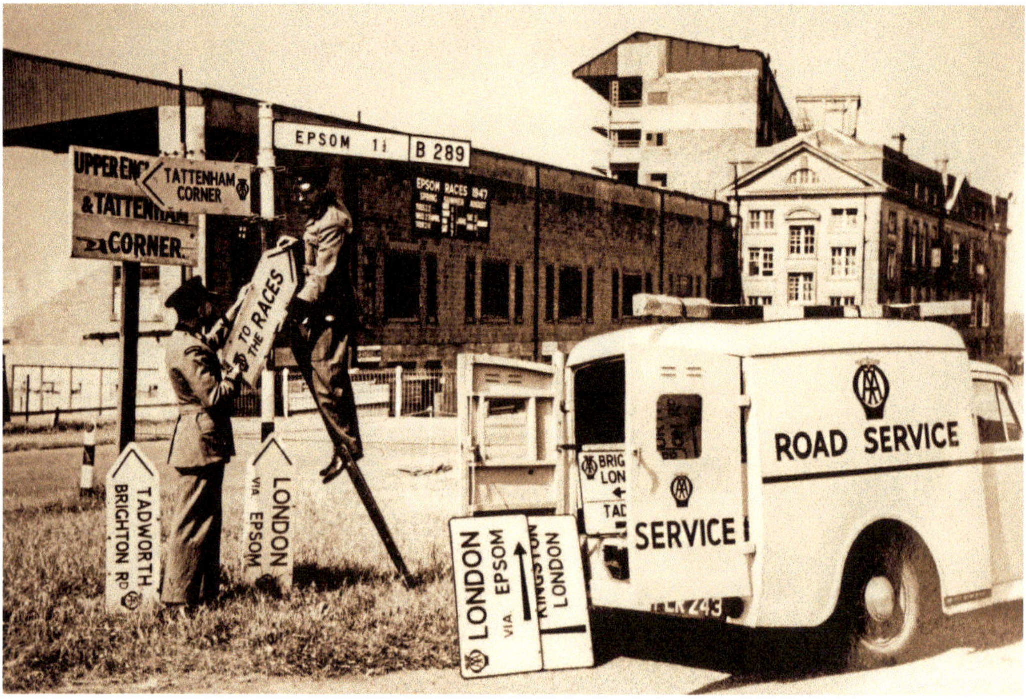

In 1947 the profit from car park fees at the Derby was £9,000, three times what it had been before the war. The AA were responsible for putting up temporary road signs.

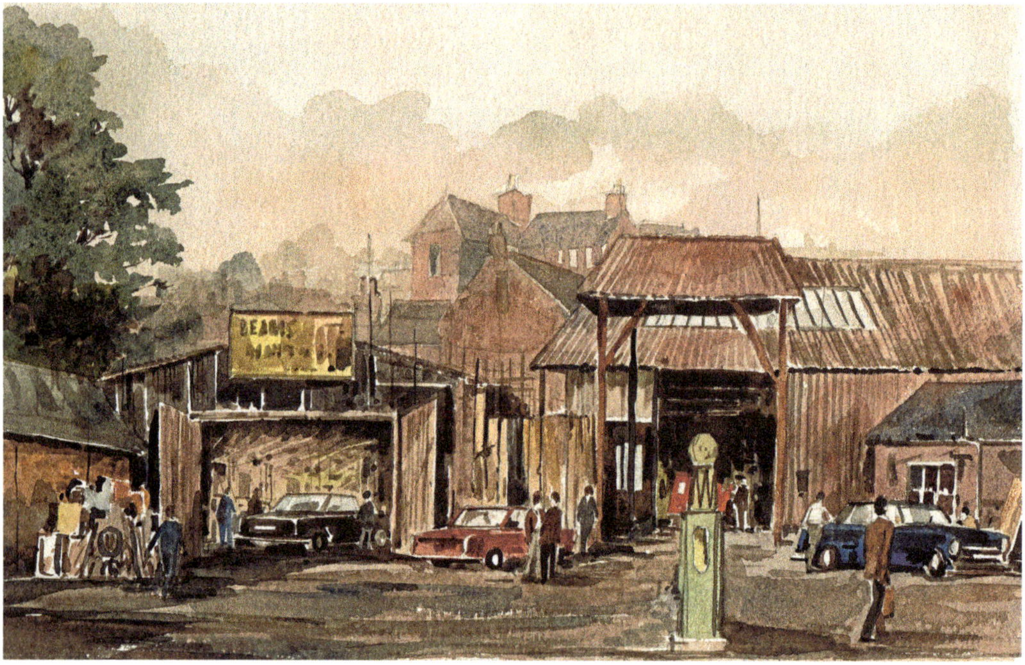

A garage stood beside the Spring Hotel, where once stagecoach horses had rested. Founded by Norman Simmons in the 1920s, it appears here in its last days in 1961.

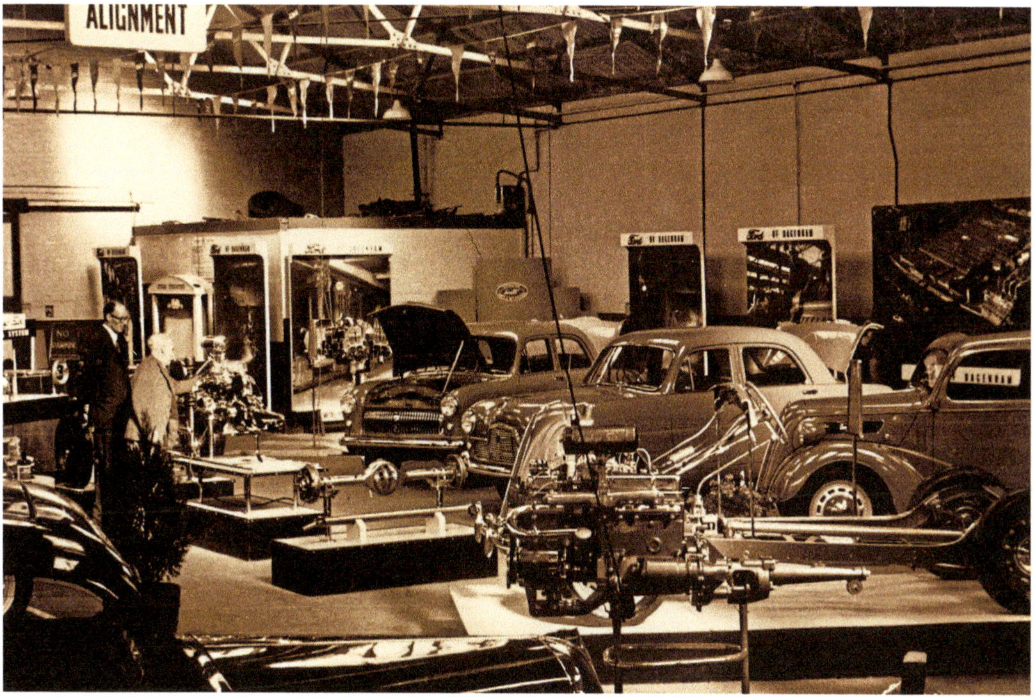

Inside the showroom at Farm Garage for Ford Service Week, September 1952. Alignment, Welding, Specialist Tools, Electrical Repair and Engine Repair were on offer.

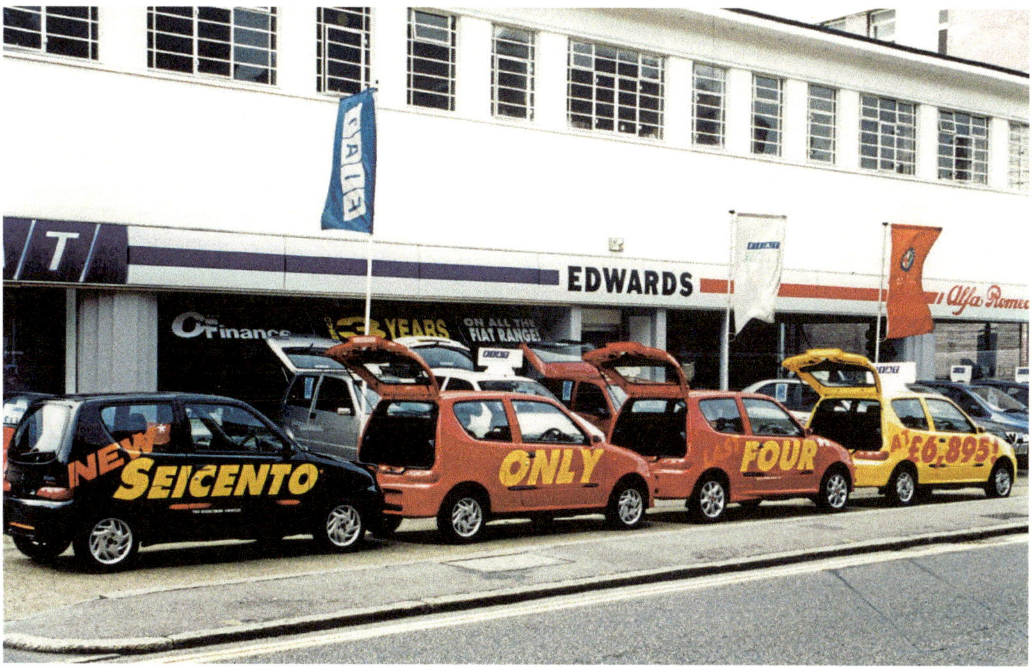

In 1935 Woodcote Motors moved to No. 6 Church Street, an art deco building by the Wallis Gilbert partnership. H. P. Edwards was running it in 1998, shortly before it closed.

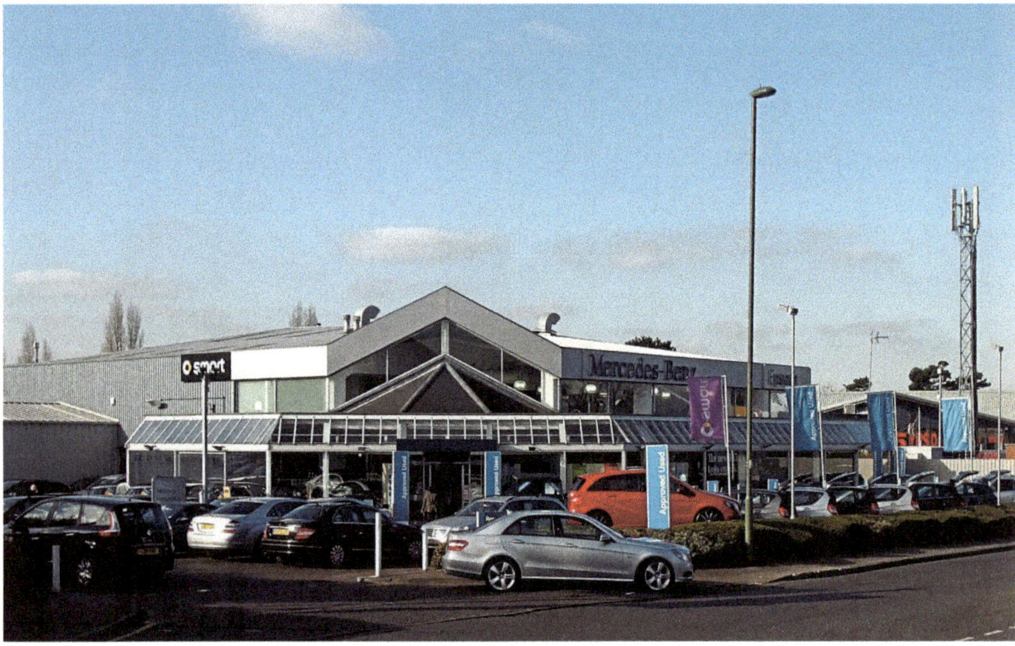

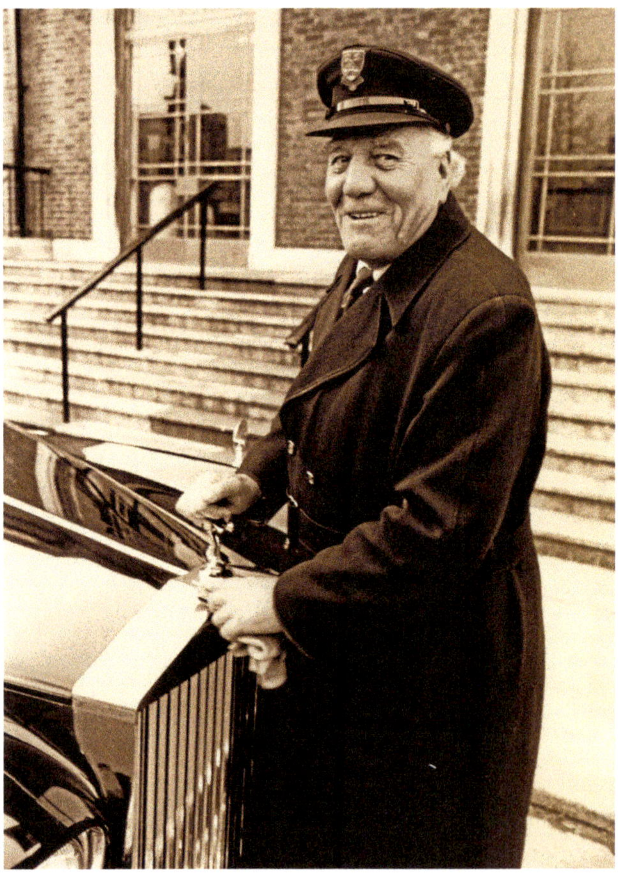

Above: Page Motors established a branch on the Kiln Lane estate when this was opened in the 1960s. When they moved to East Street, Mercedes-Benz rebuilt the showroom.

Left: The mayor's chauffeur polishes his Silver Lady outside the old Baths Hall. Rolls-Royce had a school of instruction at Seleng House off Epsom Road from 1925 to 1930.

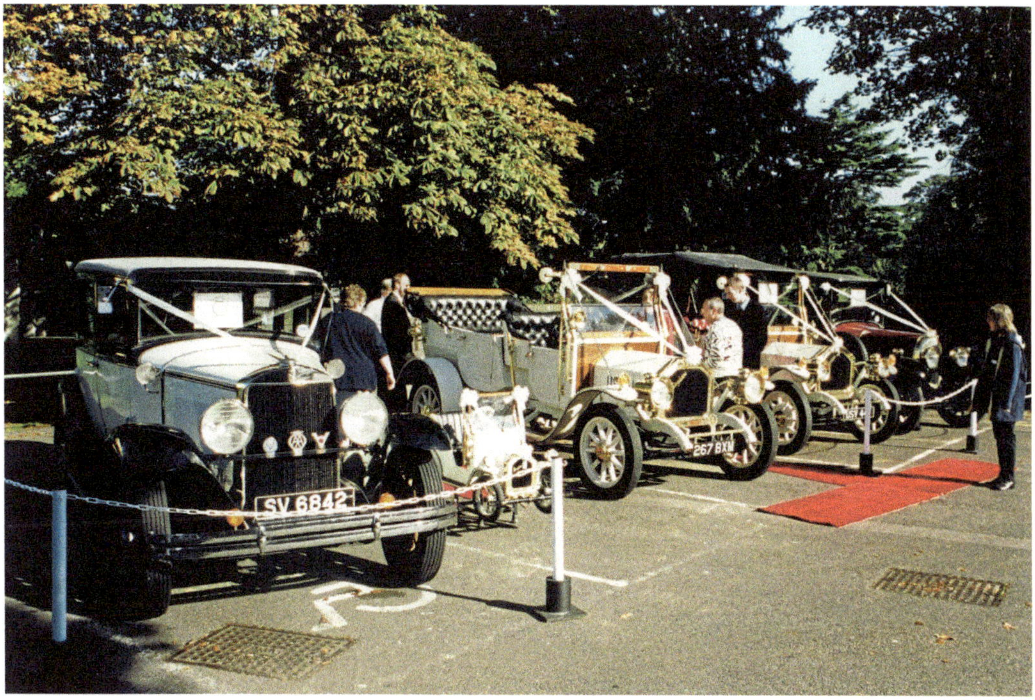

A parade of vintage cars advertising for a wedding fair outside Bourne Hall in 1999. In 2017 a classic car rally featured for the first time as part of the Derby entertainment.

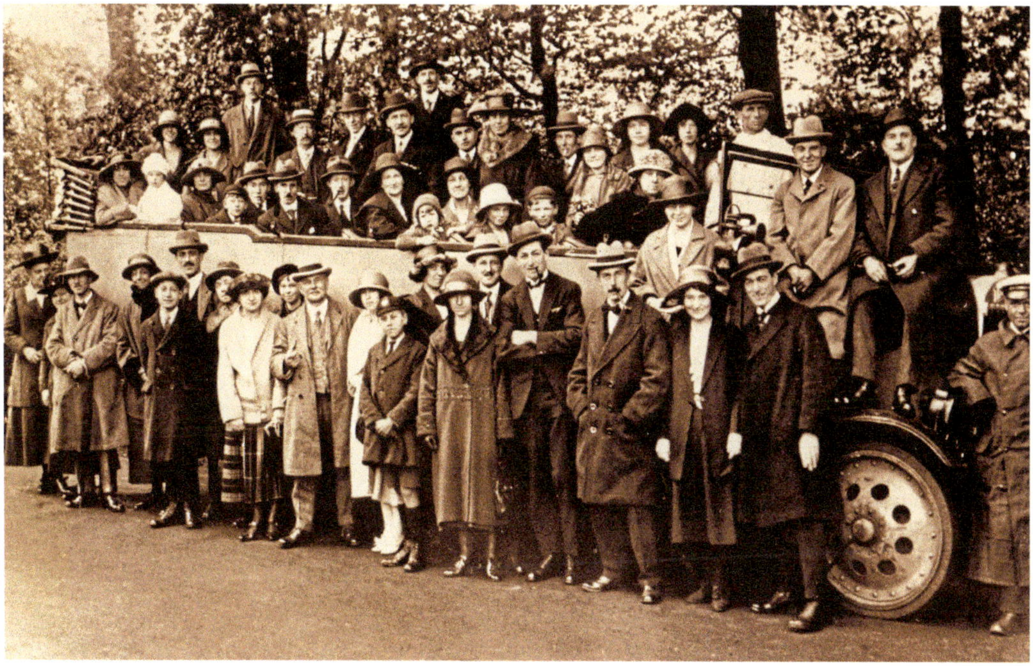

An early outing with Richmond Coaches. Roddy Richmond had set up business between Boots and a blacksmith in 1920, buying an ex-army Lancia charabanc.

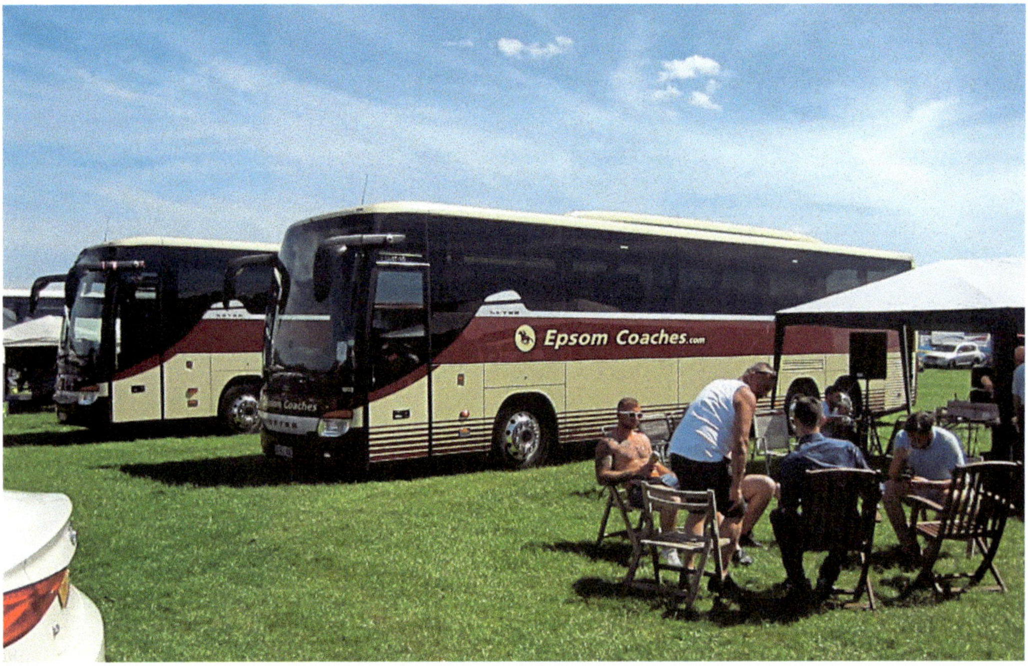

The last appearance of Epsom Coaches, at the 2017 Derby. Andrew Richmond, grandson of the founder, sold up to the RATP group, who ran down the coach service.

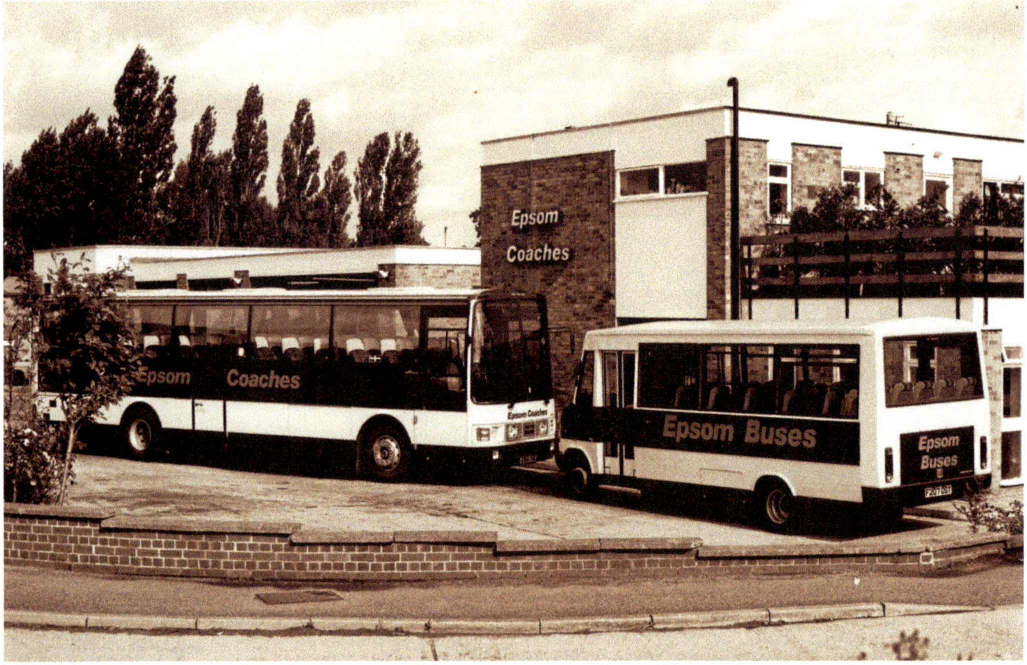

In 1971 the Richmond family, now Epsom Coaches, moved to the Longmead Estate. With the deregulation of bus services in 1986, they registered routes as Epsom Buses.

INDUSTRIAL SCALE

In 1684 the brickyard on Epsom Common was making stock bricks 'so hard, that we have laid them under a loaden cart-wheel, and yet they will not break'. Work followed an annual cycle, with the brick-earth dug at Christmas, weathered until Easter, and then tempered by the workmen trampling it. A team of three (one man tempering, another casting, and a boy to carry and stack the bricks) could make 2,000 in a day. Production followed much the same lines in the late nineteenth century when the Nonsuch Brick Works, owned by Stone & Swallow, had two sites, one at Kiln Lane, the other in London Road, just opposite the Brick Kiln pub, where the men used to sink a khaki baby – a stoneware flagon of beer – after dehydrating at work. In their leisure time the Ewell brick-makers used to make little flower vases and spittoons out of the rough clay. The most difficult productions were the chimneypots, 5 or 6 feet high, some of which can still be seen on roofs in Chessington Road.

Although these bricks were intended for local builders, other products were distributed further afield. Ewell had two ancient corn mills, but with developments in output – and the provision of two windmills, one on Epsom Common and the other at the parish boundary – it was found that the needs of the neighbourhood could be served by the Upper Mill alone. In 1732 William Jubb arrived in the village with plans to convert the Lower Mill for making paper. He built extensions to store the cotton and linen rags which constituted his raw material. Trip-hammers pounded these into pulp, which was couched and laid into sheets, and then hung to dry in a long barn. The paper was good enough to be used for a petition tendering for the manufacture of English banknotes – but not good enough to convince Parliament that this would work. When Jubb's son died in 1795, the mill went back to grinding corn once more.

Further downstream were the gunpowder mills established by Alexander Bridges in 1754. These were well away from inhabited areas, with wide stretches of water beside the buildings to absorb the blast if they blew up – a necessary precaution, because in the next 120 years there were sixteen explosions and an overall loss of twenty-two lives. The incorporating mills, where the charcoal, sulphur and saltpetre were mixed into gunpowder, were most at risk, followed by the corning house, where it was reduced to grains, and the press house, where it was prepared for transport. In 1865 Lewis Hills and William Horscroft were packing barrels in the press house when a spark caught the powder; only fragments of their bodies could be collected for the inquest. John Carr Sharpe, the foreman who had taken over from the Bridges family, realised that the mills would not meet government safety standards and had them closed in 1872.

A combination of government intervention and local feeling pushed the area into providing public utilities. After the damning health report of 1849, Epsom's local board realised that a clean supply of water was needed. They bought land in East Street and sank an artesian well in 1853, which raised 100,000 gallons a day – enough for the town's population of 5,000. Ewell people, not wanting to grow too dependent on their urban neighbour, joined up with the Sutton District Water Co. in 1871, although many continued to rely on jugs filled at the old Dipping Place by Bourne Hall. In 1896 a new reservoir in Downs Road served the growing needs of Epsom, including the mental hospitals, which took a third of the supply.

The Epsom and Ewell Gas Co. was set up in 1839, although its early prospects were dim in more senses than one – only after protests at inadequate illumination for Queen Victoria's wedding was the supply increased. By 1911 there were three gasholders between East Street and the railway line, and in the next year the undertaking was taken over by the Wandsworth Gas Co. The gasometers saw new life in the Second World War, when they stored hydrogen for barrage balloons.

The generating station in Depot Road was set up as a council undertaking in 1902, originally steam powered but later operated by diesel engines. In 1918 power was extended to Ewell, although some of the big houses had anticipated the move by laying on their own supply. Bourne Hall, the first house in the neighbourhood to have electric lighting, relied on a gas engine and a 100-volt battery, while at Ewell Castle another 12-hp engine fed the battery cells, and at Ewell Court power was supplied by a turbine housed in one of the old gunpowder mill buildings by the River Hogsmill.

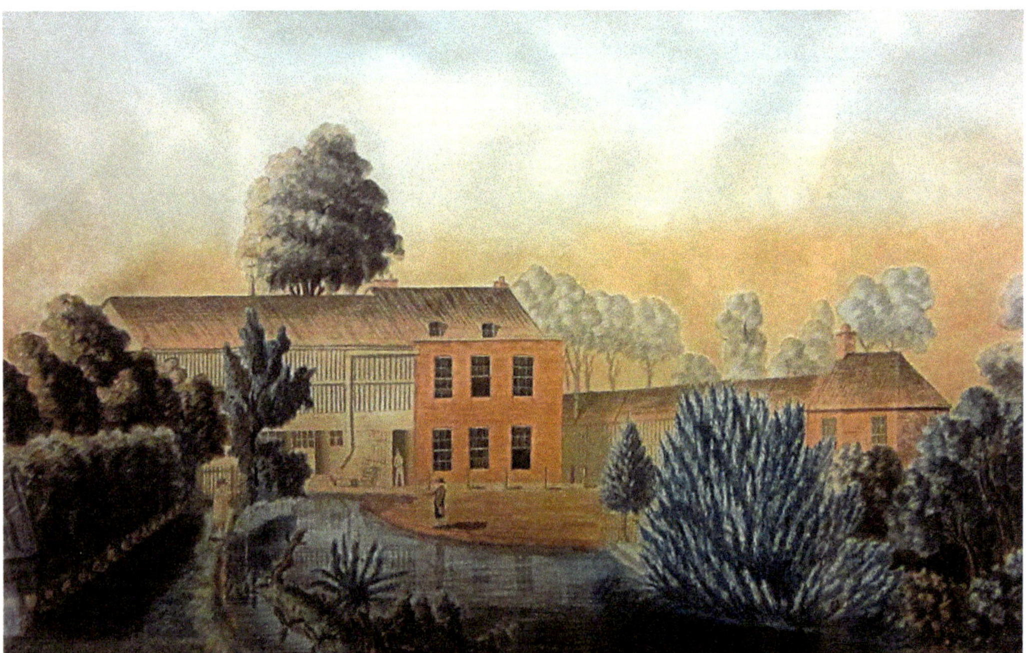

William Jubb the younger ran paper mills at Ewell from 1739, evidently with time for his garden as well: the stream in the foreground powered the mill wheel and hammers.

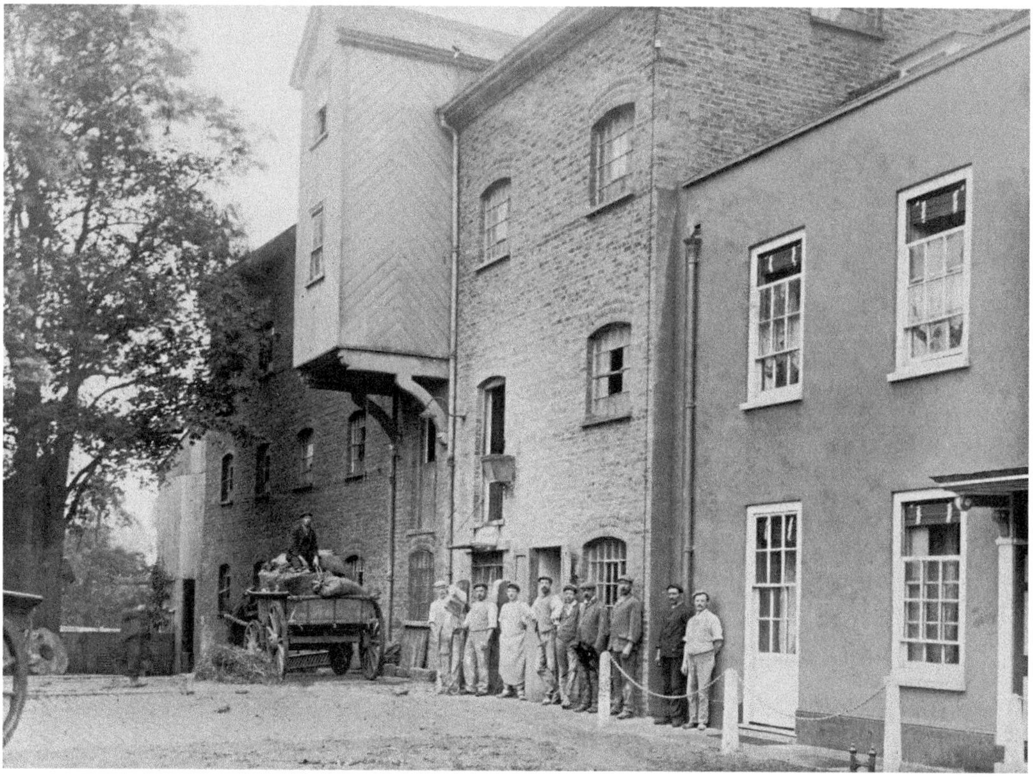

Above: In the 1870s the Lower Mill was rebuilt, to be run by two shifts of six men each. It had a private railway siding to deliver coal for the engine and take flour to London.

Right: In 1896 the Lower Mill went over to roller plant – for whiter flour – but the nearby Upper Mill (also owned by Hall & Davidson) kept its millstones for wholemeal bread.

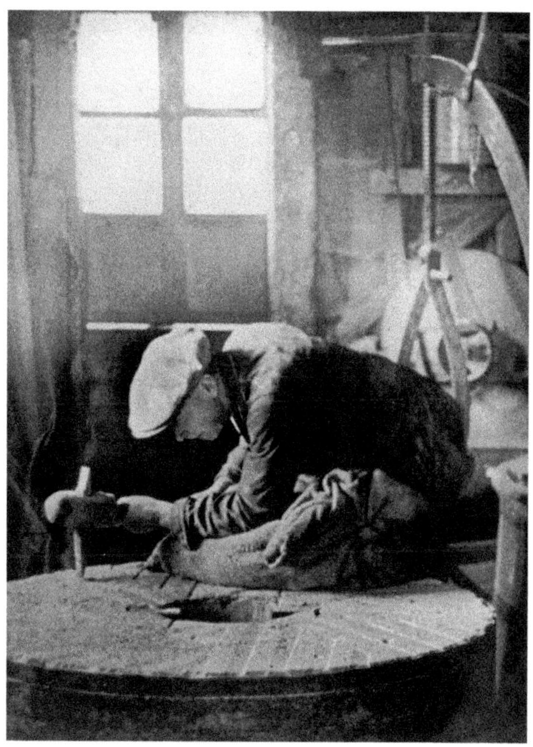

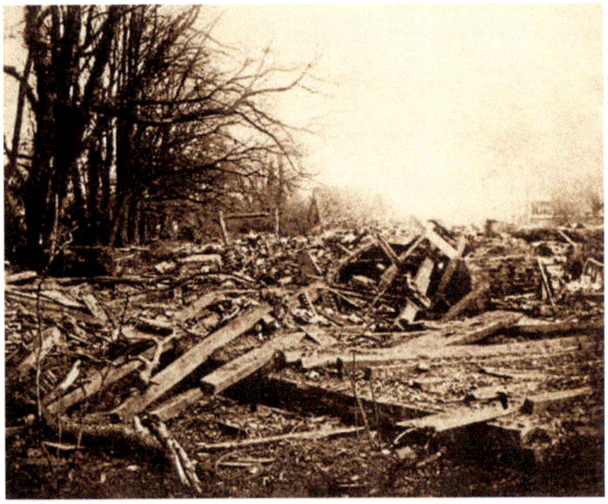

Left: The corning houses at Ewell Powder Mills held machinery for rendering the powder into pellets. One of these exploded in 1863, killing James Baker and two colleagues.

Below: Mike Ralph at Ewell Forge in 1970. His grandfather had moved here in 1914, when the previous smith signed up for the army while drunk at the Eight Bells next door.

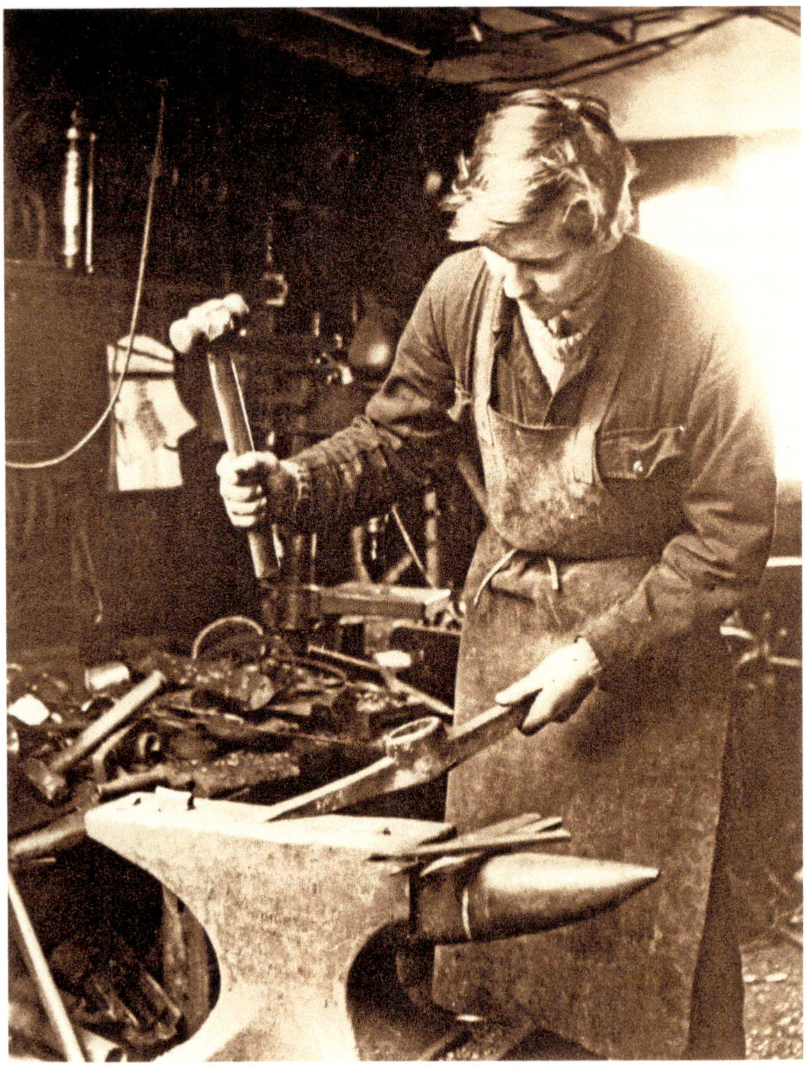

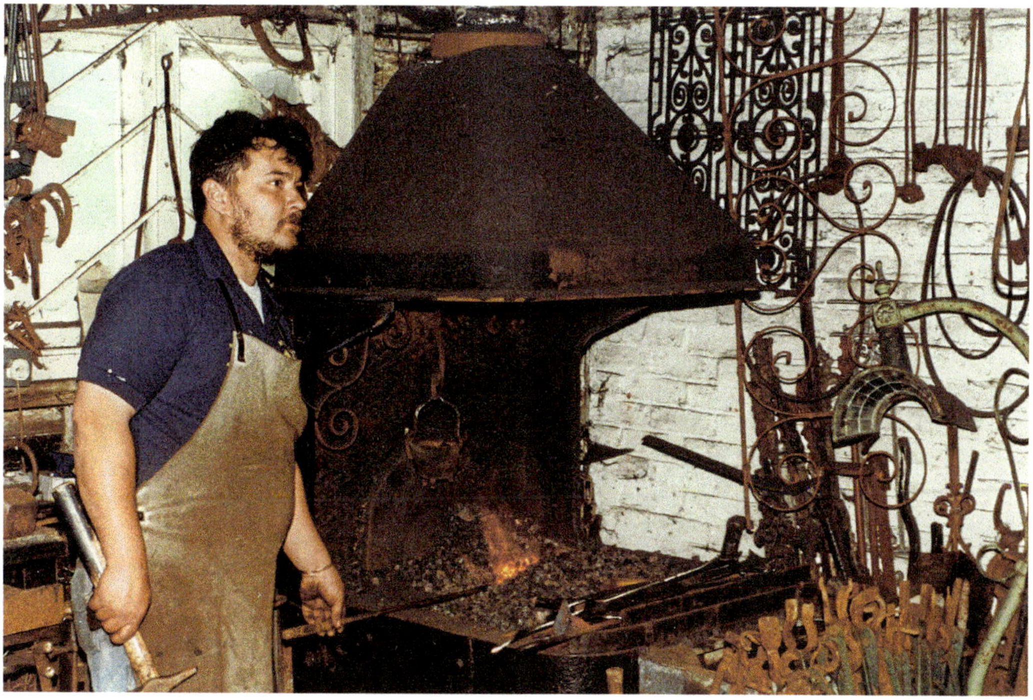

Mike Demianow at Black Barn Forge in 1994. In this building, once part of Long Grove Farm, he made Cinderella's coach for the ballet and gates for Waterloo Bridge.

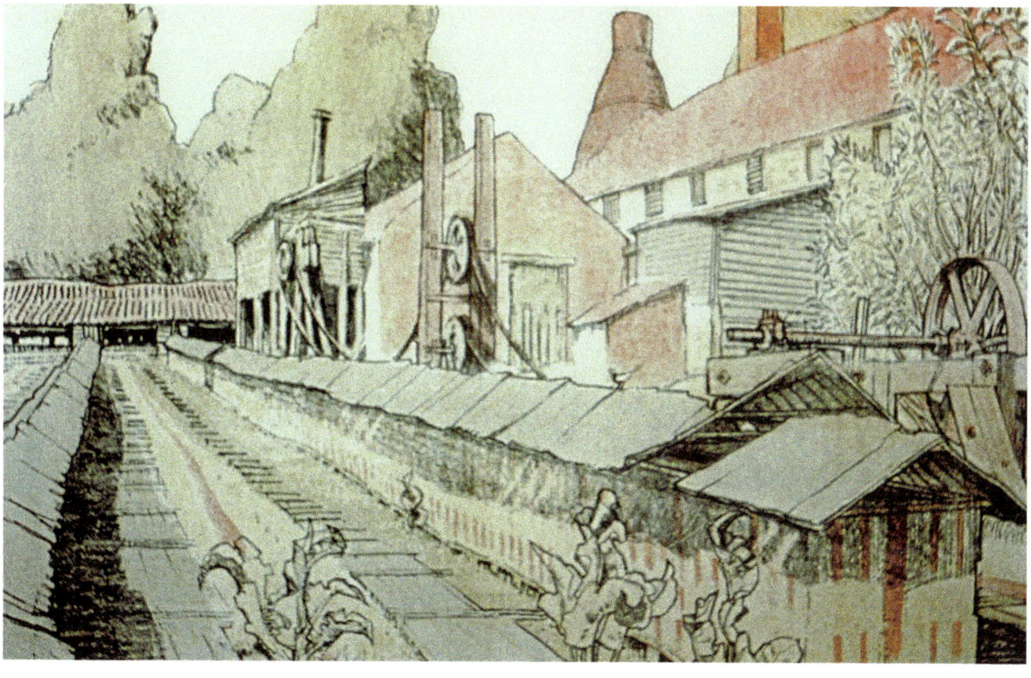

The Nonsuch Pottery was established by William Waghorn. Matthew Swallow, his foreman, went into partnership with John Stone in 1850 and ran it as a brickworks.

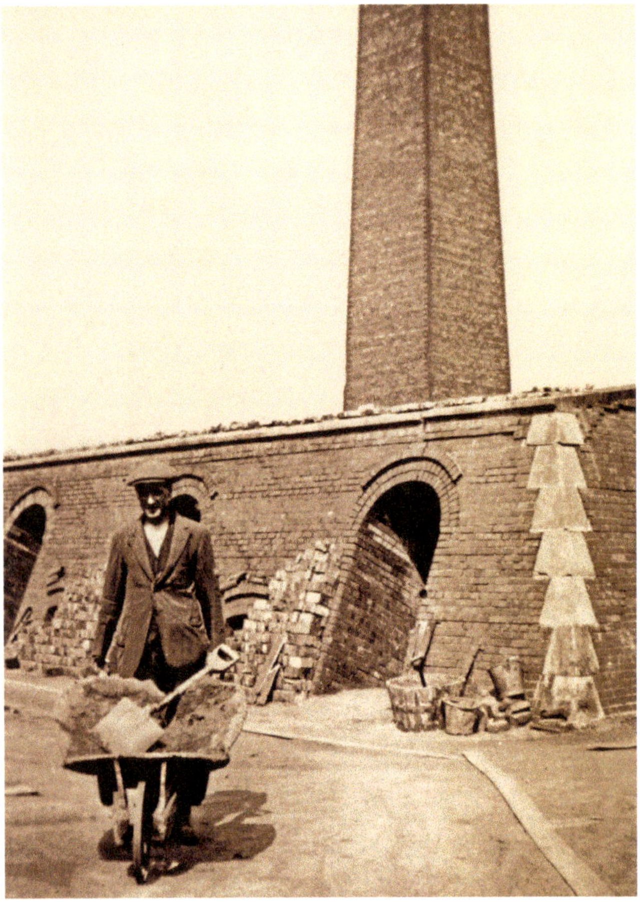

Left: Albert George Sparrow at the brickworks off East Street. Established by Stone and Swallow in 1859, when the railway came, this ran until destroyed by fire in the 1930s.

Below: In 1926 new reservoirs were built at the top of Downs Road, which had a connecting main to the waterworks. A heavy oil engine at East Street worked the pumps.

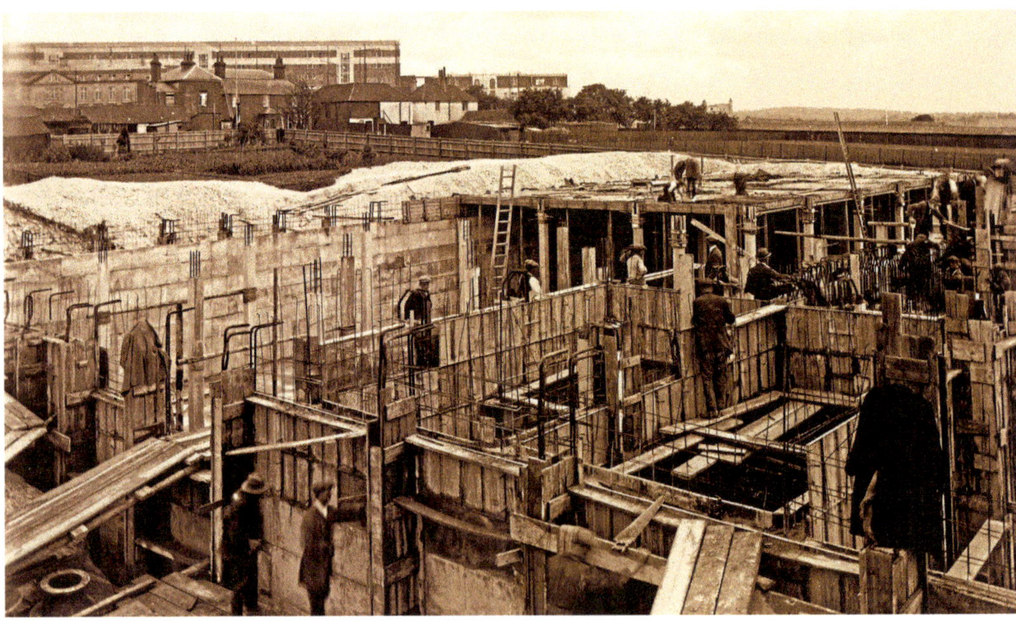

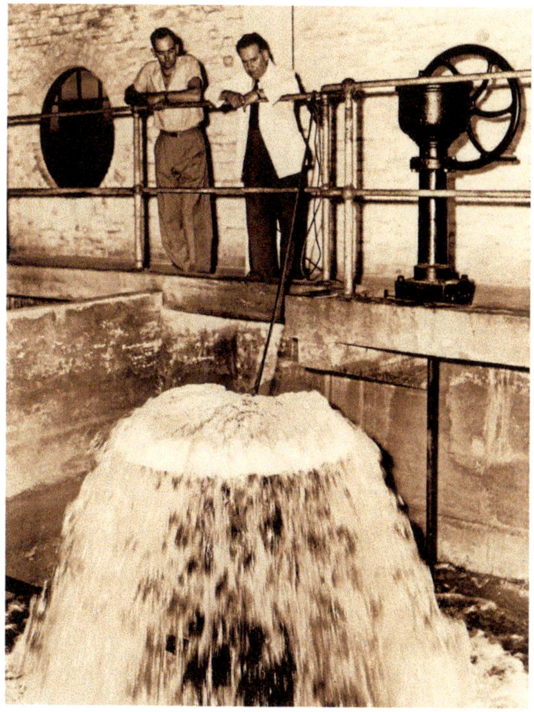

East Street waterworks in 1950, shortly after the completion of a 600,000-gallon contact tank and installation of chlorination and dechlorination plant for the hard water.

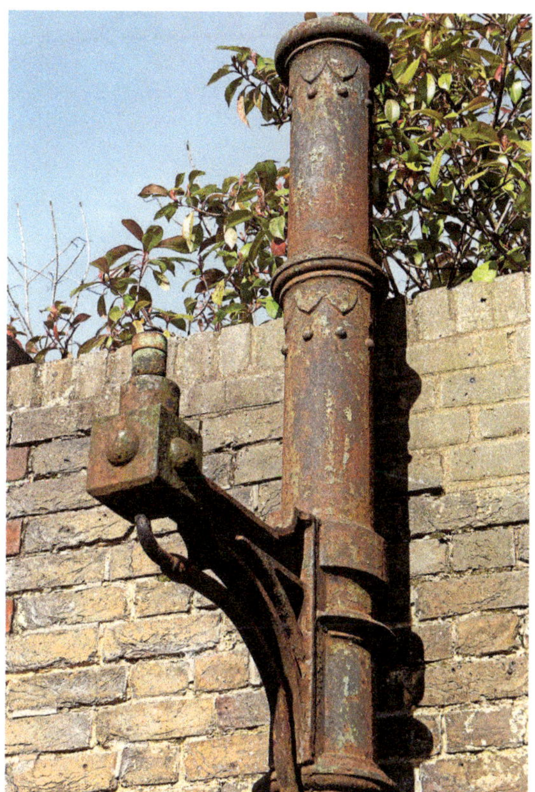

A combination lamp post and sewer vent in Downside. These were invented by G. R. Keeling the dentist and member of the Board of Health, for destroying 'fever gases'.

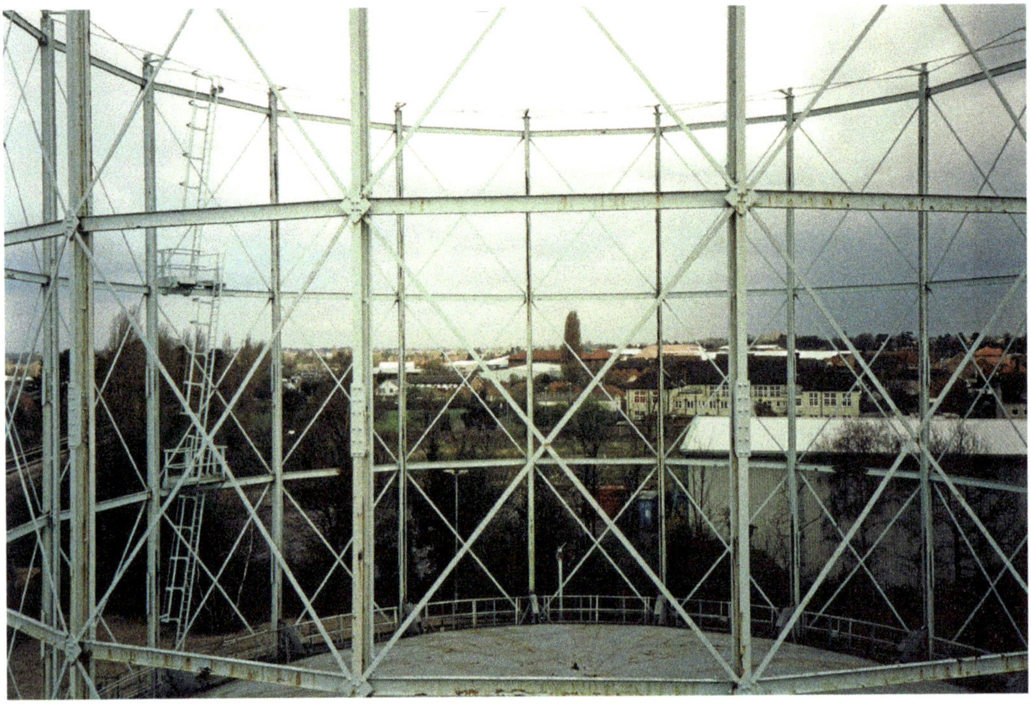

A gasometer was built off East Street in 1840. Another one soon followed, and both were enlarged in 1881. The local gas company was merged with South London in 1912.

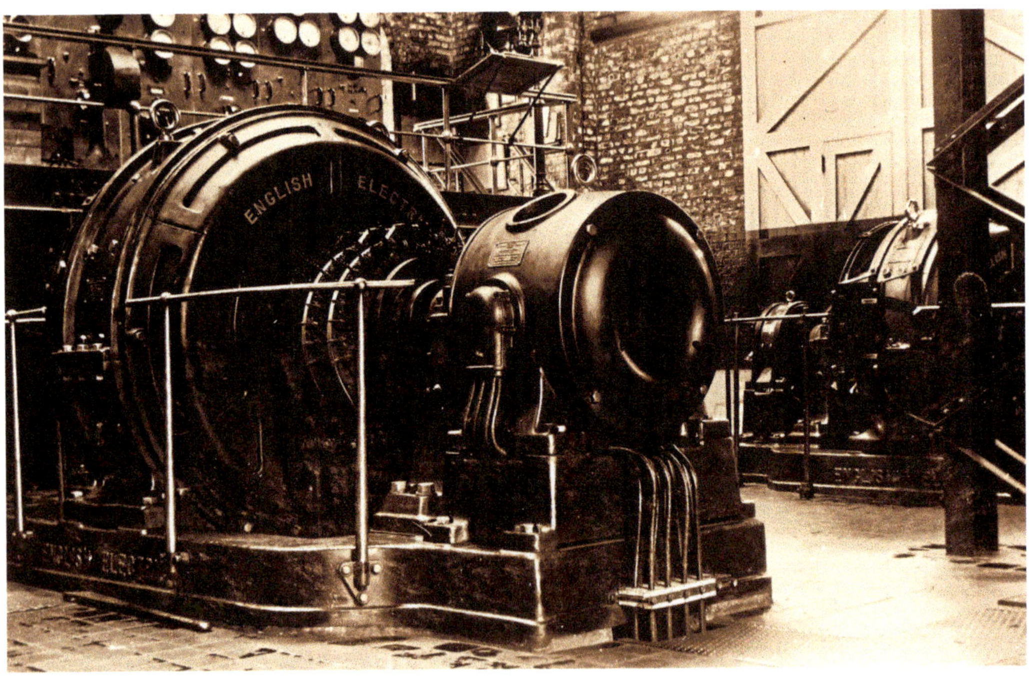

Two rotary convertors in the council's generating station at Depot Road in 1930. Epsom had just been linked to the National Grid but these were kept for standby.

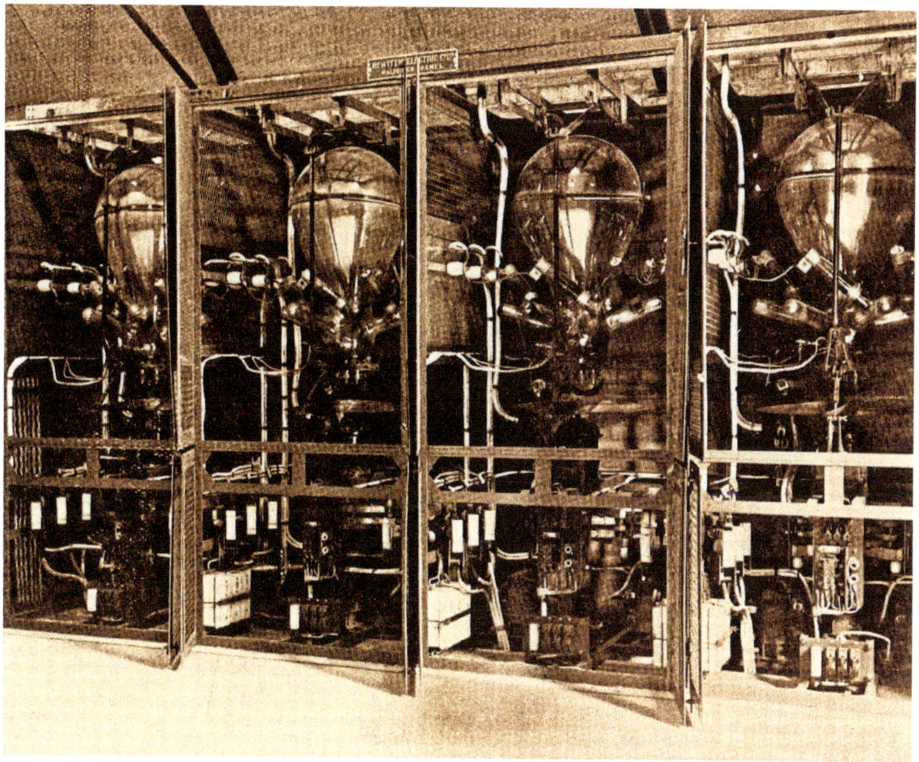

Mercury arc rectifiers at the Pound Lane substation. At first, electrical supply was for central Epsom; Ewell was added in 1918, and in 1930 cable was laid to every road.

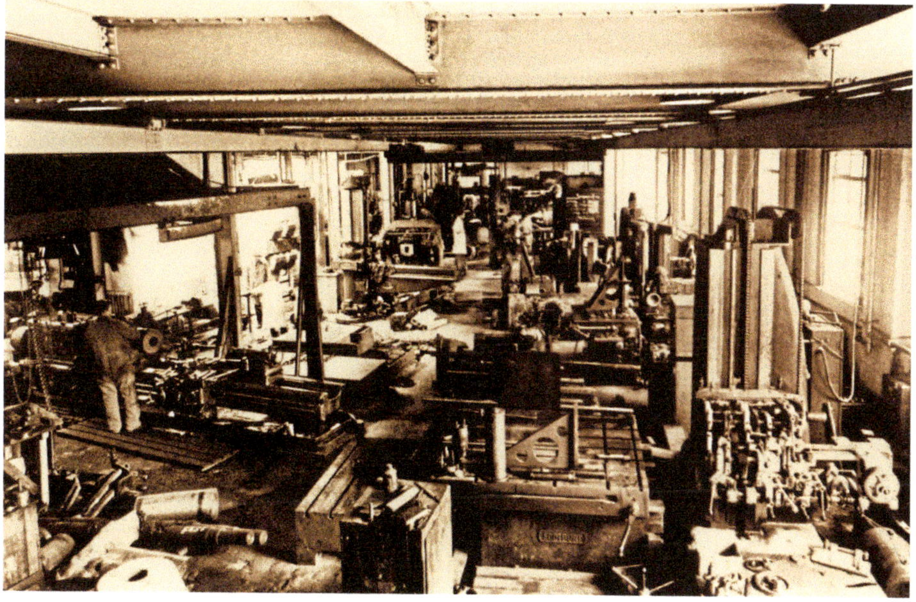

J. L. Jameson set up at West Street in 1933, making heavy-duty machine tools until the 1960s when the workshops were transferred from Ewell to their Chessington branch.

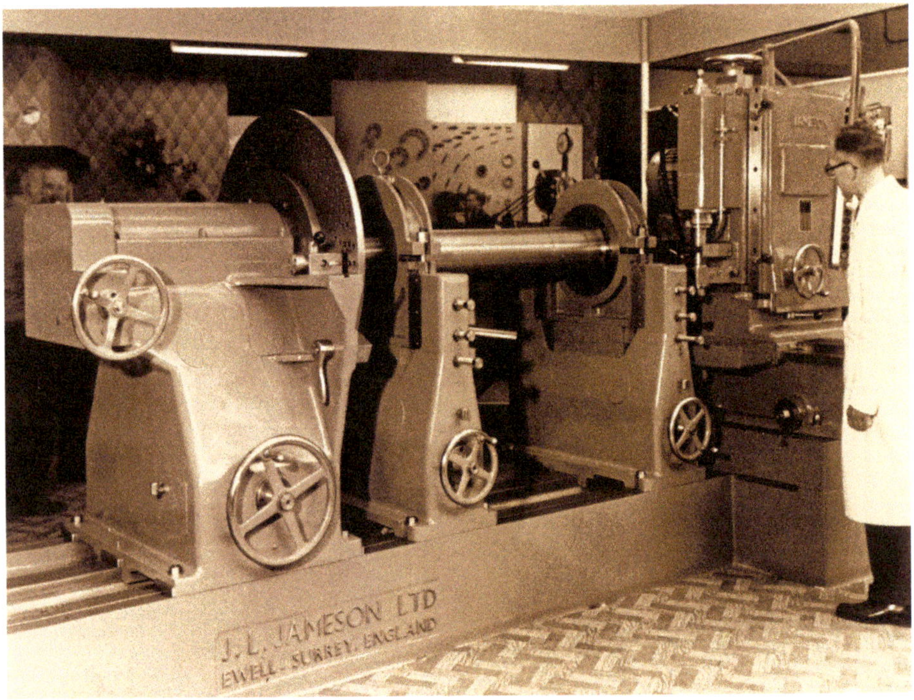

Jameson's milling machine for clutch teeth. During the war they were a shadow factory with 180 staff. Later they made the undercarriage of the Vickers Valiant bomber.

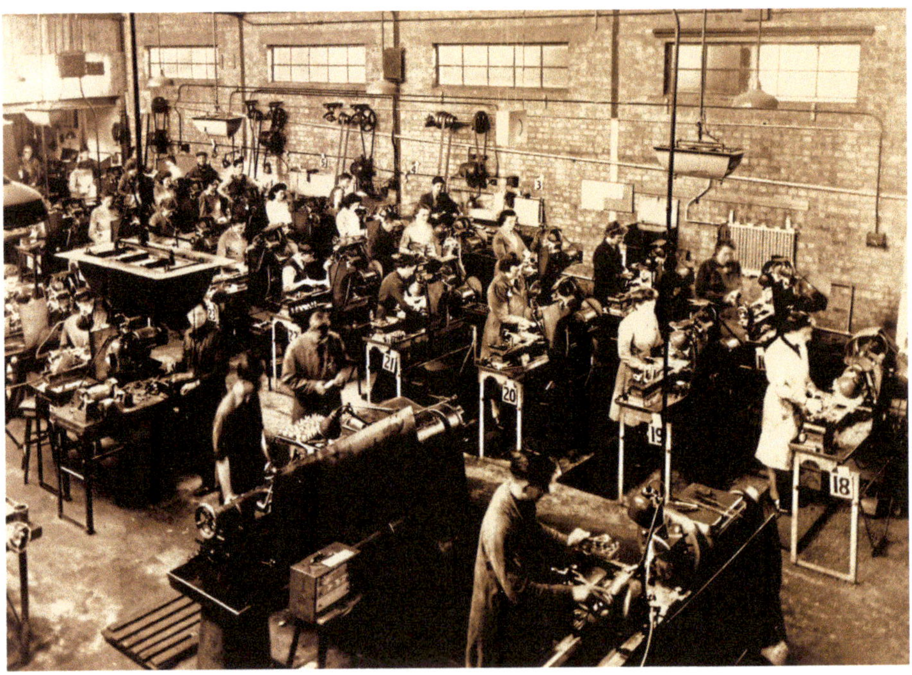

French and Belgian refugees worked in 1943 at this factory in Ashley Avenue. At the second machine from right, R. J. Webb is making parts to connect aircraft fuselage.

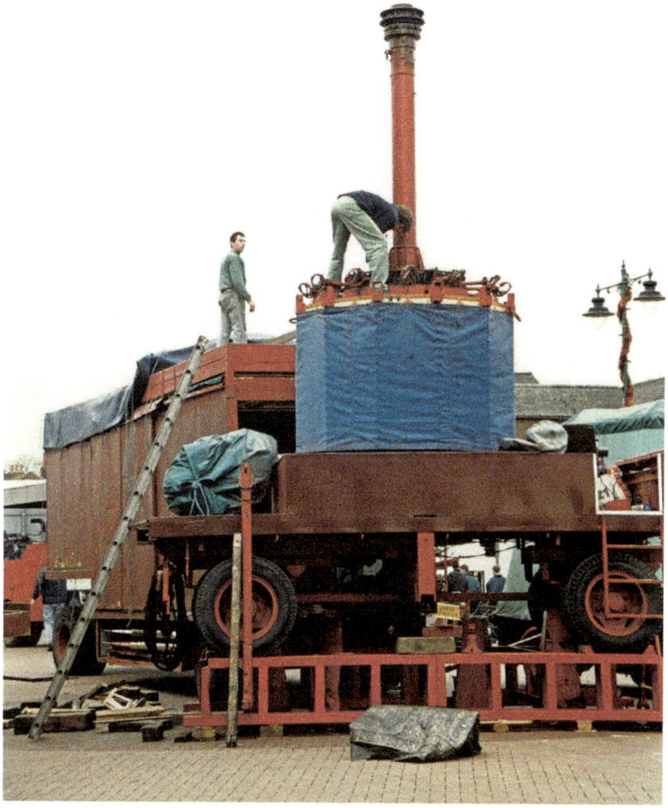

Right: Setting up the roundabout in Epsom marketplace for the Victorian evening of 1997, the Borough's Golden Jubilee year. Celebrations have been based here since 1863.

Below: Laundry staff at Epsom College in the 1910s. The new laundry had been built in the 1890s at a cost of £2,400 to allow for the expansion of the school to 200 boys.

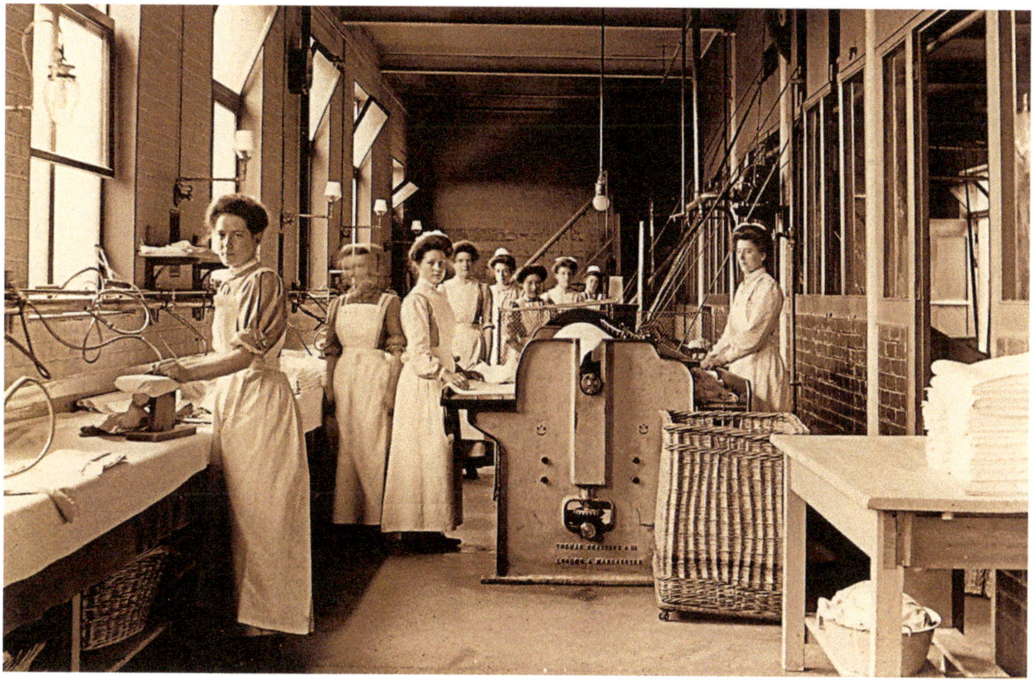

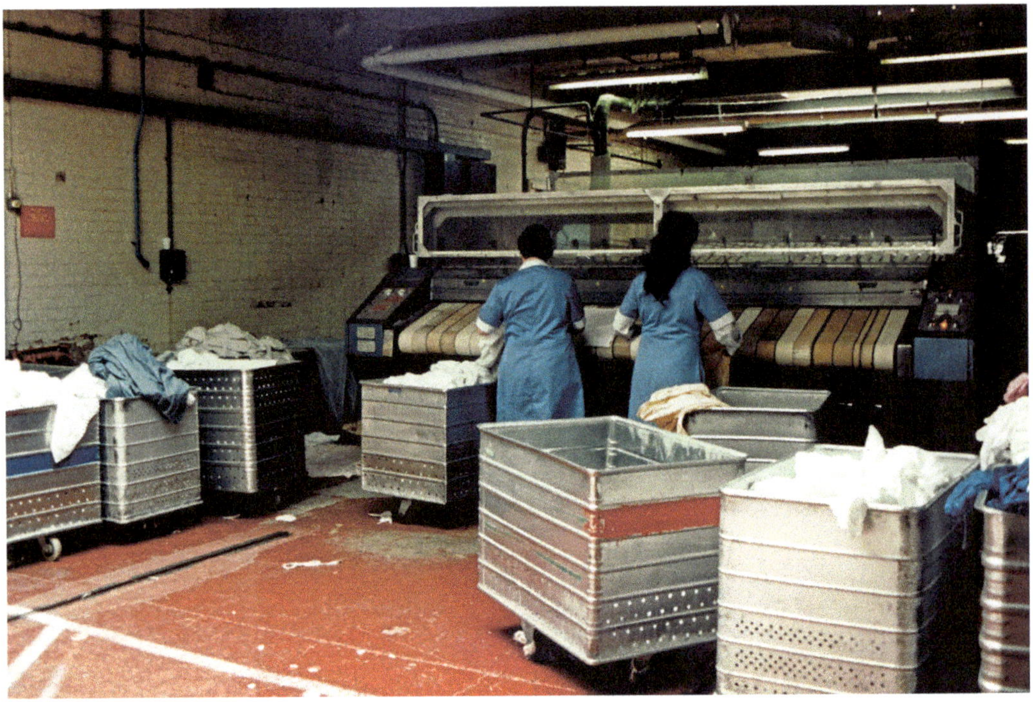

Laundry staff at Horton Hospital in 1995, just before closure. In 1909 'the veiled hostility of the laundrymistress' had caused trouble for the Physician–Superintendent.

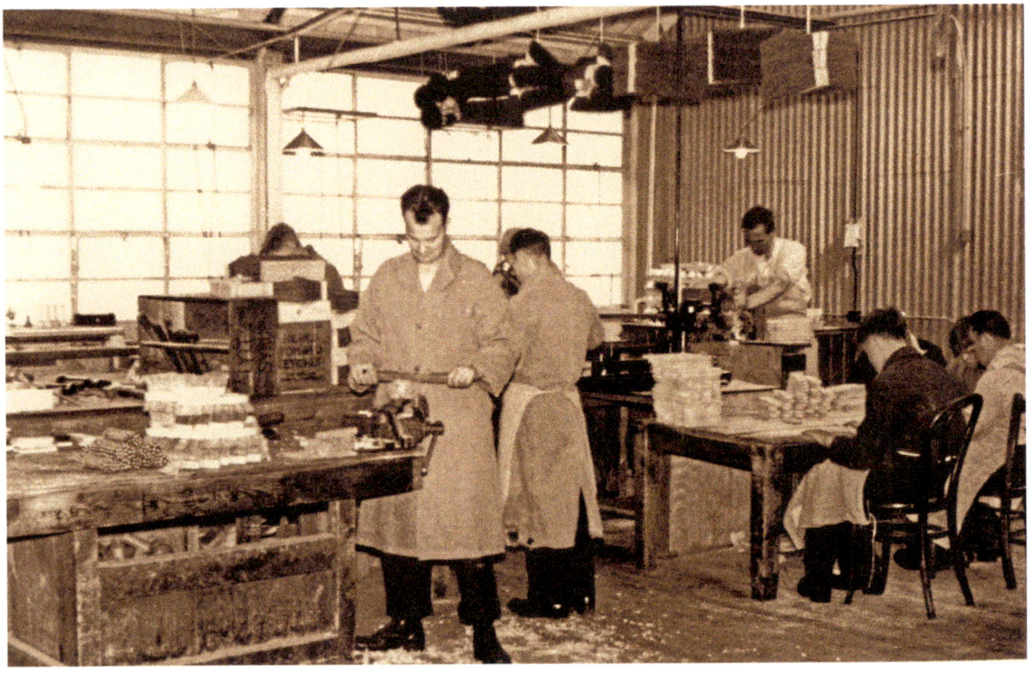

The old brush shop at the Manor Hospital. In 1965 Albert Tebbs, who trained here with his father, started Sherwood, a progressive workshop for those with a mental handicap.

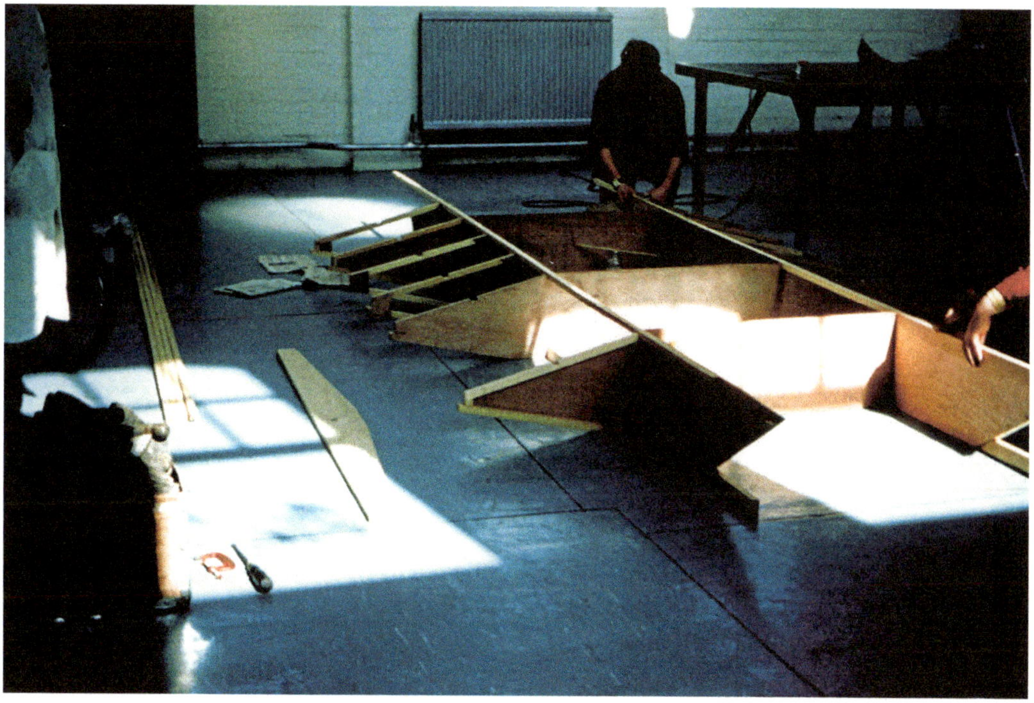

Sherwood Industrial Therapy unit produced electrical parts, spot-welding and chain-link fencing, all to commercial standards. The health authority closed it in 1985.

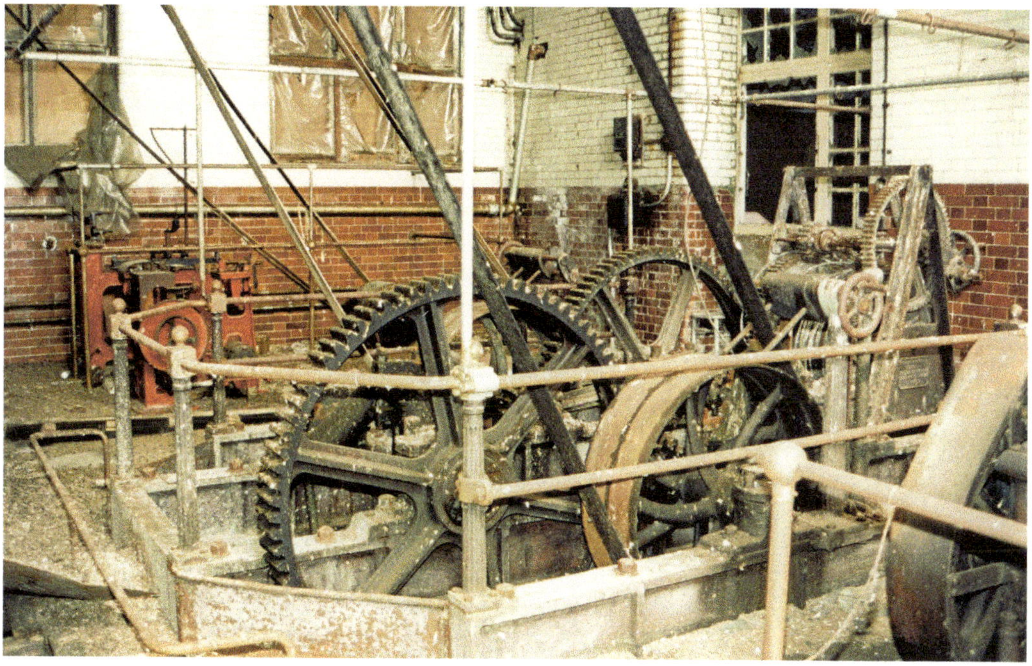

Waterworks were built in 1901 to serve the mental hospitals. These triple-throw cranks operated pumps which brought 2,000 gallons of water an hour from the borehole.

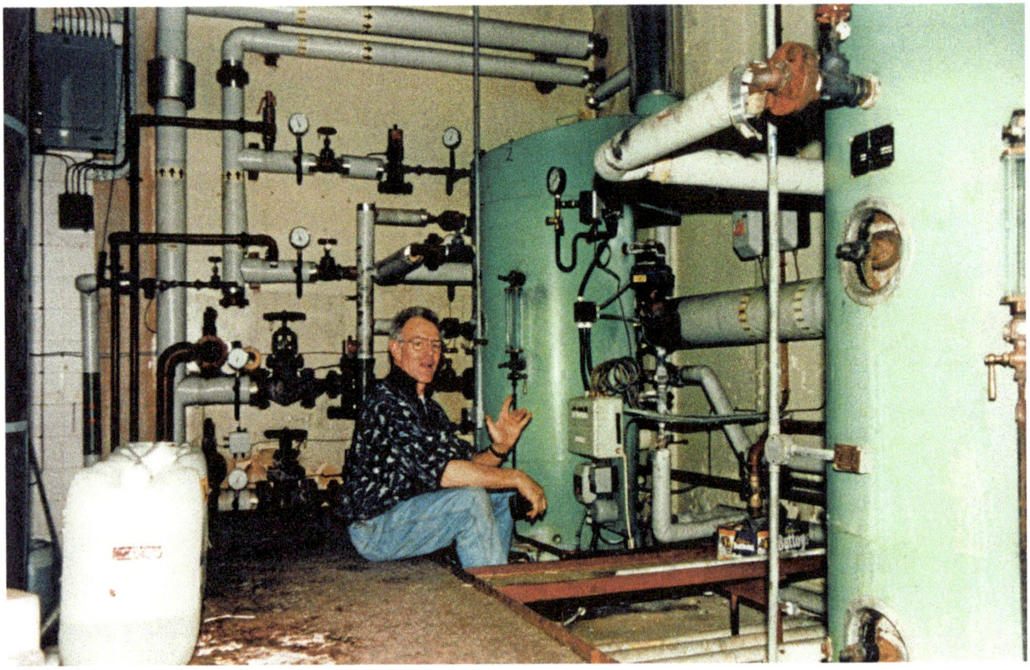

Dennis Barraclough in the boiler room at St Ebba's Hospital. From 1960 a high-pressure steam heating system was provided from the boiler house to all the hospitals.

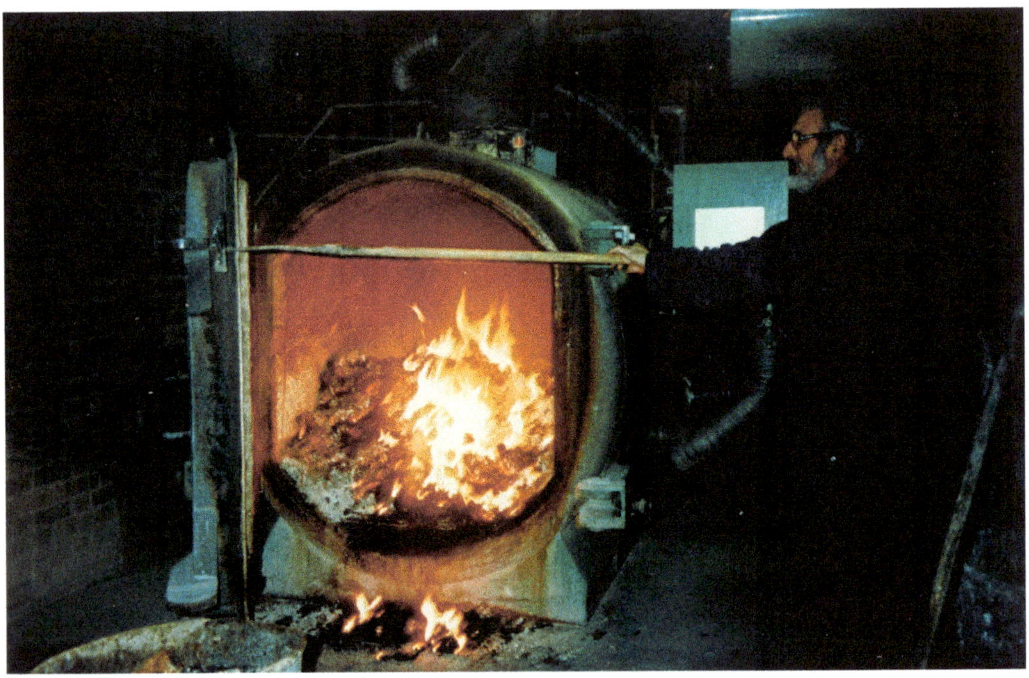

This incinerator for surgical waste was used at St Ebba's until 1993. Hospitals of the Horton Cluster were set up to be as near self-sufficient as possible, using inmate labour.

KEEPING IN TOUCH

There has always been a ready market for information. When a Derby winner passed the post in the 1840s, the last roar of the crowd would be followed by a flutter of wings as carrier pigeons were released from their cages, circling above the Downs for a few confused seconds before setting off to carry the horse's name across the country. The tradition lasted until 1853, when the Electric Telegraph Co. installed a temporary office for the race. Fifteen years later the service was taken over by the Post Office, and news of the Derby winner became available almost instantaneously anywhere in the country.

More important for gambling men was advance information on the horses' form, breeding, trainer and jockey. This had not always been easy to obtain, since racing was kept as a sport for those in the know. But when William Dorling came to Epsom and set up as a jobbing printer, he soon realised that the town offered opportunities beyond the usual routine of almanacs and auction catalogues. At the 1827 races he issued the first Dorling's Correct Card, telling punters everything they needed to know. Under the masterful eye of William's son Henry, the Derby expanded to a national institution. The old hand-operated machinery was laid aside for a rotary cylinder press housed in the Grandstand, and the card was printed in tens or hundreds of thousands.

The first local newspaper, *The Epsom Advocate and Advertiser*, ran for only three issues in 1856–57. The *Epsom Advertiser* was published more successfully from 1869 to 1988. Its rival, the *Epsom Herald*, was part of a north–east Surrey group, which began in 1878 under the care of the local MP Sir Thomas Bucknill. The *Epsom Observer*, which ran from 1901 to 1908, was the first to be printed in the town by Birch and Whittington of Upper High Street. The *Observer* was founded to promote a political career for Alfred Aston of Woodcote Grove, but he failed to win Epsom for the Liberals in the 1906 election. Birch and Whittington secured the coveted contract for printing the council's minutes, which meant that during the First World War their staff were exempt from conscription. Finally in 1937 they merged with Dorlings.

Epsom's status as a posttown went back to 1769, when John Cole was appointed deputy postmaster. His successor, John Jaquet, was also a collector of taxes and agent for Sun insurance. After his wife died in 1810, he had nine children to bring up in the house at No. 94 High Street, which left only one room free as the post office, so customers were expected to transact business through a flap in the door. Lucy Andrews, William Dorling's daughter, became postmistress in 1857 having previously run the business in her husband's name. Her daughter Mary helped as a telegraphist and later took over, persuading the GPO to build a new post office in 1898. It was designed with surplus capacity for race meetings when the eighteen tills and nine telegraph compartments were fully occupied. The sorting room at the back had booths for the sorting clerks, segregated tables for newspapers and parcels, a wire cage for the clerk incharge of registered letters, and a raised desk for the superintendent.

The Derby continued to stimulate media developments, and the finish of the 1895 race was filmed by Birt Acres for exhibition in London. By 1910 Epsom had its own Electric Theatre at the foot of East Street, and locals could watch the coronation procession of George V as easily as if they were standing by Admiralty Arch themselves. Newsreels were shared with the Sutton Electric, after the projectionist had sprinted along Upper High Street to catch the connecting train. By 1938 four more cinemas had been built, but other news media were on the rise. The newly formed BBC had provided a live radio broadcast of the Derby in 1927, with listeners consulting Eric Fraser's cartoon in *Radio Times* for local atmosphere. In 1932 John Logie Baird succeeded in televising the race, projecting the event live in a London cinema.

The first telephone service in Epsom was provided by private enterprise at Hook Road in 1893, followed in 1905 by another exchange run by the Post Office opposite the station in Upper High Street. By 1912, when the GPO was due to take over rival suppliers, there were 350 subscribers and it was decided to use Epsom as a trial location for automatic switching. Within twenty years the number of subscribers had increased fourfold and a new exchange was built in East Street, with another one for Ewell in London Road. Ironically these had both reverted to manual operation as this was the standard for anywhere more than 10 miles out of London. Subscribers did not have the convenience of an automatic STD exchange until 1965.

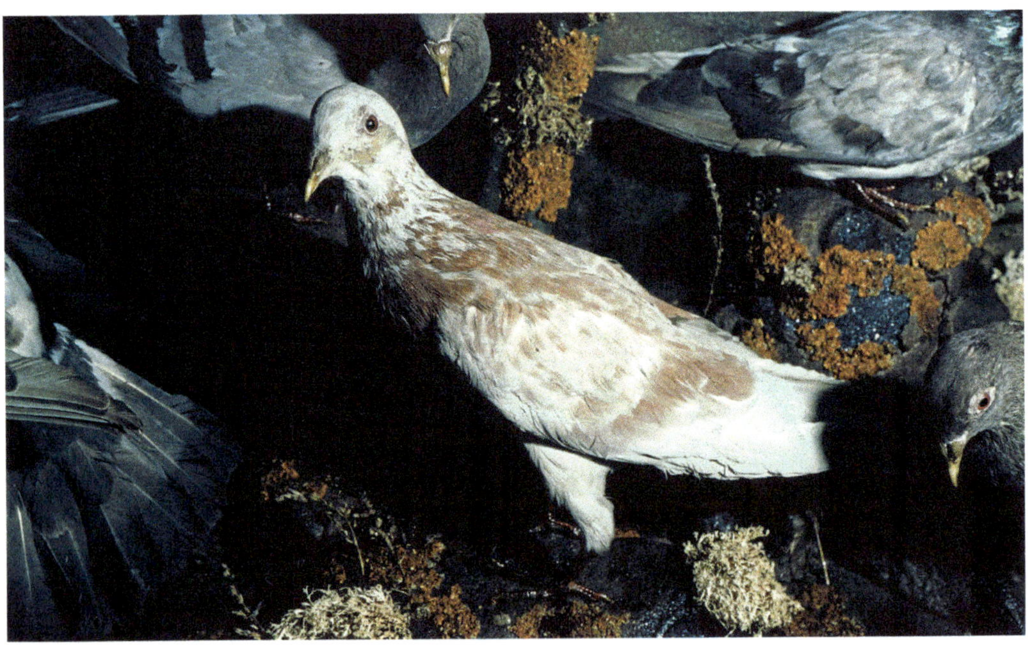

The carrier pigeon Daniel O'Rourke was named after the 1852 Derby winner, whose name he carried back to Hereford where he now rests in the office of the *Hereford Times*.

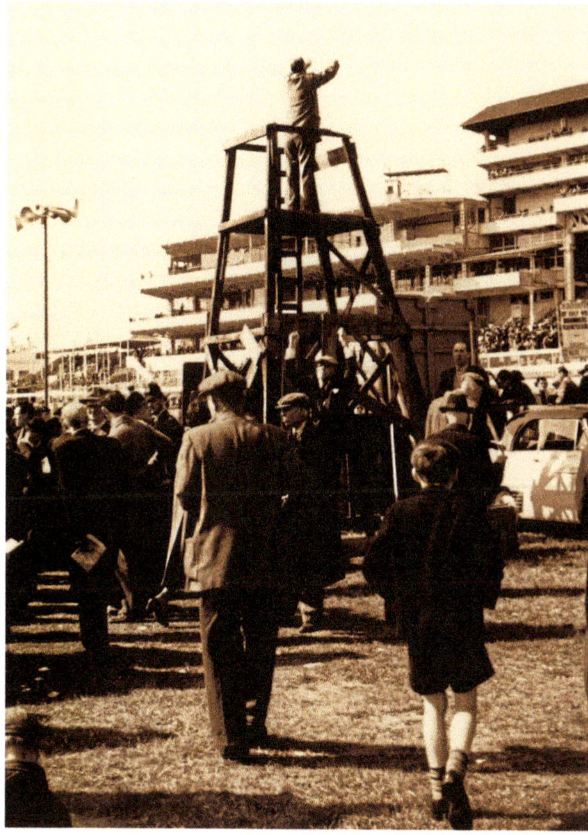

Right: A tic-tac man signing at the Spring Meeting of 1957. He is telling colleagues the changes in the odds on a horse, with white gloves to make the hand movements clearer.

Below: Epsom Post Office was built in 1898, with restrooms for the twenty-six postmen. To help at the Christmas rush, 'one of the staff would play a harmonium and others would sing'.

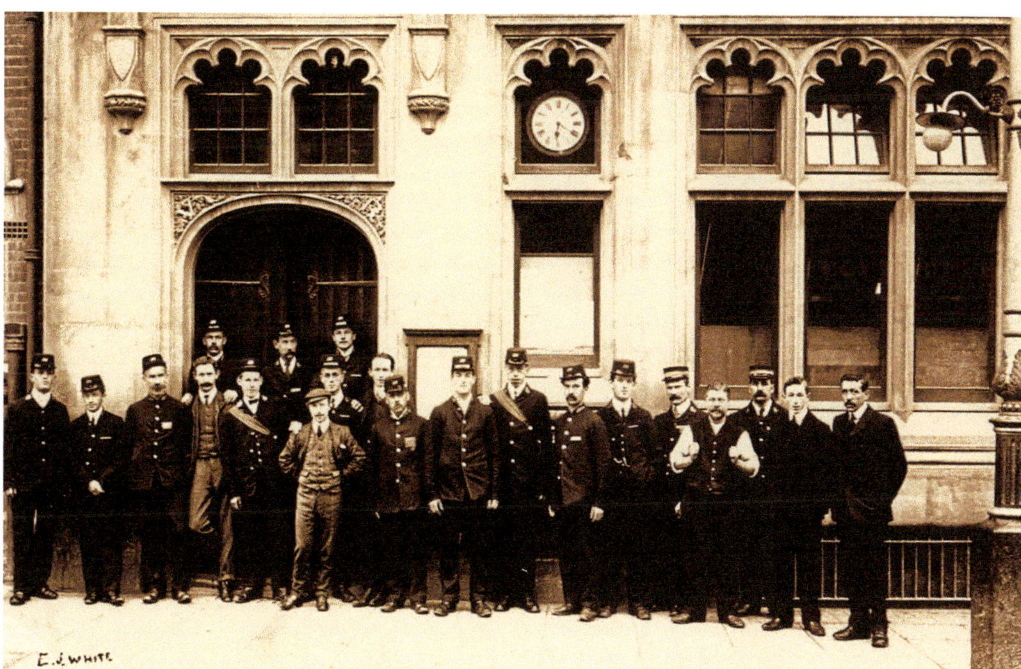

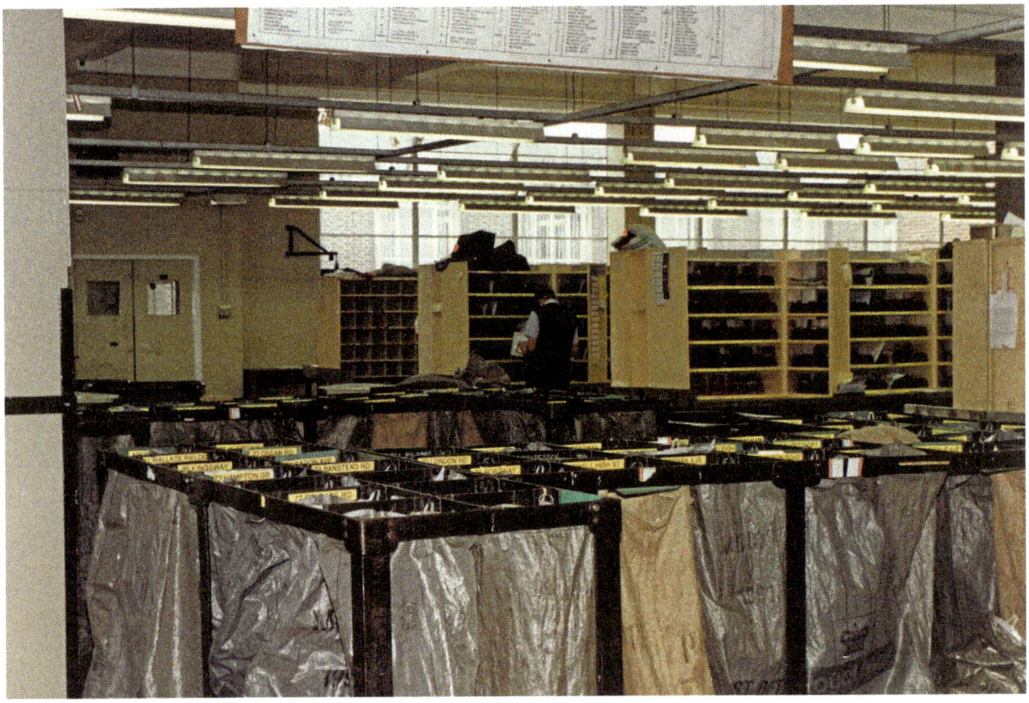

First floor at the East Street sorting office in 1994, with bins for local deliveries. Decline in demand saw the main Post Office close in 2017 and moved to Town Hall.

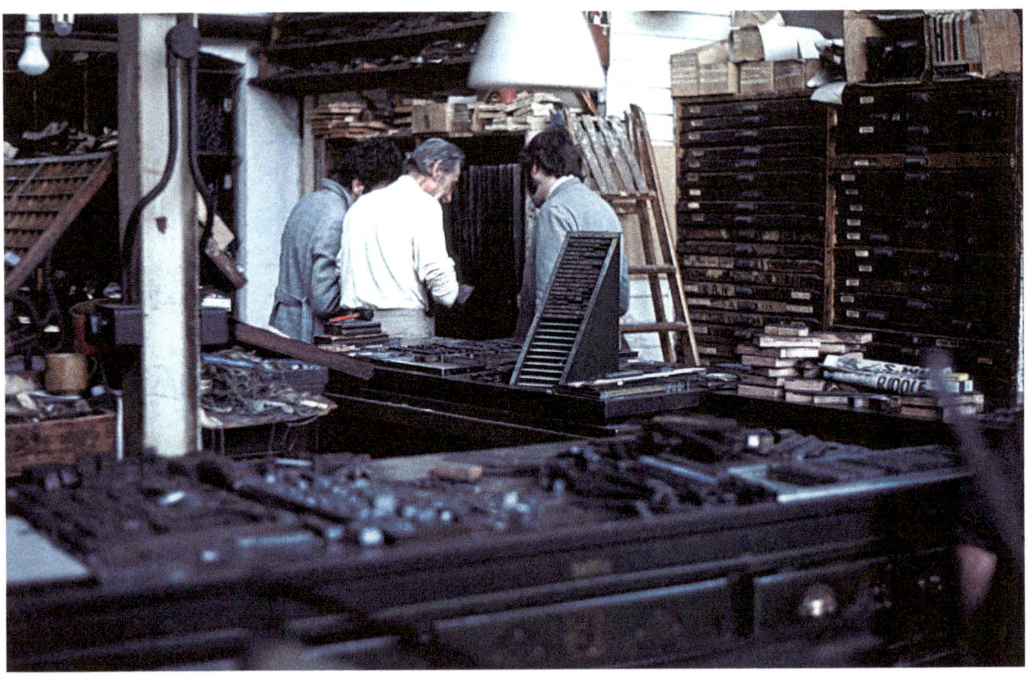

The last days of Dorlings the printers in 1978. Founded by William Dorling in 1821, the firm was operating from Depot Road in conjunction with Pullingers stationers.

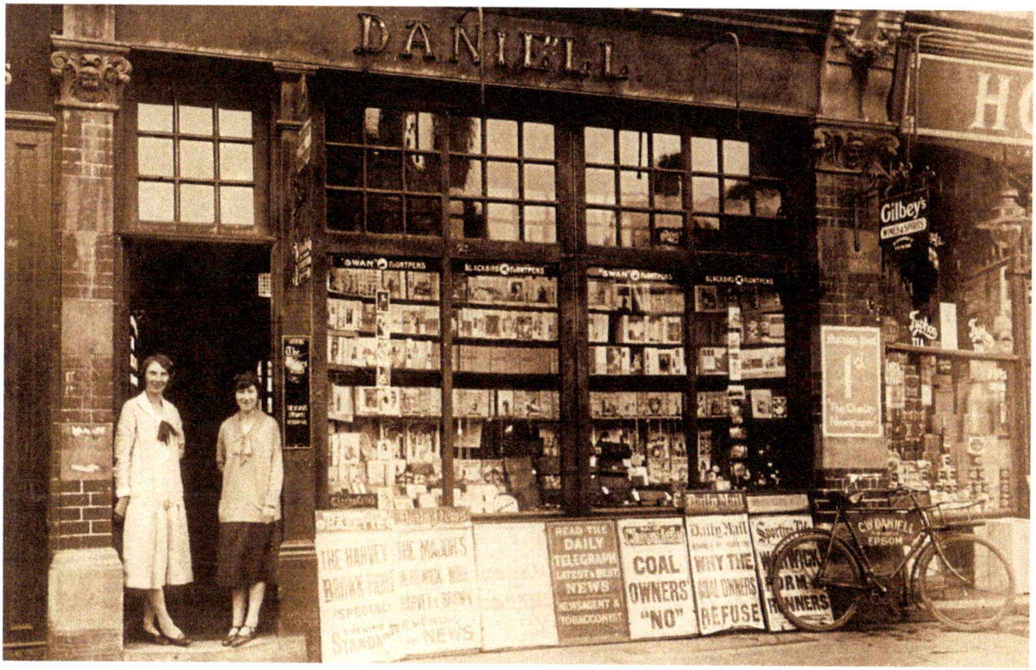

It's September 1926, Len Harvey is to fight Johnny Brown, and the miners are still locked out after the General Strike: Charles Daniell of No. 27 High Street brings all the news.

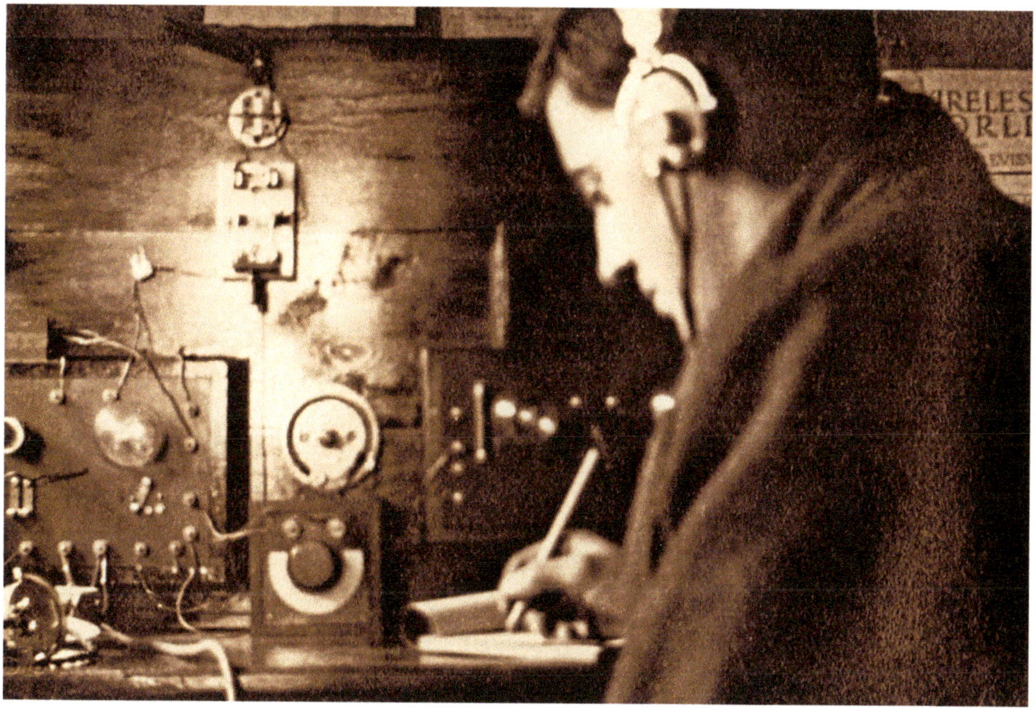

An amateur radio enthusiast at No. 35 Beech Road in the 1920s. He may have bought equipment from E. T. Turner, electrical and radio engineer of No. 77a Epsom High Street.

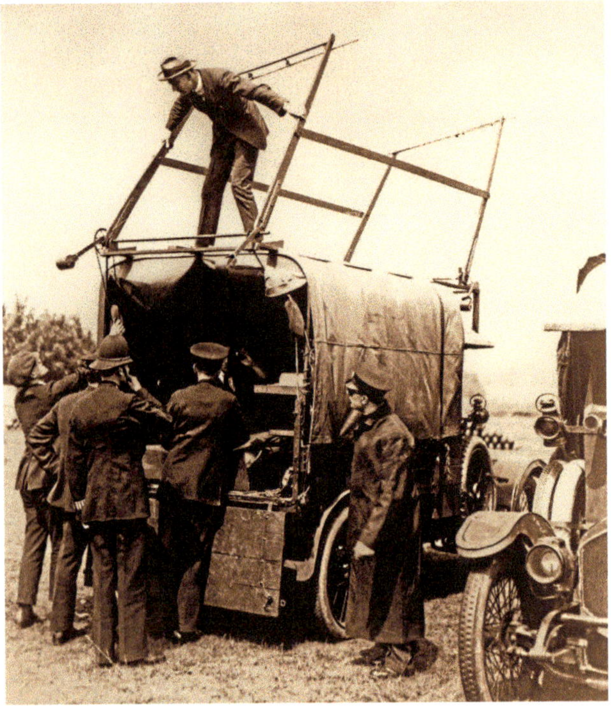

Left: Crossley Tenders, equipped with bulky radio aerials, were used by Metropolitan Police at the Derby from 1923. The 1,800 officers on road duty needed some coordination.

Below: When the Rembrandt Cinema opened at Kingston Road in 1938, it had two Super Simplex projectors, with an adjoining rewind room for the inflammable nitrate film.

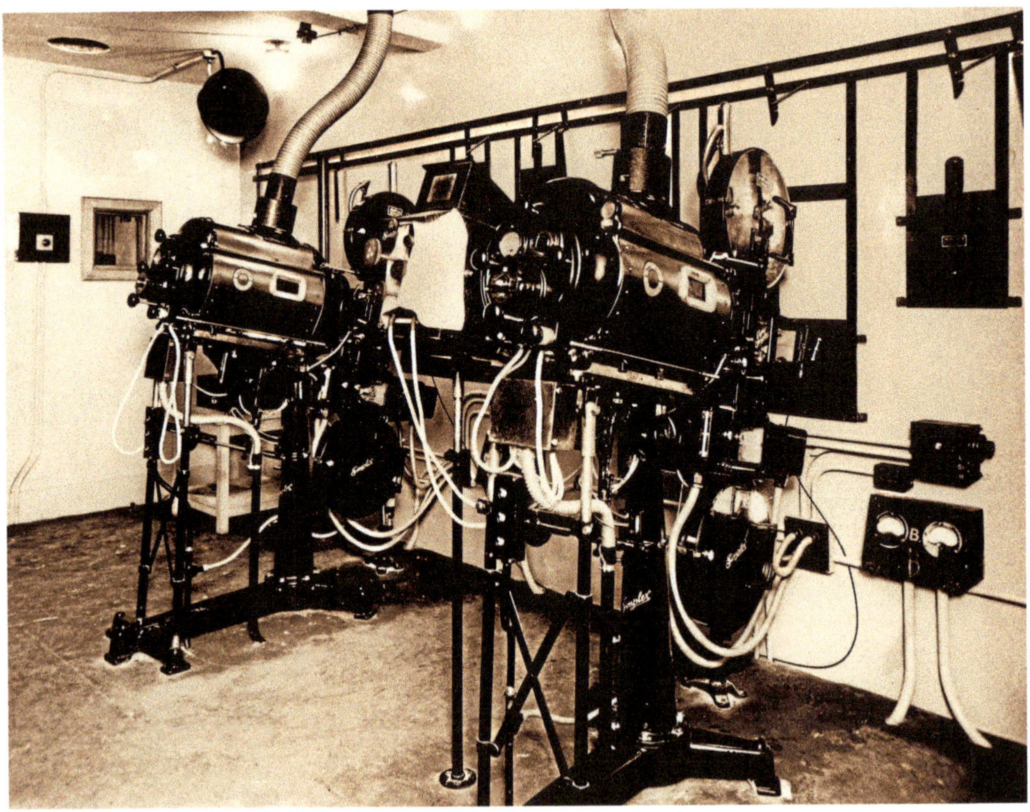

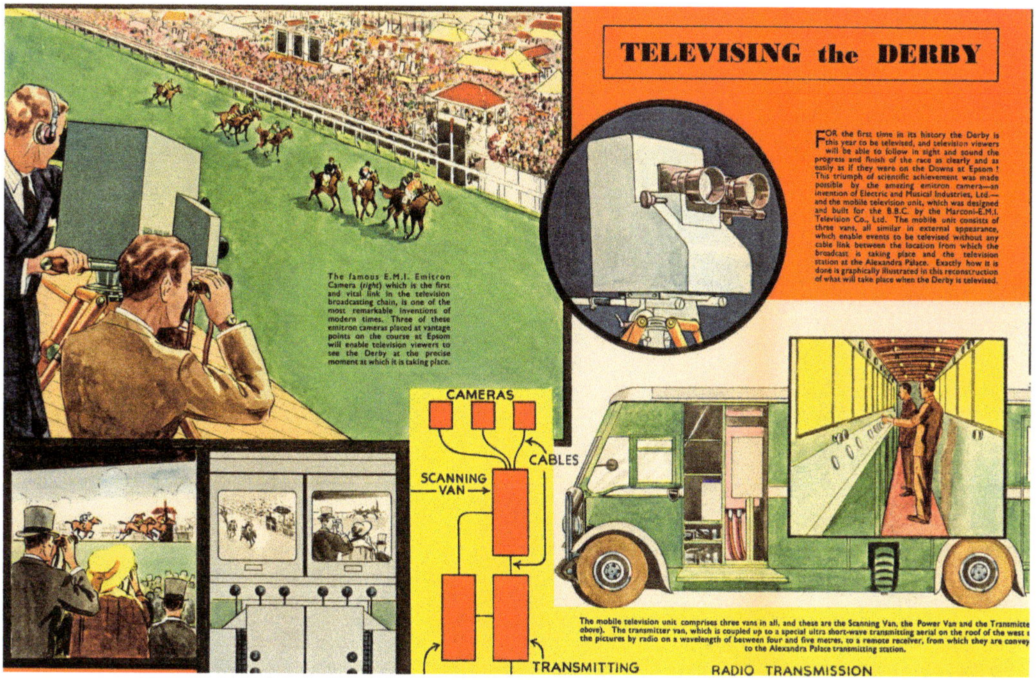

Above: TV viewers could see the 1938 Derby 'at the precise moment at which it is taking place', gasped *Modern Wonders*. John Logie Baird had trialled the technology in 1931.

Right: The test desk at Epsom Telephone Exchange in 1912. Equipment – and staff – for the Strowger system of automatic switching were brought over from America for trial.

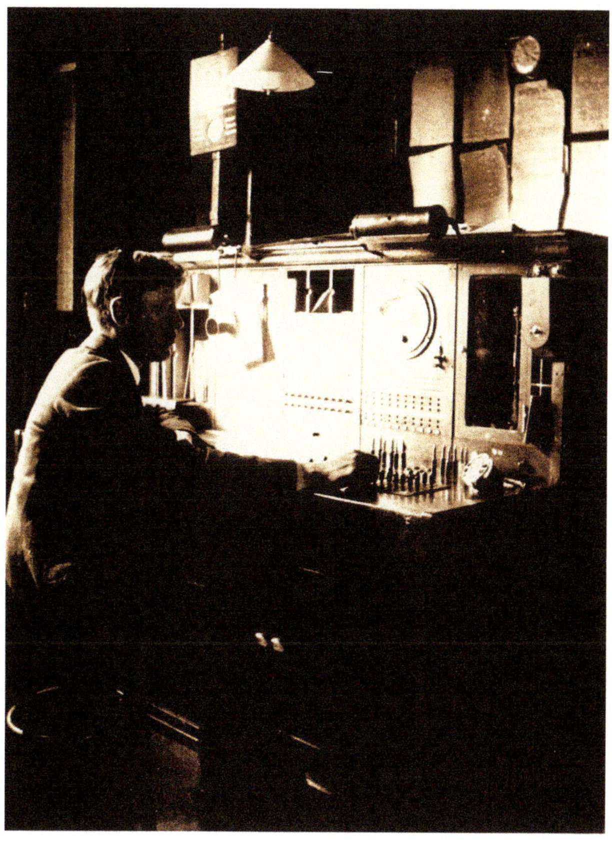

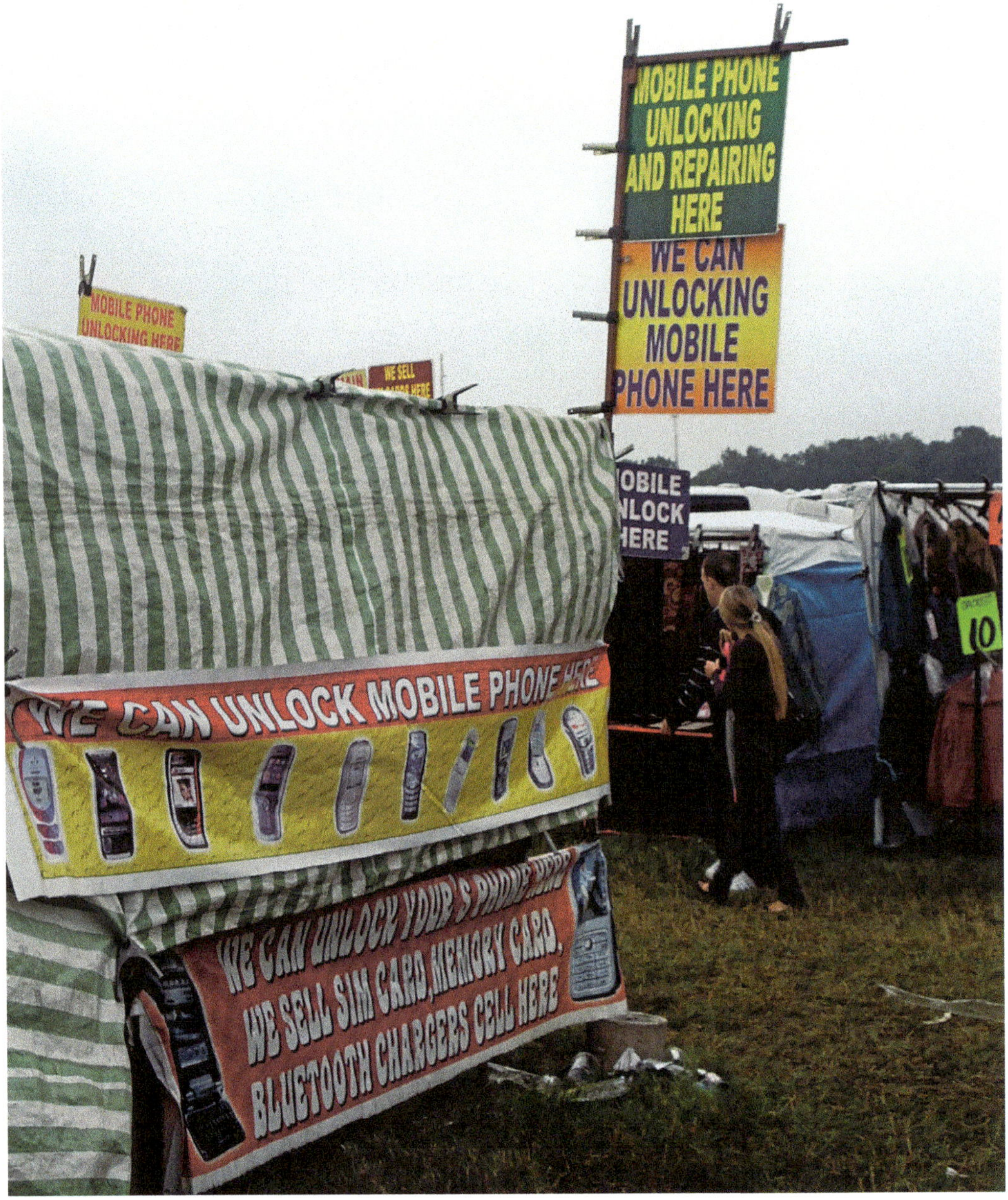

In the first decade of the new millennium, mobile phones had moved from being state-of-the-art to back-of-a-lorry purchases. A selection was on offer at the 2009 Derby.